THE CHANGING CONTEXTS
OF TEACHING

THE CHANGING CONTEXTS OF TEACHING

*Ninety-first Yearbook of the
National Society for the Study of Education*

PART I

Edited by
ANN LIEBERMAN

Editor for the Society
KENNETH J. REHAGE

Distributed by THE UNIVERSITY OF CHICAGO PRESS ● CHICAGO, ILLINOIS

LB
1025.2
.C53
1992

The National Society for the Study of Education

Founded in 1901 as successor to the National Herbart Society, the National Society for the Study of Education has provided a means by which the results of serious study of educational issues could become a basis for informed discussion of those issues. The Society's two-volume yearbooks, now in their ninety-first year of publication, reflect the thoughtful attention given to a wide range of educational problems during those years. In 1971 the Society inaugurated a series of substantial publications on Contemporary Educational Issues to supplement the yearbooks. Each year the Society's publications contain contributions to the literature of education from more than a hundred scholars and practitioners who are doing significant work in their respective fields.

An elected Board of Directors selects the subjects with which volumes in the yearbook series are to deal and appoints committees to oversee the preparation of manuscripts. A special committee created by the Board performs similar functions for the series on Contemporary Educational Issues.

The Society's publications are distributed each year without charge to members in the United States, Canada, and elsewhere throughout the world. The Society welcomes as members all individuals who desire to receive its publications. Information about current dues may be found in the back pages of this volume.

This volume, *The Changing Contexts of Teaching*, is Part I of the Ninety-first Yearbook of the Society. Part II, which is published at the same time, is entitled *The Arts, Education, and Aesthetic Knowing*.

A listing of the Society's publications still available for purchase may be found in the back pages of this volume.

Library of Congress Catalog Number: 91-066982
ISSN: 0077-5762

Published 1992 by
THE NATIONAL SOCIETY FOR THE STUDY OF EDUCATION
5835 Kimbark Avenue, Chicago, Illinois 60637
© 1992 by the National Society for the Study of Education

No part of this Yearbook may be reproduced in any form without written permission from the Secretary of the Society

First Printing, 5,000 Copies

Printed in the United States of America

*Board of Directors of the
National Society for the Study of Education*
(*Term of office expires March 1 of the year indicated.*)

DAVID C. BERLINER, Arizona State University (1993)
LARRY CUBAN, Stanford University (1994)
ANN LIEBERMAN, Teachers College, Columbia University (1992)
JEANNIE OAKES, University of California, Los Angeles (1994)
A. HARRY PASSOW, Teachers College, Columbia University (1992)
PENELOPE L. PETERSON, Michigan State University (1993)

KENNETH J. REHAGE, University of Chicago, Secretary-Treasurer

Contributors to the Yearbook

ANN LIEBERMAN, Teachers College, Columbia University, Editor

TERRY ASTUTO, University of Virginia
DAVID CLARK, University of North Carolina
MARILYN COHN, Washington University, St. Louis
LINDA DARLING-HAMMOND, Teachers College, Columbia University
PAMELA GROSSMAN, University of Washington, Seattle
JENNIFER KNUDSEN, Stanford University
GARY LICHTENSTEIN, Stanford University
JUDITH WARREN LITTLE, University of California, Berkeley
KAREN SEASHORE LOUIS, University of Minnesota
ROBERT M. MCCLURE, National Education Association
MILBREY W. MCLAUGHLIN, Stanford University
LYNNE MILLER, University of Southern Maine
GARY NATRIELLO, Teachers College, Columbia University
CYNTHIA O'SHEA, Gorham (Maine) Public Schools
JON SNYDER, Teachers College, Columbia University
PATRICIA WASLEY, Coalition of Essential Schools, Brown University
KAREN K. ZUMWALT, Teachers College, Columbia University

Acknowledgments

Professor Ann Lieberman, a member of the Board of Directors of the National Society for the Study of Education, is the editor of this volume. She is responsible for the planning of the yearbook and for soliciting the collaboration of a distinguished group of authors. All who have written chapters included here have drawn upon a rich experience in studying or participating in some of the most important developments affecting teaching today.

The Society is deeply indebted to Professor Lieberman and to each of the authors. Their work has made it possible to add a timely and provocative volume to the Society's series of yearbooks.

Professor Margaret Early, a member of the faculty of the College of Education, University of Florida, and a former member of the Society's Board of Directors, reviewed all manuscripts for this volume. Her editorial suggestions have been exceedingly helpful. H. Jerome Studer, assistant in the NSSE office, compiled the name index and assisted with the reading of proof.

KENNETH J. REHAGE
Editor for the Society

Table of Contents

	PAGE
THE NATIONAL SOCIETY FOR THE STUDY OF EDUCATION	iv
BOARD OF DIRECTORS OF THE SOCIETY, 1991-92; CONTRIBUTORS TO THE YEARBOOK	v
ACKNOWLEDGMENTS	vii

CHAPTER
I. INTRODUCTION: THE CHANGING CONTEXT OF EDUCATION, *Ann Lieberman* 1

Section One
The Changing Policy Context of Teaching

II. FRAMING ACCOUNTABILITY: CREATING LEARNER-CENTERED SCHOOLS, *Linda Darling-Hammond* and *Jon Snyder* 11

III. TEACHER EMPOWERMENT AND PROFESSIONAL KNOWLEDGE, *Gary Lichtenstein, Milbrey W. McLaughlin,* and *Jennifer Knudsen* . . 37

IV. CHALLENGES TO AN ALTERNATE ROUTE FOR TEACHER EDUCATION, *Gary Natriello* and *Karen K. Zumwalt* 59

V. A TEACHERS' UNION REVISITS ITS PROFESSIONAL PAST, *Robert M. McClure* 79

Section Two
The Changing School Context

VI. CHALLENGING THE LIMITS OF SCHOOL RESTRUCTURING AND REFORM, *Terry Astuto* and *David Clark* 90

VII. HOW TEACHERS PERCEIVE TEACHING: CHANGES OVER TWO DECADES, 1964-1984, *Marilyn Cohn* 110

VIII. RESTRUCTURING AND THE PROBLEM OF TEACHERS' WORK, *Karen Seashore Louis* 138

IX. OPENING THE BLACK BOX OF PROFESSIONAL COMMUNITY, *Judith Warren Little* 157

CHAPTER

Section Three
Changing Roles and Relationships of Teachers as Learners and as Leaders

X. TEACHING TO LEARN, *Pamela Grossman* 179

XI. LEARNING TO LEAD: PORTRAITS OF PRACTICE, *Lynne Miller* and *Cynthia O'Shea* 197

XII. A TEACHER-RUN SCHOOL: TEACHER LEADERSHIP REVISITED, *Patricia Wasley* 212

NAME INDEX 237
SUBJECT INDEX 241
INFORMATION ABOUT MEMBERSHIP IN THE SOCIETY 245
PUBLICATIONS OF THE SOCIETY 247

CHAPTER I

Introduction: The Changing Context of Education

ANN LIEBERMAN

The wave of educational reform initiated by *A Nation at Risk*[1] in 1983 called for more mathematics and science courses specifically, and a more rigorous course of studies for high schools in general. Somehow the schools were being blamed for the growing social discontent, the increasing dropout problems, the low scores on tests of higher-order thinking, and America's falling position in the international scene. A second wave of reform, however, has already shifted to issues surrounding the preparation of teachers, to a focus on teachers and students, and to the restructuring of schools. The formal beginning of this second wave could be dated from the Carnegie Commission report entitled *A Nation Prepared: Teachers for the 21st Century* and the Holmes Group Report on *Tomorrow's Teachers*, both published in 1986.[2] While the first wave was characterized by "top-down" mandates for change in curriculum standards, the second, as one might expect, was far more involved in engaging "bottom-up" participation from teachers and principals in efforts to restructure schools. Despite the pessimism of those who dismiss the current reform movement as transitory, another of the pendulum swings that happen every decade, there are many who are involved in changing their schools by investing much time, energy, and resources in the effort to fundamentally reshape American education.

There is a strong consensus in our country that something is seriously wrong with our schools and that nothing short of comprehensive change will make a difference. At virtually every level decision makers are involved in some way in debate and discussion about how to change schools. There is great fear of the loss of our economic competitiveness in the world because of the failure to

---

Ann Lieberman is Professor of Education and Co-Director of the National Center for Restructuring Education, Schools, and Teaching at Teachers College, Columbia University.

educate our students to the level needed by the work force of the twenty-first century. There is concern about the increasing numbers of poor and illiterate people in a society that needs educated workers and citizens. And there are immediate problems of teacher shortages and the inability to attract and retain teachers. All these lend an air of urgency to the ethos surrounding this era of school reform.

Unfortunately the messages are confusing and contradictory, and often in conflict. "Restructuring" is becoming the new word for reform, but the terms that are being used—including teacher professionalism, deregulation, and school choice—mean different things to different people, concealing widely differing assumptions about the purposes, functions, organization, and work of schools, teachers, and students. Calls for providing deeper and fewer experiences for students are met by continuous increases in new courses.[3] Some states are mandating shared decision making at the local level, while some researchers are providing evidence that "one can't mandate what matters most."[4] Some new organizations are pressing the old ones into new stances, while some traditional organizations are encouraging new collaborative structures to help create new roles and relationships between schools, universities, and businesses. Teachers' unions, having fought long and hard for collective bargaining agreements to protect seniority, are now suggesting that senior people should take leadership and go to the toughest schools, thereby giving up their hard won prerogatives. Research on teaching, long dominated by a view that attempted to link particular behaviors of teachers to student achievement and thus find generic rules for teachers, is now in the process of shifting its focus to observing the context of teaching, recognizing that diversity rather than uniformity may be the norm.[5] Millions of dollars have been spent on the professional development of teachers, although the evidence indicates that what "sells" best is not necessarily what is most meaningful to teachers. Some states are having severe shortages of teachers, adding further pressure to make teaching more attractive, while others offer alternative routes to becoming a teacher that often undermine the professional status that could make a teaching career more attractive. For the first time some state and federal policymakers are calling for national goals while at the same time recognizing the need for strong involvement of teachers at the local level, a reversal of the traditional state and local control over schools and curriculum.

What is the context for all this pressure for educational change? Why is it happening now? What does all this ferment mean? What persistent themes are getting replayed in this current period of school reform, and what factors are new? What new practices are being tried as a result of these reform efforts? How can we clarify these complex issues so that we can better understand the intentions and the possible consequences accompanying these changes?

It is the purpose of this book to try to frame the major themes that historically have been concerned with the nature of and support for good teaching as they relate to the current effort to restructure schools. Particular attention is paid to teacher participation and development in this changing context, highlighting the problems, paradoxes, and possibilities for significant change. Policies are changing and, presumably, that means practices will also change, so we try to see policies and practices here as separate but interconnected phenomena. Context, whether in the state house or the schoolhouse, is always significant in determining the substance and extent of school reforms.

Social and Demographic Conditions in the 1990s: Effects on Teaching

Perhaps the most dramatic differences in the schools of the 1990s are rooted in the social, economic, and demographic changes in the society. The decade of the 1980s increased the number of poor families and widened the gap between those who participate fully in the society and those outside of it. Students with social, physical, or educational problems have always been a challenge to teachers, since they need highly personalized and individualized attention, emotional sustenance, and often specialized learning tasks. But in this postindustrial society new problems have exacerbated the challenge and put increased pressure on schools and teachers. Urban school populations have not only been characterized by students who are increasingly diverse ethnically and linguistically, but by students who, in ever larger numbers, are coming to school with many more physical, social, and emotional problems that make them far from ready to learn. In fact, some of the problems are so new that they have yet to be described adequately, much less diagnosed for possible solutions.[6] For these and other reasons, schools have not been able to stem the rising tide of dropouts as reports show not only more students dropping out, but more of them leaving at earlier ages.

The educational response from schools to those with learning difficulties has been to require that students who perform poorly learn the basic skills *before* they learn anything else. Indeed, in the past decade support grew for teaching methods, particularly for disadvantaged students, that focused most on learning skills: learning them sequentially, and most definitely learning them in teacher-directed classrooms. This view, supported by "effective schools" research as well as folk wisdom,[7] means that teaching methods that are passive, impersonal, and generally print-bound have dominated many classrooms.

But the world has changed and basic skills alone are insufficient in a society heavily dominated by increased technology and the need for continuous problem solving. The view that schooling is mostly about basic skills often sets a ceiling on what teachers come to expect of students and themselves, rather than becoming a base upon which to build. This has all too often limited classroom instruction to clearing away learning deficits; the strengths that students bring to school, regardless of their home situations, are then ignored. This focus has also limited teachers' sensitivities and abilities to help students care about themselves and their participation in society, so that they might come to understand why and how schooling can be important for them.[8] Some have described the need to look at the whole child, his or her psychosocial needs, the climate of the school, the involvement of parents in the school, and teachers' greater involvement in school governance as prerequisites for success in academic work.[9] Some of these views, although familiar from past reform eras, have become increasingly relevant today. As they enlarge our understanding of the teaching context by making manifest other conditions that influence student learning, they also influence our perspective of the teacher's expanding role and changing responsibilities in the school and the profession.

Until recently, the response of the educational system to growing societal problems (e.g., poverty, homelessness, teen-age pregnancy, single-parent families, increased violence) has been to mandate increased curricular efforts, or perhaps a new bureaucratic position to handle the problem, while leaving the existing institutional forms and teaching practices in place. The results show that "more of the same" has not worked, and that teachers, beleaguered by mandates, requirements, and standards that assume uniformity rather than diversity, are themselves feeling victimized. It is not surprising then that reforms of the 1990s suggest confronting the problems of teaching by engaging teachers in fundamental ways, not only by dealing with teaching methods but also by participating in the organization of schools so as to focus better on students and involve them more effectively.

This dual agenda has become the key to developing a new context for teaching: creating learner-centered schools with teacher involvement in schoolwide decision making and program development. But it also has led to new questions. What new knowledge is being produced in the process of restructuring schools? What issues are surfacing concerning the potential for and limitations of changing teaching policies and practices? What assumptions about teaching and learning underlie both new and old views?

Teaching: Past and Present

For many years two seemingly contradictory terms—"teacher-centered" teaching and "student-centered" teaching—have dominated the literature on teaching. (Other euphemisms include: traditional and progressive, conservative and liberal, technical and professional, mimetic and transformative.)[10] In essence, these views describe different approaches to teaching stemming from conflicting sets of assumptions about student learning.

Teacher-centered teaching assumes that there is basic knowledge that must be transmitted, that teachers organize and deliver this knowledge to students, and then test them to see if the students have learned the material. In this view, teachers dominate the classroom, students are seen as recipients of the teacher's instruction,[11] and curriculum is categorized into courses and tracks—college-bound, general, and vocational. Historically this has been a generally efficient way of organizing masses of students and transmitting knowledge, and it continues to be—along with its assumptions about a teacher's control of curriculum and a more passive role for students—the dominant mode of classroom work.

In *student-centered teaching*, the teacher creates conditions to engage students in learning, interesting them in a curriculum that is problem oriented. Here the teacher becomes more of an orchestrator or artist, giving up some authority and control to gain student interest and involvement.[12] Teachers spend more time planning for student engagement with a variety of materials, some or all of it the students' choice. Learning is far more individualized, yet group oriented. Student needs are not predetermined, but rather serve as a basis for the continuous organization of what goes on in the classroom. The progressive movement and its contemporary advocates best exemplify this view.[13]

Moreover, these differences in how teachers teach and how students participate in learning have formed the basis for educational reform movements in this century that have themselves been linked to broad social movements. In the present, as the pendulum seems to be swinging back from teacher-directed to student-centered classrooms in the attempt to find the "one best way" of teaching, it is still necessary to look at teaching and teachers within a larger social and historical framework. Teaching is affected not only by what the teacher does, but by the context within which teaching takes place: the kinds of students, the content of the curriculum, and political and social forces within as well as surrounding the school. As this and subsequent chapters will show, teachers are powerfully affected by changes in context, both in their ability to be successful with students and in their own feelings of adequacy. Therefore reforms to ameliorate changed conditions must be seen as not only a set of abstract ideals, but as living ideas that must be flexible and strong enough to survive the conflicting demands placed on teachers, while enabling them to deal successfully with those demands within the context of the school organization.

Further, new research on cognition must be considered when issues of teacher or student centeredness within the changing social context are raised. Perhaps this old dichotomy is inappropriate for understanding ways to deal with the new learning tasks that we are confronting today. If we need more people able to solve the problems of an increasingly complex technological society, then we need to think about learning not simply as consumption of preexisting knowledge but also as the production of knowledge. If higher-order thinking and team work is what a postindustrial society demands, then to achieve these goals we must focus on how students learn, which may help change the way we think about teaching and learning and the organization of schools.

In her exploration of the differences between in-school and out-of-school learning, Resnick examines the dramatic differences between students' work in schools (usually individual performance) and out-of-school performance and out-of-school work (often socially shared). In school, students engage in thinking that is often symbolic, while out-of-school work occurs with objects and within particular contexts and situations. "Schooling aims to teach general skills and knowledge, whereas situation-specific competencies dominate outside."[14] These differences were as dramatic in Dewey's day, and they were the foundation of his call to make schoolwork more closely resemble "real life." Moreover, his call for creating schools and classrooms that are life rather than preparation for life, and his focus on active engagement of students, seems very much in keeping with the contemporary view of student learning that sees it as taking place in the context of the realities of social and economic conditions. But it is not only student learning that has to be understood in these ways. Indeed, how much do we understand about teachers and how *they* learn?

The Professional Development of Teachers: Some Enduring Assumptions

It is a little known fact that "staff development" (or the more recent term, "professional development") is a young idea. It was not until the 1970s that staff development and the ways in which teachers actually transform new ideas into usable practices became an area of study.[15] Early descriptions of staff development reveal that teachers upgraded their content, skills, and abilities by going to teacher institutes where, often in audiences of hundreds or more, they were lectured to by experts. The institutes were an efficient means to "teach" large numbers of teachers new methods or new curricular ideas, but no one questioned whether that "teaching" was effective.[16] Taking another approach, some educators experimented with the idea of "action research," in which teachers' own classrooms or school problems became the object of study, with teachers and academics working together. These two forms, teacher institutes (which assumed that teachers could be taught by lecture to use new methods) and action research (which projected teachers' active involvement in their professional problems) indicate two extremes stemming from entirely different sets of assumptions about how teachers learn and improve their practices. These assumptions continue to dominate the descriptions and the practice of staff development in the 1990s. Teachers' learning, complicated as it is by differing context issues and the particular styles of learning of individual teachers, is still not well understood. Even when new methods, including intense classroom modeling of and continuous support for innovative practices, have been evident, teachers' learning of new methods for working with students has been problematic.[17]

The changed social context and its demands on teachers, as well as the reexamination of assumptions about how teachers teach and learn, confront schools with critical choices that are both old and new: old, in that it has long been the view that curriculum coverage, by a combination of textbooks and lecture by the teacher, is the only appropriate way for students to learn; and new, at least since Dewey, in the view that students must be actively engaged in their own learning. "Teacher-centered" schools have been predominant because texts, lectures, and worksheets can "teach" masses of students, although it is difficult to deal with individual differences among students. Child-centered schools make heavy demands on teachers' time, judgments, knowledge, and skill in conducting classrooms because there is more project work, more research by students, and more individual and group engagement. School work is more fluid, more flexible, less dependent on the text, and often demands more resources. While teacher-centered classrooms and schools trust the system as the ultimate arbiter, child-centered classrooms trust the teacher as the final authority.[18] It should come as no surprise then that part of the changing context is a growing move to professionalize teaching further by making demands on teachers to know more, to be heavily engaged in curriculum making and instructional decisions in the school, and to be more involved in reshaping the school to focus on students.

A New Synthesis: Changed Conditions for Students and Teachers

A growing body of research into new practices is helping us to understand that schools must develop collaborative, inquiring workplace environments for teachers at the same time that they are being developed for students. Many teachers involved in restructuring schools recognize the connection between their own development and the development of the students they teach; between their increased role in decision making and providing more choices for their students. Perhaps this obvious, yet elusive idea, provides the conceptual framework for the current reform movement.

Structural changes, in some cases, have taken the form of school site committees where teachers, principals, parents (and sometimes community-based organizations) learn to work together to define the larger visions and focus of their work, as well as to plan and implement programmatic changes that focus on the particular needs of their students. For teachers, working together in whatever form is in itself a radical departure from the usual isolated working conditions of most teachers. Current research on collegiality and the building of professional community among teachers reveals the critical importance of changing from school cultures where teachers work in isolation to those in which teachers work collaboratively. The changes in the structures of school governance form surprising parallels with those changes in classroom structure that involve students in cooperative learning groups, interdisciplinary studies, and the integrated curriculum, which reflect the recent theoretical and practical work of cognitive psychologists, learning theorists, and curriculum developers alike. How this happens for both students and teachers, the forms change takes, the barriers that are in the way, and most importantly, the powerful effects on student learning and engagement, represent a whole new line of research and practice.

New roles and relationships among teachers that exemplify collaboration, colleagueship, and inquiry into teaching and learning practices and encourage informal and formal leadership within faculties are in exploratory stages. In fact, leadership, as a set of functions to be carried out solely by a principal, is itself being held up to scrutiny. Is it possible to transform leadership roles? What responsibilities can be shared by teachers? What alternative forms and structures might transform schools into more "learner-centered" cultures? Given the paucity of understanding of how teachers learn, can professional development be reconceptualized? Is it only a set of ideas to be packaged and delivered, or can it be an integral part of school life involving school staffs in working on and working through the ongoing problems of teaching and learning? If variability of schools is the norm, what will be the role of "model schools" for the twenty-first century?

Over the years, schools have shown themselves to be resistant to political forces pressing for change. Reform movements have come and gone, shifting their focus from the child to the curriculum to the "betterment of society." But in this era the changing context of teaching must be seen within a larger transformation of society that is producing vast changes in social, political, economic, and educational thought. The impetus for change is coming from all levels of the policy community and it is beginning to have effects on schools, teachers, and students. As the following chapters show, the changes are complex, the pressures are great, and the effects on teaching and learning are potentially profound.

Notes

1. National Commission on Excellence in Education, *A Nation at Risk* (Washington, DC: U.S. Department of Education, 1983).

2. Carnegie Forum on Education and the Economy, *A Nation Prepared: Teachers for the 21st Century* (New York: Carnegie Forum on Education and the Economy, 1986); Holmes Group, *Tomorrow's Teachers* (E. Lansing, MI: Holmes Group, 1986).

3. David Tyack, "Restructuring in Historical Perspective: Tinkering toward Utopia," *Teachers College Record* 92, no. 2 (Winter 1990): 184.

4. Milbrey McLaughlin, "Learning from Experience: Lessons from Policy Implementation," *Educational Evaluation and Policy Analysis* 9 (Summer 1987): 173.

5. Milbrey McLaughlin, "Test-based Accountability as a Reform Strategy," *Phi Delta Kappan* 73 (November 1991): 248-251.

6. Suzanne Daley, "Born on Crack and Coping with Kindergarten," *New York Times*, 7 February 1991, p. 24D.

7. Michael S. Knapp and Patrick M. Shields, "Reconceiving Academic Instruction for Children of Poverty," *Phi Delta Kappan* 71, no. 10 (1990): 753.

8. Ibid.

9. James Comer, "Educating Poor Minority Children," *Scientific American* 259, no. 5 (1988): 46.

10. Philip W. Jackson, *The Practice of Teaching* (New York: Teachers College Press, 1986).

11. Ibid., p. 119.

12. Ibid. See also, Eliot Wigginton, *Sometimes a Shining Moment: The Foxfire Experience* (New York: Doubleday, 1985).

13. Kathe Jervis and Carol Montag, eds., *Progressive Education for the 1990s: Transforming Practice* (New York: Teachers College Press, 1991).

14. Lauren Resnick, "Learning In School and Out," *Educational Researcher* 16, no. 9 (1987): 16.

15. For an extended discussion, see Ann Lieberman and Lynne Miller, eds., *Staff Development: New Demands, New Realities* (New York: New Perspectives, 1978).

16. See Ann Lieberman and Lynne Miller, "The Professional Development of Teachers," in *Encyclopedia of Educational Research* (New York: Macmillan, forthcoming) for a historical and contemporary view of staff development (the deficit mode and the teacher involvement mode).

17. See Ralph Fletcher, *Walking Trees* (Portsmouth, NH: Heinemann, 1991).

18. McLaughlin, "Test-based Accountability as a Reform Strategy."

Section One
THE CHANGING POLICY CONTEXT OF TEACHING

CHAPTER II

*Reframing Accountability:
Creating Learner-Centered Schools*

LINDA DARLING-HAMMOND AND JON SNYDER

In this chapter we argue that major changes in American society are producing a radically different mission for schools—a mission requiring new conceptions of accountability tied to new roles for teachers. Social requirements are pressing for forms of schooling and teaching that will ensure high levels of student learning for all rather than the traditional school outcomes of success for some and failure for many others. This means that schools must find ways to reach diverse learners effectively rather than being accountable merely for "offering education" or "delivering instruction" regardless of the outcomes.

At the crux of this new school mission is a changed conception of teaching. In a learner-centered view of schooling, the teacher is responsible not merely for "covering the curriculum" but for connecting with students in ways that actively help them to construct and use their own knowledge. If all students are to learn well, teachers must be able to meet them on their own terms, at their own starting points, and with a wide range of strategies to support their success.

These conceptions, in turn, point to new approaches for developing and maintaining school accountability. In contrast to the bureaucratic mechanisms promulgated over many decades to enforce

---

Linda Darling-Hammond is Professor of Education and Co-Director of the National Center for Restructuring Education, Schools, and Teaching at Teachers College, Columbia University. Jon Snyder is Associate Director for Research at that Center.

standardization, the challenge is to create accountability mechanisms that will support the nonstandardized, individually appropriate teaching strategies needed to produce success for diverse learners. In lieu of hierarchical decision making resting on routinized conceptions of teaching and learning, accountability will need to be based on a greatly enriched capacity for knowledgeable and responsible decision making on the part of teachers. This chapter explores the possibilities for a learner-centered conception of accountability grounded in a strengthened profession of teaching.

The Social Context for a New Mission for Schooling

The 1980s launched the most sustained and far-reaching set of efforts to "reform" American elementary and secondary education since the formation of the common school nearly a century earlier. Spurred by massive changes in the nation's economy and social fabric, these initiatives have involved alliances between chief executive officers of major U.S. corporations, the heads of teachers' unions, state governors, and progressive educators in a variety of roles.

The sense of reformers is that American public schools designed for the needs of the nineteenth century will not meet the demands of the twenty-first. Their sense of urgency comes from the convergence of a number of trends which are changing society in profound ways. In brief, these trends include:

• A rapidly changing industrial base, and the prospective loss of U.S. economic dominance in international markets;

• Major demographic shifts, including a substantial growth in the population over age 65—a population that will need to be supported by a shrinking number of young people entering the work force, more of whom are—and will increasingly be—the children of immigrants, poor families, and minorities;

• Continuing underperformance of the educational system for these same young people, who by the end of the 1990s will comprise 40 percent of the public school population and over a third of the entering workforce;

• Disappointing outcomes for the educational system more generally. (For example, the U.S. scores near the very bottom of all industrialized countries on international assessments of students' knowledge of mathematics and science. National assessments continue to show declines in students' problem-solving skills and critical thinking abilities. Dropout rates, which continue to hover at 25 percent for all U.S. students, reach 50 percent for minority youth in central cities, for whom unemployment rates remain almost that high as well.)

These concerns occur against a backdrop of dramatic economic shifts as our society moves from a manufacturing economy to a technologically based information economy. Whereas in 1900 about half the nation's jobs required low or unskilled labor, today fewer than 10 percent do. And while fewer than 10 percent of jobs at the beginning of the century were professional or technical jobs requiring higher education, more than half of the new jobs created in this decade will require education beyond high school; 90 percent will require at least a high school education.[1] The technological explosion has hastened new methods of organization for business and industry which demand better educated, more thoughtful workers for virtually all kinds of jobs.[2]

Thus, the life chances of students whom schools have failed grow increasingly dim. A male high school dropout in 1986, for example, had only one chance in three of being employed full-time—half the odds of twenty years earlier. If employed, he earned only half of what a high school dropout earned in 1973.[3] Lack of education is also linked to crime and delinquency. More than half the adult prison population is functionally illiterate, and nearly 40 percent of adjudicated juvenile delinquents have treatable learning disabilities that were not diagnosed in the schools.

In addition, the United States is entering a period of labor shortage, while the number of older Americans is growing. In the 1950s the ratio of active workers to social security beneficiaries was 10 to 1. Soon that ratio will be 3 to 1. If one-third of those three are "unemployable," not only will we have a growing class of permanently impoverished Americans, but the social contract that supports the promises to older generations of Americans will collapse.[4] In brief, there is a growing consensus that the United States cannot maintain its democratic foundations or its standard of living unless all students are much better educated. Students who have traditionally been allowed to fail must be helped to succeed; many more must become not just minimally schooled but highly proficient and inventive. This consensus creates a new mission for schools and teachers and entirely new approaches to accountability.

Creating Accountability for Students' Learning

Ideas about how to achieve accountability are in a state of flux. In recent years, the term "accountability" has been used nearly synonymously with mandates for student testing and standard setting. The idea of many legislated accountability initiatives is to bring rapid order to the educational system by setting high goals and making students, teachers, and administrators responsible for meeting them.

We argue, however, that accountability requires much more than measuring narrowly defined student outcomes. An accountability system is a set of commitments, policies, and practices that are designed to create responsible and responsive education. Each aspect of an accountable school's operations should aim to (a) heighten the probability that good practices will occur for students; (b) reduce the likelihood that harmful practices will occur; and (c) provide internal self-correctives in the system to identify, diagnose, and change courses of action that are harmful or ineffective.

Accountability is achieved when a school system's policies and operating practices work both to provide a nurturing and educational school experience and to address problems as they occur. Assessment data are helpful in this regard to the extent that they provide relevant, valid, timely, and useful information about how individual students are doing and how schools are serving them. But this kind of data is only one small element of a fully functioning accountability system.

Accountability encompasses how a school or school system hires, evaluates, and supports its staff, how it relates to students and parents, how it manages its daily affairs, how it makes decisions, how it ensures that the best available knowledge will be acquired and used, how it generates new knowledge, how it evaluates its own functioning as well as students' progress, how it tackles problems, and how it provides incentives for continual improvement.

Accountable schools establish policies and practices in all of these areas that are likely to produce responsible and responsive education for their students. Their accountability systems enable them to set goals or standards and to diagnose how they are doing; they establish processes by which these standards are likely to be achieved or maintained; and they include ways of correcting problems when they arise.

Types of Educational Accountability

In education, as in other enterprises in our society, at least five types of accountability mechanisms exist alongside each other:

- *political accountability*. Legislators and school board members, for example, must regularly stand for election.
- *legal accountability*. Citizens can ask the courts to hear complaints about the public schools' violation of laws, say, regarding desegregation or provision of appropriate services to a handicapped student.
- *bureaucratic accountability*. District and state education offices promulgate rules and regulations intended to ensure that school activities meet standards and follow set procedures.
- *professional accountability*. Teachers and other school staff must acquire specialized knowledge, pass certification exams, and uphold professional standards of practice.
- *market accountability*. Parents and students may choose the courses or schools they believe are most appropriate. They may also be involved in other more direct means of participating in school decision making.

All these accountability mechanisms have their strengths and weaknesses, and each is more or less appropriate for certain goals. Political mechanisms can help establish general policy directions, but they do not allow citizens to judge each decision by elected officials and they do not necessarily secure the rights of minorities. Legal mechanisms are useful in establishing and defending rights, but not everything is subject to court action and not all citizens have ready access to the courts.

Bureaucratic mechanisms are appropriate when standard procedures will produce desired outcomes, but they can be counterproductive when, as in the case of schools, clients have different needs. Professional mechanisms are important when, as in teaching, services require complex knowledge and decision making to meet clients' individual needs. However, these mechanisms do not always take competing public goals (e.g., cost containment) into account. Market mechanisms are helpful when consumer preferences vary widely and the state has no direct interest in controlling choice, but they do not ensure that all citizens will have access to services of the same quality.

Because of these limits, no single form of accountability operates alone in any major area of public life. The choice of accountability tools and the balance among different forms of accountability are constantly shifting as problems emerge, as social goals change, and as new circumstances arise. In education, the power of political accountability, exemplified in the authority of school boards, has waxed and waned over the past twenty years in relation to that of appointed officials. In the same period, legal forms of accountability have grown, as court cases have been used to settle educational policy; and bureaucratic forms of accountability have expanded through increased policymaking at the district and state levels.

Recently, market accountability, the least used form, has been expanded somewhat through the creation of magnet schools or schools of choice. Finally, based on an expanding knowledge base and efforts to create more meaningful standards of practice, professional accountability is gaining currency as a way to improve teaching. Nevertheless, the use of bureaucratic and legal accountability mechanisms now outweighs all others—and some experts suggest that these two forms may have overextended their reach, now hindering the very aims they are designed to further.

Bureaucratic, professional, political, and market accountability tools are all currently being proposed as strategies for school improvement. The trade-offs and tensions among these approaches are part of the balancing act that must occur in striving for a better combination of methods to promote accountability. The key question is which combination of approaches is most likely actually to *strengthen* schools' and teachers' capacities to meet students' needs rather than merely measuring and monitoring what they do.

BUREAUCRATIC ACCOUNTABILITY

The intention of bureaucratic accountability is to ensure equal education through the development of uniform, standardized procedures. The view underlying this approach to school management is as follows: Schools are agents of government to be administered by hierarchical decision making. Policies are made at the top of the system and handed down to administrators who translate them into rules and procedures. Teachers follow these rules and procedures (class schedules, curriculum guides, textbooks, rules for promotion and assignment of students, etc.), and students are processed according to them.

Bureaucratic accountability offers the hope of finding the "one best system," codified by law and specified by regulations, by which all students may be educated. When applied directly to teaching practices, bureaucratic forms of accountability assume that (a) students are standardized so that they will respond in identical and predictable ways to the "treatments" devised by policymakers and their principal agents; (b) sufficient knowledge of which treatments to prescribe is both available and generalizable to all educational circumstances; (c) this knowledge can be translated into standardized rules for practice, which in turn can be maintained through regulatory and inspection systems; and (d) administrators and teachers can and will faithfully implement the prescriptions for practice.

The validity of these assumptions, though, is questionable. Research and the wisdom of practice have demonstrated that student diversity demands responsive, reciprocal teaching practices. In order for individual school children to be treated equally and appropriately, they must be treated differently in response to their talents, interests, experiences, and approaches to learning.[5] The bureaucratic strategy of using mandates and monitoring to insure standard practice has neither helped teachers meet the needs of diverse students nor has it attracted and held highly trained, talented, and committed teachers in the numbers required.[6]

In the bureaucratic model, teachers are held accountable for implementing curricular and testing policies, most often prescribed at the district and state levels, whether or not the prescriptions are appropriate in particular instances for particular students. Their own knowledge about learning theory and pedagogy may actually be a liability if it conflicts with these policies. In fact, current knowledge about learning suggests that this will frequently occur, since students learn in different ways and at different rates under different circumstances, and effective teaching strategies must be flexible, adaptive, and nonuniform to meet these needs.

However, the bureaucratic model does not seek to ensure that teachers are highly knowledgeable, since it presumes that many important decisions will be made by others in the hierarchy and handed down to teachers in packaged form. In this system, teachers cannot be held accountable for meeting the individual needs of their students; they can only be held accountable for following standard operating procedures.

In addition, the assumption that rules for practice can be enforced through regulatory and inspection systems leads to a massive investment in monitoring that, given the impossibility of its task, is an expensive exercise in futility. The increased use of bureaucratic accountability mechanisms has produced layer upon layer of "overseers" responsible not to children or families but to insuring that rules are followed. Throughout the last three decades, the rate of growth in administrative positions has far outstripped the rate of growth in the number of teachers employed by schools. By 1986, school districts in the United States employed approximately one administrative staff person for every 2.5 teachers and spent only 38 percent of their total budgets on teacher salaries.[7] Having produced a system in which one out of every two educational dollars is now spent outside the classroom, bureaucratic accountability tools have reduced investments in the actual activities of teaching and learning.

Another aspect of bureaucratic monitoring is the remote control of teaching through heavy emphasis on standardized test scores. Given the nature of tests currently used in the United States—primarily norm-referenced, multiple-choice basic skills tests—focusing on test scores as the primary outcome of schooling inhibits teaching aimed at higher-order skills and the development of genuine performance abilities.[8] Current tests are based on an outmoded theory that views learning as the accumulation of tiny bits of information, a view compatible with bureaucratic efforts to break tasks up into their smallest discrete parts as the basis for organizing work and learning. Bussis explains how early reading instruction, now aimed at the production of good scores on basic skills tests rather than the development of good readers, actually impedes students' efforts at learning to read:

Instructional programs in U.S. schools focus on "essential" reading skills; yet these skills have no demonstrable relationship to learning how to read books, and they impose definitions of reading and standards of reading progress that are contrary to common sense. . . . Presenting children with written language in piecemeal fashion . . . actually imposes formidable burdens on the learner.[9]

The end result can be that both teachers and students fail to develop the skills they need to engage in productive teaching and learning together. "Because multiple-choice testing leads to multiple-choice teaching, the methods that teachers have in their arsenal become reduced, and teaching work is deskilled. . . . Over time and with increased testing stakes, teaching becomes more testlike."[10]

In addition to missed opportunities for productive learning, this kind of monitoring system poses heavy costs in time and money. An estimated twenty million school days are spent each year by American students just taking tests.[11] Smith found in one state that one hundred hours per classroom were devoted to preparing for and recovering from state-mandated criterion-referenced tests.[12] The National Commission on Testing and Public Policy estimates that testing and related costs present taxpayers with a bill of nearly a half billion dollars annually.[13]

These costs might be justified if the use of the tests improved teaching and learning. Current evidence suggests they do not. Based on two decades of research, officials of the National Assessment of Educational Progress, the National Research Council, the National Council of Teachers of English, and the National Council of Teachers of Mathematics, among others, have all attributed the decline in students' performance on problem-solving and critical-thinking tasks to schools' overemphasis on multiple-choice tests of basic skills.[14] While offering certain superficial comforts, the current overreliance on bureaucratic forms of accountability appears to be imposing costs that are greater than the benefits secured for education.

PROFESSIONAL ACCOUNTABILITY

Professional accountability starts from assumptions very different from those of bureaucratic accountability. It assumes that, since decisions about different clients' needs are too complex and individualistic to be prescribed from afar, the work must be structured to ensure that practitioners will be able to make responsible decisions. It aims to ensure professional competence through rigorous preparation, certification, selection, and evaluation of practitioners, as well as continuous peer review. It requires that educators make decisions on the basis of the best available professional knowledge; it also requires that they pledge their first commitment to the welfare of the client. Thus, rather than encouraging teaching that is procedure-oriented and rule-based, professional accountability seeks to create practices that are *client-oriented* and *knowledge-based*.

In short, professional models propose to meet the obligation of accountability by ensuring that (a) all individuals permitted to practice are adequately prepared to do so responsibly; (b) existing knowledge concerning best practices will be used, and practitioners, individually and collectively, will continually seek to discover new knowledge and increasingly responsible courses of action; and (c) practitioners will pledge their first and primary commitment to the welfare of the client.

Professional accountability acknowledges that, since children are not standardized, it is unlikely that uniform prescriptions for practice can be effective across vastly differing contexts for learning. To treat each student differently yet equally is a challenging responsibility for the teacher. As Shulman states:

The teacher remains the key. The literature on effective schools is meaningless, debates over educational policy are moot, if the primary agents of instruction are incapable of performing their functions well. No microcomputer will replace them, no television system will clone and distribute them, no scripted lessons will direct and control them, no voucher system will bypass them.[15]

Since only teachers can manage the complex decisions of classroom life, they must be able to stay abreast of and apply their constantly expanding knowledge of how children learn while coping with the ethical dilemmas resulting from conflicts between legitimate educational goals. Ethics, knowledge, and the wisdom required to use knowledge ethically can be neither generated nor prescribed from afar.

Clearly, the quality of staff hired and retained is a key component of professional accountability. Rather than aiming to regulate practices, this model assumes that the most important thing parents and students have a right to expect from their schools is that the persons charged with the care of children will be highly knowledgeable, competent, and committed. Rather than investing in better regulations, professional accountability seeks to invest in better teachers, supporting their preparation and their ongoing professional growth. Thus, a professional accountability system must pay particular attention to personnel policies governing the preparation, hiring, and evaluation of teachers and other staff, the support given to their ongoing learning, and the assessment vehicles that exist for evaluating classroom and school practices as well as student progress.

To be successful, professional accountability requires (a) teacher preparation and socialization aimed at knowledgeable and ethical teaching, (b) the establishment and transmittal of standards for practice, and (c) school structures that provide for consultation and collaboration.

Preparation and socialization. For educators to make the intellectual and ethical decisions inherent in professional accountability, they must have the knowledge, skills, and attitudes that will support responsible decision making. They must also work under fewer rules about what is taught, when, and how, so that decisions can be made in response to students rather than in response to regulations.

This is the chicken-and-egg dilemma. Teachers cannot teach responsively unless regulations requiring uniform (hence frequently inappropriate) practices are removed. Regulations cannot be decreased unless teachers can be trusted to make responsible decisions. At the same time, knowledgeable and ethical individuals will not suddenly and magically populate all classrooms without changes in the policies and conditions that currently create an uneven teaching force.

Professional accountability will require changes in the attractions to teaching, so that a steady supply of talented recruits is available; in the standards for teacher licensure, so that they better reflect a knowledge base appropriate to learner-centered practice; in schools, in teacher education institutions, and in the nature of the relationship between the two, so that they provide and support the acquisition of skills and dispositions suited to student-centered, reflective teaching.[16]

The systematic and continuous improvement of the quality of education cannot occur until education becomes a progressive profession rather than a tradition-based craft. And education cannot become a progressive profession until those who prepare educators and those who practice in the field are bound by a common culture.[17]

The transmission and enforcement of professional norms of continual learning, reflection, and concern with the multiple effects of one's actions upon others "require a certain convergence of knowledge, view, and purpose among those who set and enforce standards, those who train practitioners, and those who practice."[18] Within a professional accountability framework, the preparation and socialization of teachers must become the responsibility of the educational establishment as a whole—including schools, universities, districts, and unions. Throughout the course of preservice preparation, induction into teaching, and ongoing professional development, teachers should be engaged in research, inquiry, and reflection as well as the acquisition of knowledge about learners and learning, curriculum, pedagogy, and teaching.[19]

Standards for practice. Professions seek to guarantee the competence of members in exchange for the freedom to control their own work structure and the responsibility to establish and uphold standards of practice. Professional autonomy does not establish a right to practice in any way one pleases. On the contrary, it commits members of a profession to practice in ways that are collectively determined to be safe and defensible.

The application of standards of practice rests on the appropriateness of particular approaches to the needs of students and the goals of instruction. Thus the exercise of professional standards of practice will often contradict the standardized practice required by some bureaucratic mechanisms. A professionally responsible teacher may decide that some or all of her students would be better taught using books other than a mandated text that is poorly constructed, at the wrong reading level, or biased in its depiction of certain racial, ethnic, or cultural groups. She may be aware that the learning styles of some of her students would be better addressed by one set of teaching methods or materials than another prescribed for general use. She would insist, in line with professional knowledge about assessment, that no decision about any student be made solely on the basis of a single test score or other standardized measure.

The potential benefit of professional accountability is a focus on the appropriateness of decisions for students' needs. The potential pitfall is that, if professional standards are not rigorously enforced for preparation and ongoing practice, educators' individually oriented decisions may become idiosyncratic rather than well-grounded in professional knowledge and ethics. Thus, the enforcement of standards through vehicles like peer review of practice and ongoing evaluation of individual and collective work are critical to the effectiveness of professional accountability strategies.

School structures for consultation and collaboration. Some aspects of professional accountability focus on the individual teacher. But without institutional changes in schools to support appropriate practices, such practices wither and the individuals thus prepared either succumb to environmental pressures or desert teaching as a career. Chief among required institutional changes are supports to insure that teachers have the skills needed to accept the responsibilities required by learner-centered practice and the collegial time needed to develop the shared norms and values that support professional practice and effective schooling.

A major aspect of school accountability is the effort to establish an inquiry ethic and a commitment to collective problem solving that will permeate the school. Such an ethos must be supported by methods for continually evaluating what is going on, asking not just *what* is occurring but also *why* it is happening and *whether* existing practices are accomplishing what the school community wants to accomplish. These questions should not be raised only once or twice a year, when the students are tested or the annual needs assessment form is filled out. They should be raised in every faculty and team meeting, on every occasion when faculty and students are striving to meet their goals, at every juncture when any kind of stock taking occurs.

In a few schools, this kind of collective questioning and reflection is frequent. In most schools, it rarely occurs. Teacher isolation has worked against collective accountability, while centralized planning, decision making, and evaluation have often removed occasions as well as incentives for this kind of activity at the school level.

Yet if schools are to become more responsive and open to change, they must find ways—as other professional organizations do—to make evaluation and assessment part of their everyday lives. Just as hospitals have standing committees of staff which meet regularly to discuss the effectiveness of various aspects of the hospital's functioning (surgery, pathology, epidemiology, etc.), so schools must have regularized occasions for examining their practices. And just as lawyers, doctors, psychologists, social workers, and other professionals use case conferences and other forms of consultation as opportunities to share knowledge and solve problems on behalf of their clients, so teachers must have opportunities to profit from their colleagues' knowledge and perspectives on behalf of their students.

School-level accountability requires both of these kinds of mechanisms. Mechanisms for peer review of practice establish regularized evaluation activities that create opportunities for using assessment data and other feedback to inform decision making. Consultation structures, such as staff reviews of individual students' progress or collective planning activities, provide a second kind of mechanism for accountability. Building institutional capacities for learner-centered teaching must include the creation of these opportunities for teachers to jointly plan and evaluate their work; to reflect together about the needs and progress of individual students and groups of students; and to share teaching ideas, strategies, and dilemmas for collective problem solving. Organizational supports for collegial work and learning are critical for the implementation of new educational practices.[20] Schools that want to support learner-centered practices must establish structures for ongoing consultation and collaboration among teachers and other school staff.

COMBINING ACCOUNTABILITY TOOLS TO ACHIEVE EQUITY AND PRODUCTIVITY

In deciding which aspects of education should be relegated to bureaucratic accountability and which to professional accountability, it is useful to distinguish between concerns for equity and for productivity. Equity issues generally must be resolved by higher units of governance, because they "arise out of the conflicting interests of majorities and minorities and of the powerful and powerless," and because local institutions are often captive to majoritarian politics and "intentionally and unintentionally discriminate."[21] Matters such as the allocation of resources and guarantees of equal access can and should be bureaucratically regulated and monitored.

On the other hand, productivity questions cannot be solved effectively by bureaucratic regulation, since at its best teaching knowledge is context- and content-specific. Thus, uniform policy decisions about teaching methods and school processes cannot meet the needs of varying school and student circumstances. Improving student and school achievement demands discretionary decisions safeguarded by professional accountability.

Wise and Gendler offer a specific example of the equity/productivity distinction.[22] When a state attends to equity by guaranteeing equality of financial resources, it encourages local initiative, equalizes the capacity of poor districts to secure a sufficient and highly qualified teaching force, and permits schools from poor districts to choose among curriculum and equipment options, just as wealthy districts do. When a state regulates outputs (a productivity concern) by mandating achievement outcomes defined by standardized tests, its "effort to produce equal education ends up degrading learning for all. Individuality, creativity, and depth are lost; all that is retained is uniformity, conventionality, and trivial skills."[23]

This argument suggests that state- and district-level bureaucratic accountability mechanisms are appropriate for the equitable allocation of resources, but not for defining educational processes or as a single standardized approach for measuring effectiveness. Yet some methods must exist to evaluate how well schools are meeting their obligation to provide a nurturing and educational school experience for all students. We present next a framework for approaching that task.

The growth of bureaucratic forms of accountability in recent decades has made it clear that top-down decision making cannot solve all problems, and that overregulation may actually undermine accountability in some ways. In addition to prescribing practices that are bound to be inappropriate for some students, hierarchical decision making often leaves no one accountable for results. When school-level staff are not responsible for making decisions, they also do not become responsible for finding solutions to school problems.

The fact that different needs and circumstances require different strategies has brought renewed attention to methods for lodging greater authority and responsibility at the school level. Two concepts currently receiving a great deal of attention are school choice, which aims to create more market accountability, and school-based management, which relies on greater political accountability. To be successful, both would require enhanced professional accountability.

Market mechanisms are intended to make schools more accountable in at least two ways: (a) by letting "customers" choose, schools are expected to work harder to provide services that parents or students want, and (b) by allowing choice, the market should reveal for policymakers that there are problems they need to address in those schools that are undersubscribed. For choice to produce better schooling for most children, however, it will have to be combined with methods to upgrade the quality of instruction in all schools so that they are worth choosing. Otherwise, market accountability will merely produce greater inequity rather than greater quality.

Other proposals, such as those for school restructuring and new forms of school management, suggest that responsiveness to clients could also be promoted through school structures for shared governance, accessible review and appeals processes, and parental involvement in decisions about their own children. Most school-based management proposals call for shared decision making among faculty, staff, parents, and students. They presume that better decisions will be made when those who are closest to the situation and who must live with the decisions are involved. Where parent and student participation are called for, these initiatives introduce a form of political accountability that is otherwise very weak in large, impersonal school systems. The greater authority vested in school faculties suggests that professional accountability mechanisms, which aim to ensure the competence and commitment of staff, should also be strengthened so that the authority will be well used.

As these new ideas are explored, each level of the system should assume its appropriate share of responsibility. *States* should be responsible for providing equal and adequate resources to schools and for ensuring the enforcement of equity standards and standards of professional certification. *School districts* should be accountable for the policies they adopt (including everything from standards for hiring staff to paperwork requirements), for equity in the distribution of school resources, and for creating processes that make them responsive to the needs and concerns of parents, students, and school-level staff. *Schools* should be accountable for equity in the internal distribution of resources, for adopting policies that reflect professional knowledge, for establishing means for continual staff learning, for creating processes for problem identification and for problem solving that drive continual improvements, and for responding to parent, student, and staff ideas. *Teachers* should be accountable for identifying and meeting the needs of individual students based on professional knowledge and standards of practice, for continually evaluating their own and their colleagues' practices, for seeking new knowledge, and continually revising their strategies to better meet the needs of students.

For the protection of children, it is most important to attend to the balancing of different accountability mechanisms as changes are sought. If schools are to rely less on hierarchical regulation to define school processes, then other forms of accountability must be strengthened to protect students' welfare. Greater guarantees of staff competence and commitment would accompany more stringent professional accountability mechanisms. Greater voice for parents and students would accompany more powerful political accountability mechanisms involving participatory decision making at the school-site. Greater incentives to attend to consumers' wishes might result from enhanced market accountability mechanisms involving school choice within the public sector. The key is to find the right mix of tools to provide support for school improvements that will encourage responsible and responsive education.

What Might a Learner-centered Accountability System Look Like?

Although there are widespread concerns that schools find better ways to attend to student learning, nonbureaucratic ideas about how to both stimulate and measure school improvement are still in their infancy. We have stressed that accountability involves much more than mandating school procedures and measuring the "outputs" of teaching. An accountability system uses a range of tools to create practices that are likely to be beneficial for students, to evaluate how well these practices are working, and to address problems as they occur. Among other things, an accountability system must attend to the following:

- how schools hire, support, and evaluate their staff;
- how teaching and learning are structured;
- how decisions are made about curriculum, student and teacher assignments, student responsibility and discipline;
- what mechanisms are established for communication among and between teachers, students, and parents; and
- what structures exist for continual inquiry and improvement.

The ways in which schools conduct their affairs in these matters will result in more or less responsible practices and greater or lesser responsiveness to the needs and views of students, parents, and staff. Accountability is achieved only if a school's policies and practices work both to provide an environment that is conducive to learner-centered practice and to identify and correct problems as they occur.

In this view, accountability is embedded in (a) school *policies*, the statements of commitments a school adopts arising from the values, goals, and norms it holds for itself; (b) the *structures* by which policies are pursued (e.g., methods of organization, consultation, and action that operationalize the commitment); and (c) the *processes* used to engage members of the school community in enacting their commitments in practice. To ensure that these are working as intended, accountable schools institute practices for *feedback and assessment*, *safeguards* to prevent students from "falling through the cracks," and *incentives* to encourage all members of the school community to focus continually on the needs of students and the improvement of practice. All these features of an accountable school should reflect the goals, norms, and values of the members of the school community, translating community desires into actions that make good on the rhetorical promises schools make to their publics. (See Figure 1.)

It is worth noting that much frustration with today's bureaucratically managed schools occurs because they frequently lack several of these elements which would allow them to make good on the rhetorical promises typically embodied in legislation or their local mission statements. While promising to attend to the learning needs of all children, schools often lack the structures and processes by which to identify those needs or address them in a concerted fashion. While hoping to support student success and prevent student failure, schools typically lack assessment tools that would give them usable information about students' abilities and performances. While intending to stimulate improvements, schools generally provide few incentives for the activities needed to motivate and sustain ongoing inquiry and change. As static institutions divided into egg-crate compartments among which little collective discourse about problems of practice occurs, bureaucratically managed schools lack an engine for accountability.

The ongoing interaction of these six elements (policies, structures, processes, feedback and assessment mechanisms, safeguards, and incentives) constitutes a model of a learner-centered accountability system. The concentric circles in the figure indicate that accountability cycles must exist for all significant educational players (e.g., students,

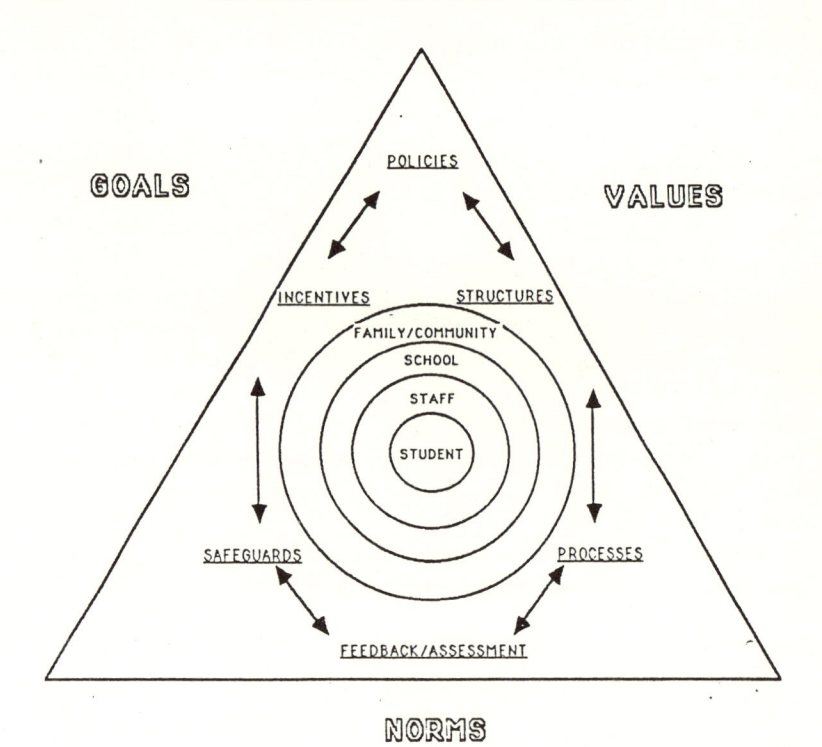

Fig. 1. A model of an accountability system.

staff, school, family, and larger community). This model suggests that learner-centered schools will hold themselves accountable for:

• relationships and voice in the school—e.g., governance, decision making, and communication mechanisms developed to ensure that important needs and issues are raised and addressed;

• school organization that helps to personalize relationships, ensure attention to student needs and problems, and bring coherence to teaching and learning;

• vehicles for staff interaction, shared inquiry, and continued learning which strengthen practice and create opportunities for continual evaluation and improvement of teaching (e.g., teacher evaluation, professional development opportunities, structures for consultation);

• forms of student assessment that reveal student strengths, talents, abilities, and performance capacities, including methods by which teachers observe and evaluate student growth along with formal exhibitions, performances, examinations, and portfolios;

• strategies to promote ongoing evaluation of school functioning utilizing input from parents, students, staff, and external reviewers.

A learner-centered system of accountability must acknowledge that the quality of measures used to evaluate student and school progress—and the ways in which these measures are used in decision making—have major effects on the quality of education itself. It will wrestle with important issues including who chooses what measures of educational achievement are to be used to assess students and schools, and whether the measures are valid and useful for the different purposes they may be asked to serve.

School accountability thus conceived requires numerous interconnected accountability cycles. We present now an example of one such accountability cycle currently in place in an inner-city elementary school that is succeeding with students where many others have failed.

AN EXAMPLE OF LEARNER-CENTERED ACCOUNTABILITY IN ACTION

The Brooklyn New School (BNS) in New York City's Community School District 15 has articulated its academic curricular commitment as the empowerment of students so that they are able to face the challenges and problems of life and can realistically say, "I can do it."

Structures and processes. The staff and parents at BNS have created and implemented many structures and processes to increase the probability that the school will meet its goals. In the general category of relationships and voice in the school, these include:

• collaborative governance of the school by a steering committee of parents, teachers, and the school director;

• a lottery admission system creating an equal ethnic mix of children in classrooms and parents on the steering committee;

• joint teacher/director participation in the selection of staff;

• decision by consensus (with the time and the training in the needed skills provided);

• an annual survey of parents regarding concerns, comments, and compliments;

• weekly school and classroom newsletters;

- twice yearly family conferences;

- extensive narrative report cards which include a rich, descriptive report from the teacher along with both the student's and parents' comments, concerns, and compliments;

- numerous classroom opportunities for guided student choice to operationalize students' dual needs for freedom and structure.

These strategies enact the school's goals of empowering students by ensuring voice and engagement of students and their families in aspects of classroom and school life ranging from information sharing to decision making and evaluation.

To support student learning within a personalized school organization, BNS has created and implemented a curriculum that is active, explorative, manipulative, and emphasizes critical comprehension. The curriculum as enacted is always built from a starting point of student strength and interest. The school also places students in classes where they spend two years with a teacher in a multiage grouping. This arrangement encourages and allows teachers to be more accountable for student learning as it permits them to come to know well the minds and needs of their students.

To encourage consultation and collaboration among staff and to enhance teacher learning, BNS has established a number of structures and processes that go far beyond the opportunities for discourse and reflection available in most schools. These include:

- weekly two-hour staff meetings structured to ensure active and equal participation by inviting each individual staff member to raise ideas or concerns in turn (e.g., rotating chair, jointly established and prioritized agenda);

- use of the "descriptive review" process[24] in which staff discuss the status and progress of an individual child with an eye toward identifying strengths and capabilities on which to build and environmental supports that might further nurture growth and development. This process is designed to meet the needs of "reviewed" children directly and the needs of all children indirectly by enhancing teacher observational skills and sensitivity to the unique abilities of each child;

- use of one weekly staff meeting each month for "staff development" (i.e., presentations by specialists in such topics as reading assessment, reporting to parents, language development, etc.).

- teacher evaluation based on weekly half-hour conferences between the director and each individual teacher;
- opportunities for peer coaching and counseling;
- close working relationships with local colleges (e.g., collaboratively planned professional development, placement of student teachers, and opportunities to attend seminars).

Together, these structures and processes provide an organization designed to focus on students' needs, which organizes teaching and learning in ways that support student growth and development, provides multiple occasions for communication and learning among staff, as well as between staff and parents, and continually encourages all members of the school community to reflect on how things are going, while empowering them to raise and pursue ideas for changes that might produce even better outcomes.

Feedback and assessment. BNS is not afraid of assessing itself or of having others evaluate its work. This past year, for instance, the staff not only undertook a year-long self study. They also utilized an evaluation facilitator from the central office as well as the services of a national research and documentation center to help them examine how they might strengthen their teaching practices as well as their capacity to hold themselves accountable. BNS constantly asks itself:

- How do we know how well we are achieving what we want?
- What happens at our school? With what effects upon whom?
- What approaches to assessment do—and can—we use to help us answer these questions?
- Are these approaches appropriately matched to our values and goals?
- Do these approaches give us information that helps us understand, explain, and improve upon what we do?

In seeking answers to these questions the BNS community uses as many and as wide a range of feedback tools as possible. Parents provide input on report cards, in family conferences, PTA meetings, and at steering committee meetings; student views are expressed in the student newspaper, in responses to report cards, and in interviews; teachers engage in self-study and in ongoing assessment conferences.

Similarly, in evaluating student performance, a wide range of tools are used in conscious and deliberate ways. For example, to gauge students' progress in reading, teachers use informal reading inventories to keep track of what and how students are reading; miscue analysis that provides information about how students are interacting with text; records of student book choices; a wide array of learning activities that themselves provide information about student capabilities—oral reading, written and oral book reports, art projects based upon books, research projects; interviews with parents about the child's literacy development at home; individual and group conferences with children about the books they read; student surveys conducted to create a summer reading list; student reading logs; and questions asked by students.

These varieties of student and school assessment tools inform the learning and problem-solving activities that occur in the settings described earlier: faculty meetings, descriptive review sessions, peer coaching activities, and other structures established to ensure ongoing attention to student needs and school improvement.

Safeguards and incentives. Many of the preceding structures, processes, and feedback mechanisms function as safeguards and incentives. The descriptive review, for instance, is a safeguard for those children who are nearing potentially critical moments of their school experience. It is also an incentive for teachers in that it promotes a rewarding sense of staff cameraderie as well as increased individual efficacy. In addition, the BNS staff "does something" with the data they gather. They refine and recreate safeguards and incentives to enhance the possibility that no student, teacher, or family slips through the cracks. Accepting that the primary goal of accountability is to take action to improve, BNS views change as a desirable programmatic and behavioral regularity in the school.

In the past two years alone, BNS has undertaken many activities aimed at enhancing feedback and strengthening accountability for student performance and well-being. Some of these activities have resulted in new structures and processes for maintaining the inquiry ethic that permeates the school. Among them are:

- a schoolwide curriculum development project that has helped clarify joint expectations for learning;
- individual and small group tutorials for students in need of extra help;
- hiring a reading specialist and a resource room teacher;
- conducting research comparing and contrasting teacher-generated reading data with reading data from standardized tests to provide a better understanding of what each is measuring;

- inclusion of parents in the staff retreat;
- conducting parent workshops on curriculum issues;
- revision of governance procedures;
- experimenting with the time, location, and function of parent committees to better support participation.

While all of these activities strengthen the safeguards in the accountability system, they also help to provide incentives for continued efforts toward maintaining a learner-centered school. Staff at BNS point to outcomes of these practices such as positive interactions with students and families, self-respect and the respect of others, freedom and responsibility, collegiality, and opportunities to share skills as motivating their efforts. In addition, staff value the networking opportunities they are afforded with like-minded schools and practitioners, along with professional development opportunities such as the Primary Language Record Project which, with the facilitation of external experts, is seeking to improve assessment skills and mechanisms for reporting to parents.

When described in this manner, an accountability system for a learner-centered school may seem like "pie in the sky." What human organization can be expected to do all these things? It is worth restating that BNS is not a hypothetical example. It is a real school operating under the kinds of adverse conditions that characterize many central-city schools. By the reports of school community members, the efforts to engage in responsible and responsive practice bear their own rewards.

Teachers do not leave the school, but rather enjoy "the permission to do what we know how to do." Parents from all socioeconomic levels report being pleased with how their children are developing, the relief of knowing that "my child is being treated with respect," and knowing "for the first time what and how my son is doing in school." The District 15 School Board, the Superintendent, and the district office, confronted by many plausible bureaucratic reasons for not supporting the school and surmounting considerable pressure from existing power structures, have recognized excellence at BNS by locating a larger physical site for the school. Most important, the students themselves are happy, secure, and learning:

"Whatever work you do the teacher explains."

"You can talk to the teachers when you have a problem."

"In the Brooklyn New School if you do something wrong, they sit you down and explain it to you."

"The school is much more together, like one family."

"BNS is the best school I ever went to. It helps you to do for yourself and makes it easier to get along with others."

Clearly, learner-centered accountability is possible, but that does not mean it is easy. Many changes in state and local policy along with school practices are needed to make schools like BNS one of many, rather than a rare oasis of enlivened learners in a desert of deadening bureaucracy. As we have discussed, both the profession of teaching and the schools within which teaching occurs must be restructured.

The many efforts of today's reformers offer reason for hope. On one front, organizations like the Holmes Group, the new National Board for Professional Teaching Standards, a growing group of state professional standards boards, accrediting agencies, and teacher education organizations are working to strengthen the profession. On another, restructuring efforts like the Coalition for Essential Schools, the Foxfire Project, Project Zero, James Comer's School Development Program, the Education Commission of the States' Re:Learning Project, and many others are working to build schools' capacities to focus on the needs of learners. On a variety of fronts, states like New York, California, Minnesota, and Connecticut are working to transform the governance and regulatory structures shaping school possibilities.

Perhaps in this era of school reform we will realize the "Copernican revolution" that John Dewey hoped for when he proclaimed the advent of a "new education" at the turn of the last century—an era in which all of the "appliances of the school will revolve around the child." One major stimulus for such a revolution will be the effort to establish learner-centered accountability systems at every level of educational governance and in every school.

Notes

1. Hudson Institute, *Workforce 2000: Work and Workers for the 21st Century* (Indianapolis, IN: Hudson Institute, 1987).

2. Peter F. Drucker, *The Frontiers of Management* (New York: Harper and Row, 1986).

3. Commission on Youth and America's Future, *The Forgotten Half: Non-College-Bound Youth in America* (Washington, DC: William T. Grant Foundation, 1988).

4. Linda Darling-Hammond, "Accountability for Professional Practice," *Teachers College Record* 91 (Fall 1989): 59-80.

5. Kenneth Sirotnik and John I. Goodlad, eds., *School University Partnerships in Action: Concepts, Cases, and Concerns* (New York: Teachers College Press, 1988); Gary Sykes, "Public Policy and the Problem of Teacher Quality: The Need for Screens and Magnets," in *Handbook of Teaching and Policy*, edited by Lee Shulman and Gary Sykes (New York: Longman, 1983), pp. 97-125; Phillip Schlechty, "Inventing Schools" (Presentation at the 1989 MSSC Spring Conference, Riverdale, NY, 1989); Darling-Hammond, "Accountability for Professional Practice"; Rensis Likert and Jane G. Likert, *New Ways of Managing Conflict* (New York: McGraw-Hill, 1976); Lee Shulman, "Autonomy and Obligation: The Remote Control of Teaching," in *Handbook of Teaching and Policy*, edited by Lee Shulman and Gary Sykes (New York: Longman, 1983), pp. 484-504; Holmes Group, *Tomorrow's Teachers: A Report of the Holmes Group* (East Lansing, MI: Holmes Group, 1986); idem, *Tomorrow's Schools: Principles for the Design of Professional Development Schools* (East Lansing, MI: Holmes Group, 1990); Donna Kerr, "Teaching Competence and Teacher Education in the United States," in *Handbook of Teaching and Policy*, edited by Lee Shulman and Gary Sykes (New York: Longman, 1983); Arthur E. Wise and Linda Darling-Hammond, *Licensing Teachers: Design for a Teaching Profession* (Santa Monica, CA: Rand Corporation, 1987).

6. Lee Shulman, "Autonomy and Obligation"; Kerr, "Teaching Competence and Teacher Education in the United States"; Linda McNeil, *Contradictions of Control: School Structure and Social Knowledge* (New York: Routledge and Kegan Paul, 1986); Linda Darling-Hammond, "Valuing Teachers: The Making of a Profession," *Teachers College Record* 87, no. 2 (1986): 205-18; idem, "Achieving Our Goals: Superficial or Structural Reforms?" *Phi Delta Kappan* 72, no. 4 (1990): 286-295; Karen K. Zumwalt, "Are We Improving or Undermining Teaching?" in *Critical Issues in Curriculum*, edited by Laurel N. Tanner, Eighty-seventh Yearbook of the National Society for the Study of Education, Part 1 (Chicago: University of Chicago Press, 1988), pp. 148-174; Carl D. Glickman, "Pushing School Reform to a New Edge: The Seven Ironies of School Empowerment," *Phi Delta Kappan* 72, no. 1 (1990): 68-75.

7. Darling-Hammond, "Achieving Our Goals."

8. National Research Council, *Ability Testing: Uses, Consequences, and Controversies*, edited by Alexandra K. Wigdor and Wendell R. Garner (Washington, DC: National Academy Press, 1982); Lauren B. Resnick, *Education and Learning to Think* (Washington, DC: National Academy Press, 1987); Daniel Koretz, "Arriving in Lake Wobegon: Are Standardized Tests Exaggerating Achievement and Distorting Instruction?" *American Educator* 12, no. 2 (1988): 8-15, 46-52; Ernest Boyer, *High School* (New York: Harper and Row, 1983); John I. Goodlad, *A Place Called School: Prospects for the Future* (New York: McGraw-Hill, 1984); Linda Darling-Hammond and Arthur E. Wise, "Beyond Standardization: State Standards and School Improvement," *Elementary School Journal* 85, no. 3 (1985): 315-336.

9. Anne M. Bussis, "Burn It at the Casket: Research, Reading Instruction, and Children's Learning of the First R," *Phi Delta Kappan* 64 (December 1982): 239.

10. May Lee Smith, "Put to the Test: The Effects of External Testing on Teachers," *Educational Researcher* 20, no. 5 (1991): 10.

11. Scott G. Paris, Theresa A. Lawton, Julianne C. Turner, and Jodie L. Roth, "A Developmental Perspective on Standardized Testing," *Educational Researcher* 20, no. 5 (1991): 15-20.

12. Smith, "Put to the Test."

13. National Commission on Testing and Public Policy, *Reforming Assessment: From Gatekeepers to Gateway to Education* (Chestnut Hill, MA: Boston College, 1990).

14. Linda Darling-Hammond, "The Implications of Testing Policy for Educational Quality and Equality," *Phi Delta Kappan*, in press.

15. Lee Shulman, "Autonomy and Obligation," p. 504.

16. Martin Haberman, "Twenty-three Reasons Universities Can't Educate Teachers," *Journal of Teacher Education* 22, no. 2 (1971): 133-141; Wynn De Bevoise, "Collaboration: Some Principles of Bridgework," *Educational Leadership* 43, no. 5 (1986): 9-12; Linda Darling-Hammond, "Policy and Professionalism," in *Building a Professional Culture in Schools*, edited by Ann Lieberman (New York: Teachers College Press, 1988), pp. 55-77.

17. Phillip C. Schlechty and Betty Lou Whitford, "Shared Problems and Shared Vision: Organic Collaboration," in *School-University Partnerships in Action: Concepts, Cases, and Concerns*, edited by Kenneth Sirotnik and John I. Goodlad (New York: Teachers College Press, 1988).

18. Darling-Hammond, "Policy and Professionalism," p. 68.

19. Holmes Group, *Tomorrow's Teachers*; idem, *Tomorrow's Schools*; John I. Goodlad, "School-University Partnerships for Educational Renewal: Rationale and Concepts," in *School-University Partnerships in Action: Cases, Concepts, and Concerns*, edited by Kenneth Sirotnik and John I. Goodlad (New York: Teachers College Press, 1988).

20. Michael Fullan and Alan Pomfret, "Research on Curriculum and Instruction Implementation," *Review of Educational Research* 47, no. 2 (1977): 335-397; Judith Warren Little, "Norms of Collegiality and Experimentation: Workplace Conditions of School Success," *American Educational Research Journal* 19, no. 3 (1982): 325-340; Thomas Timar and David L. Kirp, "State Efforts to Reform Schools: Treading between a Regulatory Swamp and an English Garden," *Educational Evaluation and Policy Analysis* 10, no. 2 (1988): 75-88.

21. Arthur E. Wise, *Legislated Learning: The Bureaucratization of the American Classroom* (Berkeley, CA: University of California Press, 1979), p. 206.

22. Arthur E. Wise and Tamar Gendler, "Rich Schools, Poor Schools: The Persistence of Unequal Education," *College Board Review*, no. 151 (Spring 1989): 12-17, 36-37.

23. Ibid., p. 36.

24. Patricia Carini, *The Prospect Center Documentary Processes: In Progress* (Bennington, VT: Prospect Archive and Center for Education and Research, 1986).

CHAPTER III

Teacher Empowerment and Professional Knowledge

GARY LICHTENSTEIN, MILBREY W. MCLAUGHLIN, AND JENNIFER KNUDSEN

"Teacher empowerment" became a catchphrase in the late 1980s. At that time, policy analysts began to worry that the ambitious reforms they conceived during the decade would come to little if teachers' classroom practices were ineffective. Policymakers acknowledged that successful outcomes of more courses, longer school days, tougher graduation standards, or "back-to-basics" curricula all hinged on the attitudes and capacities of classroom teachers implementing those reforms.

Two general strategies were advanced to attack the "teacher problem." One strategy involved raising standards for individuals entering the profession. This response targeted teacher licensure, including programs for preparation and certification. The second strategy focused on ways to enhance the status and practices of teaching professionals. Doing so, it was reasoned, would reshape teachers' conception of their own role in a way that would boost morale, generate intrinsic and extrinsic incentives to improve their job performance, and increase professional autonomy. It was out of the debates about this latter strategy that notions of teacher empowerment emerged.

Proponents of teacher professionalization cited a backbreaking educational bureaucracy as a critical impediment to the success of reform efforts.[1] Many analysts and reformers claimed that a top-heavy educational system constrained teachers' effectiveness by reducing or eliminating their professional discretion. In this view, the bureaucratic structures of the educational establishment restricted teachers' ability to operate according to their own professional notions of best practice.

Milbrey W. McLaughlin is Professor of Education and Director of the Center for Research on the Context of Secondary School Teaching at Stanford University. Gary Lichtenstein and Jennifer Knudsen are doctoral students at Stanford University.

Recognition of these constraints quickly shifted emphasis of public education reform from devising strategies of control and oversight to designing initiatives meant to empower teachers.[2] Reformers and practitioners alike embraced the concept of teacher empowerment as being fundamental to an enhanced sense of professionalism and, ultimately, to better teaching.

The concept of empowerment used most commonly in policy discussions derives from the literature on organizational management and on the sociology of work, and connotes alteration in the distribution of power in the workplace.[3] Central to talk about empowered teachers is enhanced control over decisions that affect the school workplace generally, and the classroom in particular. Most of these conversations highlight organizational arrangements for decision making and teachers' institutional authority. For example, Sara Lawrence Lightfoot defines empowerment in terms of the opportunities an individual has for "autonomy, responsibility, choice, and authority."[4] Or, Floretta Dukes McKenzie summarizes: "Empowering teachers most commonly appears to refer to 'allowing' classroom teachers to participate more directly in their schools' decision making."[5]

A conclusion many have drawn from the discussions of the 1980s is that empowerment is something *given* to teachers by shifting institutional lines of authority. And, at both local and state levels, restructuring schemes or site-based management strategies that allow classroom teachers direct influence over decisions have gained popularity as a promising means to improve the quality of classroom practice.[6]

With this authority-based, institutional conception of empowerment in mind, we set about to locate settings that had initiated strategies to empower teachers by changing their roles and responsibilities. We sought to understand the consequences of these new organizational arrangements for teachers' conceptions of their jobs and classroom practices.[7] Did reputedly empowered teachers indeed relish their new authority? Did they feel better about themselves and their professional life? Did the classroom of an empowered teacher look more effective—or at least different—from that of teachers operating under traditional institutional arrangements?

Our candidate sample comprised schools and districts in California that claimed to be restructured (or restructuring), or that expressed commitment to site-based management. We also searched the literature to find examples of new institutional arrangements and empowered teachers.[8] Despite the visibility of a few districts prominent in the school restructuring movement (Dade County, Florida, or Santa Fe, New Mexico, as examples), or individual schools operating in innovative and effective educational settings with teachers in charge (Central Park East in Harlem, most specifically), we found little to suggest that decentralization or enhanced teacher authority was necessarily or systematically associated with teacher empowerment, at least as conceived of by teachers themselves.

Instead, we observed and read about instances in which site-based authority resulted in little of consequence to the classroom. Rather than feeling empowered to exercise greater authority in their teaching, many teachers found their time bound up with committees wrestling with decisions about what color to make the curtain on the auditorium stage, or whether to spend $500 on a slide projector or bookcases. In some cases, we discovered that "restructuring" mandates provided weak school administrators an excuse to delegate significant responsibilities to teachers who then floundered because of insufficient orientation, resources, support, and expertise.[9] Further, we saw instances where efforts to expand teachers' authority without also attending to their capacity resulted in the ironic outcome of *diminished* performance of school, classroom, or system.

In short, we were not successful in locating consistently well-developed operating examples of "new roles and responsibilities" that made teachers feel empowered in terms of their pedagogy, practice, or their professional development. In part, this shortfall reflects the newness of these formal institutional reforms. The full effects of these structural reforms are yet to be realized. One district known nationally as a "restructuring district," for example, is still soliciting active school participation. Many schools in this district, officials readily admit, are restructured in name only. Other schools in the district that have implemented restructuring are still working out internal routines and processes. In another district, teachers entering the third year of restructuring continue to duplicate old materials orders and curricular plans because, they admit, they lack the expertise or time or support to change traditional routines. Our initial interviews, observations, and literature review led us to three general conclusions: (1) it is too early to tell how the many and diverse restructuring efforts will turn out, for they have yet to be fully implemented; (2) the success of structural reforms in any event depends fundamentally on the capacity of those teachers who have been given new roles and responsibilities, since even the best conceived plans turn on teachers' capability; and (3) knowledge is an elemental, irreducible aspect of teacher empowerment.

Consequently, after a year of examining structural, formal, and institution-based efforts to empower teachers, we shifted our research to look at knowledge-based reforms. This approach did indeed lead us to teachers who believe they are fundamentally empowered in principle and practice, whose attitudes about teaching are upbeat, hopeful, in many cases enthusiastic, and who believe that their practice represents a model of professionalism that ought to be widely developed. In addition, we saw that knowledge carries its own authority. We met teachers working in "unreconstructed" or "unrestructured" settings who reported that they were revitalized—professionally empowered—through access to professionally relevant knowledge. Our research led us to a conception of empowerment that expands upon authority-based definitions and that implies new approaches to empowering strategies.

This chapter elaborates this conception with the related goals of (1) presenting a view of teacher empowerment which recognizes the essential role of professional knowledge, and (2) redefining existing notions of what comprises "professional knowledge" for teachers. Our objective is not to disparage structural or authority-based reforms as such, but to argue that changed authority or institutional relations alone are likely to prove disappointing. Further, we aim to present a view of teachers' professional knowledge that extends beyond notions evident in staff development efforts or even in many knowledge-based empowerment strategies.

Rethinking Professional Knowledge

Expanding teachers' roles and responsibilities too often does nothing to enhance teachers' sense of power unless teachers feel capable of managing their new roles and responsibilities and have the time and support to work through the conflict that inevitably accompanies any real change. We have seen that capacity to manage expanded notions of teachers' roles and responsibilities resides in knowledge—knowledge relevant to professional practice.

Teacher knowledge includes knowledge of content and method, to be sure. But it also includes knowledge of policy systems, of professional organizations, and of a professional dialogue pertinent to teachers' work. We learned that the "knowledge" that empowers teachers is not the stuff of the weekend workshop or the after-school in-service session. The knowledge that empowers teachers to pursue their craft with confidence, enthusiasm, and authority is knowledge of the teaching profession, in the broadest possible sense.

We distilled the essential kinds of knowledge that empowered teachers possessed into three overlapping areas: (1) knowledge of professional community; (2) knowledge of education policy; and (3) knowledge of subject area. In the remainder of this chapter, we develop these aspects of teacher knowledge and their relationship to teacher empowerment. First, we briefly discuss the sample from which our conclusions were primarily drawn.

We conducted interviews with thirty members of the Los Angeles and San Francisco projects of the Urban Mathematics Collaborative (UMC). The UMC is a ten-year-old project seeded by the Ford Foundation and administered by the Educational Development Center in Boston. The UMC mission is to empower teachers by developing teacher networks that include professionals in industry and academia. The Los Angeles and San Francisco Collaboratives, which have been operating since 1985, are two of fourteen branches the UMC coordinates.

Each project is structured differently according to local preferences and imperatives. In Los Angeles, for example, the organization is called PLUS (Professional Links with Urban Schools) and includes from 400 to 500 participants from over fifty-two schools across the expansive Los Angeles area. PLUS runs a number of activities and programs. We studied secondary school teachers who participated in a program designed to implement changes in school curriculum and/or pedagogy. In order to be considered for membership, the mathematics department at a school must vote to participate, and school administrators must demonstrate support. Then, department faculty collaborate on writing a grant proposal that identifies a specific problem and approaches for solving it. PLUS staff help the department create the proposal, but an award is by no means guaranteed. Upon acceptance of the proposal, the department is given $2,500 to help implement changes they have proposed; more significantly, they become official members of an active professional network that operates throughout the city, state, and nation. In 1990, 375 teachers representing twenty-one mathematics departments participated in this facet of PLUS.

In San Francisco, 500 K-12 teachers have participated in Collaborative events in the past year. Events include workshops, speaker series, forums, and other activities. Our sample focused on high school mathematics teachers, fifty of whom could be considered active (there are approximately 180 throughout the district) in the sense that they attend more than one or two events per year. The Collaborative sponsors programs and activities in which individuals participate.

Our sample is a particular one in a number of respects. First, it is composed of secondary school teachers. The subject matter emphasis of the Collaborative may be the most appropriate means to hook secondary school teachers, but may function differently for elementary school teachers, who tend to be more interested in pedagogical ideas. Second, California's mathematics teachers are in the midst of implementing a new state-mandated curriculum; thus, teachers' interest in examining current practice and new ideas may be artificially high. Third, the teachers we interviewed were recommended to us by the Collaborative's program director, who chose them for their consistent involvement and support of the program's goals.

Obviously, this is a biased sample, representative of only a limited population, even among Collaborative members. However, in other respects, our respondents are "typical" teachers in the varied motivations, capacities, and points of view they brought to the Collaborative. This is not a sample composed entirely of "superstars" or of teachers teaching in especially supportive schools or departments. Indeed, our respondents believe firmly that their experience in the Collaborative provides the basis for constructing a generalizable model of teacher empowerment and important direction for policy. We concur.

Empowering through Knowledge

KNOWLEDGE OF PROFESSIONAL COMMUNITY

The isolation of the classroom teacher is a professional commonplace.[10] Breaching that isolation was tremendously important to teachers we interviewed. Each of the teachers with whom we spoke stressed the significance of the professional community they encountered through participation in the Urban Mathematics Collaborative. Teachers from a variety of settings and all levels of mathematics described new energy and confidence that they brought to their mathematics classrooms and departments as a result of meeting other teachers and learning about the many human resources and ideas available to them. Marsha McGregory's[11] comment about attending a

National Council of Teachers of Mathematics (NCTM) conference in Orlando is typical of many teachers' enthusiasm about becoming plugged into a professional network:

... I talked to people from Alaska, talked to people from the South, and I saw things from North Dakota. I mean, I didn't know anybody even lived in North Dakota! And there was someone there who was talking about doing these math things up in North Dakota and then they have this big presentation. I end up bringing that back to my classroom. I'm still excited about all this stuff I picked up there (BA014).

Marsha's comment reflects the value teachers feel in participating in such a network. They see their out-of-classroom experiences as essential for building their capacity to be effective in their classrooms and schools. One of Charles Sorensen's comments reiterates the value of networking with other teachers in order to improve classroom practice:

I know dozens of teachers now, across Los Angeles and Los Angeles County—in fact across the United States now.... And if I have a problem now with a particular curriculum concept, I can dial on the phone or on our computer network, and connect to fifteen teachers who could help me now, outside my own school (BA003).

Charles had been teaching for twenty-one years before becoming involved with PLUS. Like most teachers, he could have gone his entire career without making the professional contacts that the Mathematics Collaborative affords. Such professional affiliation is certainly helpful to these teachers for solving immediate classroom problems; having access to such a strong resource base is empowering. Professional communities such as those of the Urban Mathematics Collaborative give teachers access to knowledge they desire, when they need it; they no longer are at the mercy of district in-service efforts for professional growth and stimulation.

Beyond the immediate practical value of these networks, however, teachers reconceptualize their roles and responsibilities as a result of their new affiliations. Further, they do so in ways that enhance their identification with the profession. We identified two ways that knowledge of professional community empowers teachers. First, it helps them recognize their own expertise. Second, it expands teachers' notions of what is possible within their own practice and the profession as a whole.

Knowledge of professional community helps teachers recognize their expertise. Teachers' learning about their own competence bolsters their confidence in front of students and other professionals. Kirk Torrence provides a particularly striking example. An eighth-year teacher, he decided to teach geometry without the textbook, having students instead work in groups to create their own geometry. It was a daring experiment, one that daunted even him. He recalls how support from other teachers strengthened his resolve:

I was at PLUS with people like Brad Franklin (BA002), and [others]. Every time there was an event that had anything to do with PLUS, these guys would be there telling me how great the geometry class was and what good stuff was going on. . . . All these guys from PLUS thought [my class] was a great idea. . . . For me, PLUS just said—it was the kind of place which said— "Okay, go ahead and do that. And you don't have to hide it" (BA012).

Patricia Hudson discussed how her interactions at a workshop helped her realize that knowledge she took for granted might be valuable to other teachers. Patricia had been teaching for twenty-one years when she attended a week-long mathematics workshop at the University of California (Los Angeles) in 1984. She admits going only upon the insistence of her principal, who wanted to send another teacher but could not unless the teacher had a partner. One of the requirements of the program was to deliver a sample lesson. Much to her own horror, Patricia volunteered to go first. She had always dreaded such presentations and knew that putting it off would be agonizing. As Patricia relates the story, we get an insight into the beginning of a newfound confidence and reconceptualization of her professional role in training other teachers:

The rest of the class went out for lunch. I didn't because my presentation was due right after lunch, and I was getting all set up. I was literally shaking, my hands were shaking. But I did it, and they liked it. Some members of the class convinced me to speak at the Los Angeles County Math Association, the local math organization. Their conference is in February. And that went well. So then the CMC (California Math Council) asked me to speak, and I guess, and it was downhill from there! Now I spend half of my Saturdays working (BA017).

Once Patricia discovered she liked teaching teachers, she sought opportunities that expanded her professional role. Not all teachers experience a shift as observable as this. Harriet Rodriguez-Douglas describes how her professional affiliation solidified her identity as a teacher relating to administrators and business professionals:

> In times past, if the superintendent were to come into this office, I would have felt really intimidated by his presence and by his authority. I'm no longer intimidated, because I grant him his experience—he has knowledge that I don't have. But I have something he doesn't have. And so I'm willing to come into dialogue and to exchange with him ideas and concerns I have, knowing that I speak from a very strong base of experience and sensitivity to classroom teachers that he does not have. The Collaborative was my training ground for that. I was forced into speaking with CEOs and, I mean, all of a sudden at a dinner meeting, I was seated next to the superintendent of schools, and some vice-president from an international bank. . . . For the first time, I was expected to have something, you know, an idea to share. And I found I could and I found I did and I found I had experience and expertise (LP008).

Harriet, like others we interviewed, recognized that her expertise as a teacher distinguished her among other professionals. This awareness increased her confidence both in and out of the classroom. Nancy Bruckner's example shows how knowledge of professional community can enhance a teacher's sense of efficacy by highlighting the commonalities among teachers:

> Because we began to talk [with other teachers in the district], we began to recognize that we had similar experiences. Our needs might be different in certain areas, but overall—discussing the process of how you teach something, the materials that you use, where you get your resources from—that kind of cross-pollination is very productive. You don't feel like you're low man on the totem pole. That there are others that have similar experiences and as strong a belief in education as you have, and in that sense it does empower who you are (BA015).

For these teachers and others, notions of empowerment include knowledge of colleagues' practice. Such knowledge creates and reinforces camaraderie by providing a web of shared experience. But knowledge of what others are doing does more than make teachers feel good. Recognizing one's own expertise can bolster one's confidence before students, colleagues, and other professionals, thus enhancing self-esteem and beliefs in personal efficacy.

Knowledge of professional community expands teachers' notions of what is possible. Recognizing one's own expertise is valuable. However, identification with a professional community provides the basis for an even more significant benefit. Interaction with other professionals—in schools, businesses, and universities—shakes up static norms of pedagogy and practice. Almost all the teachers we interviewed related examples of how knowledge of others' practice expanded their beliefs about the possibilities within their own practice and within the profession. Discussing the results of a sabbatical year during which he taught on a university campus, Oliver Reed, in his twenty-third year of teaching, remarks:

... It was this contact with UCLA which sort of changed things for me and made me part of a larger picture. Perhaps a more interesting picture, certainly more dynamic. And made me more willing to think about, you know, changing the way I do things and so forth (BA016).

A number of teachers discussed coming to understand "the larger picture." Paradoxically, glimpsing the larger picture made dilemmas teachers faced seem more, rather than less, manageable. Teachers who felt validated in their expertise in the eyes of their colleagues also felt secure acknowledging what they did not know. Gail White exclaims, "I don't know where we got the idea that we're supposed to know all the answers!" (LP007). Recognizing their expertise encourages teachers to risk practices they might not otherwise attempt. Charles explains:

[Because of the community created through PLUS] we've become less afraid to share our failures. I think most teachers want to lessen [their responsibility]. They say [when a lesson fails] "Oh, those damn kids didn't pay any attention," or "It's the kids' fault." I think that [now] we're much more willing to say, "Well, how could I restructure . . . how can I get them to buy into what I want them to do?" (BA003).

Teachers like Charles Sorensen, who are in touch with a professional community that validates their expertise, stand on solid enough ground to risk change. Edward Thurrow summed it up well in answering the question, What difference does it make to be in PLUS?:

Hope . . . it's possible to change. You can keep on moving. I don't feel stagnant. I feel that it's frustrating, but it's possible to change (BA007).

Knowledge of others' practice reestablishes professional norms that cannot be imposed by nonpractitioners. By talking with and observing others, teachers develop expectations against which they evaluate their own practice. Patricia Hudson's comments yield some insight about heightened professional norms:

> When you're with a group of people like the PLUS people, and you go to the teachers' meetings and the council meetings, and they're all out there—you're in with a lot of people who are willing to try and put themselves on the line and give this thing a shot and try something new and something different. It makes you want to do more of that (BA017).

The safety, support, and stimulation provided by the Collaborative empowers teachers to extend themselves professionally because it validates their risk-taking. Teachers become less intimidated about experimenting in the classroom and in other professional arenas, because they can gauge whether the educational choices they make will be considered sound within their respectful, tolerant, yet critical professional community. Such knowledge bolsters teachers' confidence to engage other professionals, such as district administrators, university professors, or representatives from the business community. Involvement with a professional community enables teachers to acknowledge that the knowledge, experience, and wisdom they have is specific to teaching, and not only useful, but essential, for developing meaningful reform.

KNOWLEDGE OF EDUCATION POLICY

Participation in the Urban Mathematics Collaborative connects teachers to the broader policy system and makes them aware of the policy debates at district, state, and national levels. Teachers attend conferences, workshops, and speaker-evenings, as well as read trade journals and the Collaborative newsletter. These policy-related activities are new to most of them. And, as a result, teachers are alert to and participate in policy discussions within their schools and elsewhere. They also report feeling less "victimized" by policymakers, and better able to plan their classroom activities. As Lorraine Evans puts it:

> That's another thing PLUS is good about. It keeps us informed about what [policy] changes are taking place [on state and national levels]. Otherwise, the normal teacher doesn't get an opportunity to know what's happening (BA013).

Textbook selection is a major outcome of policy decisions. As a result, teachers in the Collaboratives were especially concerned about textbook selection, because it has such a great impact on their mathematics curriculum. Concerns about textbook choices were generated by these teachers' knowledge that National Council of Teachers of Mathematics standards are being adopted nationwide. Further, teachers keep a close eye on state curriculum guidelines, which also change. Teachers want to make sure that the textbooks they will have to choose from support the newest state and national policies and represent approaches that suit their pedagogical styles. Teachers' knowledge of curriculum policy at state and national levels prompts them to become actively involved in textbook selection. Darlene Jennings describes how teachers in one district rallied:

This year we really infiltrated the geometry textbook selection committee and exerted all the pressure we could to get PLUS teachers on the committee. And they adopted six books, which is more than they normally do, more variety. And two of them are very discovery-oriented, that have never been adopted before (BA005).

Nancy discusses how her knowledge of curriculum policy affects textbook selection at the school level and has given her new authority in conversations about instructional texts and materials:

When the [salesman] came today with this Scott Foresman geometry book, one of the teachers asked, "Well, have you done the matrix so we can see how much of the [state] framework is already there for us so we don't have to do it ourselves . . .?" And he is going to get his math researcher to call us back [with the matrix information]. Those are things we've learned. We've learned to use the experts better (BA015).

Those are two examples of how knowing about imminent changes in district and state policies has prompted teachers to act. But teachers are keenly aware of academic and political implications of curriculum policy within their own schools and districts—teacher and student course assignment policies being the prime example. The UMC has provided teachers the information and background to press for curriculum change within their own instructional settings. For example, Lorraine told us:

[When we know more,] we can demand more. . . . For instance, many of us across the district are very frustrated with the fact that they push us to put kids into Algebra 1, without the prerequisite skills. And [the students] flounder, and they fail. And the failure rate is going up. And [departments across the district] are attempting different things. Well, between the different experiments going on and PLUS, I think we'll have enough data within a year or so to prove to [district administrators] that there have to be changes made in policy (BA013).

The result of teachers' policy knowledge is empowerment—a sense of authority and a belief that they can make a difference. Charles underscores his new sense of authority based in this expertise:

[The district's] approach has always been, "We will decide what's wrong, we will decide the solutions and then we will tell you what to do." It's always been a top-down administration.... Now there seems to be a genuine effort to listen to what's happening down here [because we are informed] (BA003).

Knowledge of education policy empowers teachers because it provides access to the broader policy system of which they are a part. This access dispels their perceptions of teachers as "outsiders" and enables them to be proactive rather than reactive both in the classroom and in the broader policy arena. It permits them to make professional decisions based on awareness they have of curriculum issues both inside and outside the school. In this way, teachers' knowledge of curriculum policy works both up and down the system. Knowledge of curriculum policy filters down the system when teachers bring policy knowledge to bear on decisions affecting classroom practice. Curriculum knowledge works up the system when teachers bring their knowledge of classroom culture to discussions about curriculum policy at district, state, and national meetings.

KNOWLEDGE OF SUBJECT AREA

It seems a truism that knowing more about a subject should make it easier to teach that subject. Yet contradictory evidence exists in anecdotes about very good scholars who have great difficulty communicating what they know to students. The experiences of teachers participating in the UMC compels us to move beyond this limited and possibly tenuous connection between knowing and teaching a subject to develop a more complex view of the relationship between subject matter knowledge and teacher empowerment. We see that breadth and depth of disciplinary knowledge empowers teachers in three ways: (1) it provides the foundation of their authority and thus their professional discretion; (2) it can provide a basis for involvement in a professional community; and (3) disciplinary knowledge has direct relevance in policy decisions.

Strong disciplinary knowledge provides a foundation for authority and professional discretion. Knowing a subject well entails knowing information about many topics in the discipline, having an awareness of connections between those topics, and demonstrating facility in the methods and ways of thinking commonly used within the discipline. For teachers, it also includes knowing different approaches to teaching students about these topics, connections, and ways of thinking. In addition, teachers need to know how the subject might be used by students after they leave school, and what current technologies are available as teaching tools. All this knowledge becomes integrated as teachers learn their craft. This integrated picture becomes a "map" by which teachers are able to navigate their way through the maze of decisions they must make each day: what to emphasize in a particular lesson, how to help a student who is having trouble with a particular topic, what questions to ask to stimulate students to explore their developing notions further, or how to stimulate the obviously bright but perhaps bored student in the back of the room. Some other decisions that are guided by subject-matter knowledge are: which curricular or pedagogical trends to support and which to ignore, or which textbooks to select.

Teachers we interviewed shared a desire to be creative in the classroom in order to meet the needs of students better. Deep and broad knowledge of mathematics was key for these teachers to act effectively on their desires. Charles's comments highlight the way in which subject-matter expertise renews options for teachers and students in the classroom. After several comments revealing his love for mathematics, Charles states:

We [Charles and his colleagues] are interested in math. We still look at interesting problems and then try to take those problems to class and share them with our students. We like to play with math, too. I've just taken the lap top computer to class and put on the IBM Tool Kit and started playing around with a function. Kids will look over and ask, "What are you doing" and they'll get involved. Pretty soon I can walk away and they are in there banging away at the computer. . . . I love having them [his students] give me questions I can't answer, or that we can struggle on together. I love that (BA003).

Charles is comfortable setting up situations in which he and his students can explore mathematics spontaneously. The sense of play he speaks of arises from confidence in his mathematical facility, and results in a strong expression of this confidence: the willingness to say to students, "I don't know, let's find out together."

Marsha's integration of knowing and teaching mathematics stems from her interest in current applications of mathematics:

[Math] has the mistaken reputation of being ancient, . . . [but] it's used everyday in science. I try to bring up articles that are about research on AIDS and the mathematicians involved. . . . I happened to tell some [Collaborative] people that I was interested in finding the real practical applications for the ellipse, hyperbola, and parabola. One of the guys copied off about fifteen pages on it and handed it to me the next Saturday. I immediately took that back to my classroom with specific problems that I could use when students ask, "When do you ever use this stuff?" (BA014).

Marsha felt a need to have a relevant and educational response to students' eternal (and justified) question, "Why do we have to learn this?" From Collaborative contacts, Marsha picked up subject-matter knowledge that enabled her to provide student-ready activities demonstrating the use of mathematics in real situations. Not only was she able to tell her students that mathematics is useful, but she was able to show them how they could use it.

Nancy, a mathematics department head, speaks of her department's goal to involve all students in conceptually oriented mathematics learning, in contrast to a tracked system where some students spend their high school years practicing antiquated calculation methods they failed to master earlier, while others are preparing for college-level mathematics:

Our challenge is looking at our curriculum for our freshmen and not putting kids in courses based on what they have learned in junior high. Our goal is to introduce these students to some of the ideas behind mathematics that make it interesting to us: teachers who really like mathematics (BA015).

Harriet's comments echo this concern for opening mathematics learning to all and show how a new view of mathematics enabled her to do something about her concern:

It wasn't until I started my experience with the Collaborative that I started evaluating what I was really trying to do in the classroom. What mathematics really is. . . . Now I'm convinced it's a process we're trying to teach. We're trying to create situations and experiences for the students (LP008).

Harriet's and Nancy's comments and further discussion of the curriculum each had developed illustrate the connection between teachers' affinity for and knowledge of mathematics and their desire and ability to serve all students equitably. In both cases, teachers must have a sufficiently integrated knowledge of their subject to be able to meet their students where they are, and take them where these teachers want them to go. Teachers could not do this without a sufficiently charted map of the disciplinary terrain.

In the sophistication of the map lies the power of teachers' professional authority. A sophisticated view of what constitutes mathematical thinking allowed these teachers to weigh the value of proficiency in calculation against other kinds of mathematical thinking in order to decide which is more important to their students, and when. Knowing mathematics well enough to teach it conceptually and heuristically (as opposed to algorithmically) enabled teachers to tailor a curriculum for their students.

In and of itself, subject-matter knowledge is empowering because it provides the foundation for authority essential for classroom efficacy. However, in expanding our notions of subject-matter knowledge and teacher empowerment, we now turn attention to how such authority is linked to knowledge of professional community and educational policy.

Subject-matter knowledge provides a basis for collegiality. The connection between disciplinary knowledge and professional collegiality is obvious enough. Nevertheless, we highlight that connection here because of the importance that sharing subject-matter knowledge with colleagues had for the teachers we interviewed. Of course, the relationship is reciprocal; teachers' involvement in a professional community fosters their engagement with the discipline. Since teachers often enter the profession because of their love of a discipline, engaging in the subject at new and deeper levels is rejuvenating. Teachers feel empowered as a result of acquiring or reorganizing discipline-related knowledge. Harriet, for example, describes how Collaborative events provided new ways of thinking about mathematics:

Because of my involvement with the Collaborative, I became involved and met many educators of mathematics and little by little they opened my eyes to a new way of looking at mathematics. And a different way of teaching (LP008).

Chris Chambers recalls Collaborative events where exchange of mathematics problems supported a sense of professional community:

[In addition to the regular program], we also had a chance to talk about math, too. We math teachers can give each other problems we've heard. It's almost like at a party where the person who tells the best jokes always gets the most attention. And at a math meeting, it's the person who has the best problems that gets the most attention (LP003).

Subject-matter expertise was a special facet of professional community for Collaborative teachers precisely because the Collaboratives we studied were organized around subject matter. Affiliation in the Collaborative presumes a capacity, and thereby an authority, upon which participant bonds are built.

Disciplinary knowledge informs policy decisions. Subject-matter knowledge has clear relevance to involvement in policy decisions. A number of teachers in the mathematics Collaboratives related variations on this theme: learning more about mathematics provides a broad and deep view of what constitutes mathematical activity and ways of thinking. Once teachers have developed this view, their vision of what they can do with students shifts, often leading to dissatisfaction with the traditional curriculum, or, at least, to ideas for how it could be enhanced. This prompts efforts to get involved with educational policy, i.e., organize new courses, fight for adoption of innovative textbooks.

Darlene's story provides an extended example of how subject-matter knowledge is subtly connected to policy involvement on the school, district, and state levels. Her awareness of timely and useful mathematical topics that are well within the grasp of high school students yet are completely omitted from the traditional high school mathematics curriculum led her to seek a place for these topics to be taught. Darlene tells of her first PLUS workshop, on finite mathematics, which she enrolled in to get needed credits and a little surplus cash:

I took a bunch of papers to mark and planned on sitting there and marking papers. I really did. That was my goal, was to get a set of trig papers marked, I think, while I was there, and sat in the back. But I really did get hooked! . . . It was the first time I'd been intellectually stimulated in a long time, mathematically. You know, you tend to teach high school geometry and it gets pretty boring, at least the old, traditional way. I was really searching for some challenge (BA005).

Among the topics covered in the finite mathematics workshop were probability and statistics, combinatorics and network theory. Finite mathematics usually refers to a collection of topics that diverge from the traditional algebra-geometry-trigonometry-calculus sequence and that have current applications in computer science and operations research. Much of the work done on these topics is recent in the history of mathematics; that is to say, most of the ideas were developed in the twentieth century.[12]

Darlene then talks about the difficulty of using the finite mathematics she had learned in her classroom:

There was practically no way of fitting [finite math] into the curriculum as it existed. It's real tight; our curriculum is based on everybody taking calculus. It's not for enjoying math or for any of the millions of things you can do with math without knowing geometry and trig (BA005).

This leads to a discussion of her hopes for state-level curricular changes that will make room for the finite mathematics topics in which she had developed an interest. Darlene speaks about integrating the curriculum, that is, teaching a little bit of geometry, algebra, and trigonometry, along with finite mathematics, probability, and logic, in each of the high school courses:

The trend in California is to integrate the curriculum so that you can teach algebra and geometry and trig and all those other things at the same time at different levels. I hope it [the state framework] goes through. The math teachers in the state have been working on it for five years (BA005).

In the meantime, Darlene created a way within her school to implement her new knowledge of finite mathematics topics:

So anyway, what I did was, I went back and fought. I spent two years at it before it ever happened. I tried to get the district to put a finite math course in the curriculum as an option for the twelfth graders. We [her school] finally did it through a loophole. We've taken [the course entitled] Math Analysis B and . . . [turned it into] finite math. A lot of kids take it (BA005).

Additionally, Darlene discussed her finite mathematics course in light of current trends in college-level mathematics education, where discrete mathematics, a more complex version of finite mathematics, is being offered as an alternative to calculus as a beginning mathematics course. So, in addition to deepening her involvement in policy issues, Darlene's expertise in finite mathematics made another connection for her to the broader community of mathematicians and mathematics educators.

Darlene's story demonstrates a chain of connections between subject-matter knowledge and policy involvement. Her broadened knowledge of mathematics resulted in the desire to share this new knowledge with students. When the current system made this difficult, Darlene set about changing it. Her most intense effort took place at the school level, but Darlene also spoke of her awareness of and involvement in district- and state-level movements for change.

In sum, broad and deep knowledge of subject matter improves daily decision making in the classroom; it allows teachers to convey mathematical ideas in diverse and creative ways to their students. Disciplinary knowledge informs decisions about what and how to teach to best serve student needs. In addition, disciplinary knowledge forges connections to a professional community of teachers and others who study and use mathematics, and relates to teachers' policy knowledge and involvement. Subject-matter knowledge thus empowers by enhancing teachers' capacity both in and out of the classroom.

Professional Knowledge and Empowerment

The Urban Mathematics Collaborative teachers we interviewed were empowered in the most essential sense of the word—they were genuinely inspired to perform their best because they believed they could make a difference. The Collaborative provided the setting, resources, and opportunity that enabled this to happen. Knowledge of professional community, policy, and subject area has sparked UMC teachers' examination of traditional methods and materials. Teachers participate in animated discussions in their schools, relying on their knowledge of the broader education policy arena and new ideas gained through involvement in the Collaborative's extended professional community. Teachers are also empowered in the wider policy system as they bring effective voice to policy debates at district, state, and even national levels. These teachers possess an overall confidence in their own judgment, a strong belief in their ability to make intelligent and appropriate decisions in the classroom, and professional self-esteem. And it was not always so, they say.

The experience of Urban Mathematics Collaborative teachers suggests a weakness inherent in many reform efforts that aim to empower teachers solely by increasing their participation in decision making. Delegation of expanded roles and responsibilities predictably will disappoint if bureaucratic authority is not accompanied by professional knowledge and capacity.

We do not mean to suggest that providing opportunities for knowledge should supplant opportunities for expanded institutional authority. Ideally, enhanced professional knowledge and institutional authority will occur together. And, it may be that enhanced authority catalyzes interest in acquiring new knowledge or perspective. However, we argue that professionally relevant knowledge carries its own kind of authority that has the potential to empower teachers. Our point is that notions of empowerment evident in current decentralizing reforms misconstrue the essential spirit of empowerment when they delegate to teachers authority they may not seek or define empowerment in narrow bureaucratic terms.

We also saw that, once provided opportunities for developing professionally relevant knowledge, teachers' interests emerge idiosyncratically. Some teachers with whom we spoke sought to build program continuity within their departments. Others chose to focus solely on experimenting with new pedagogical techniques. Some devoted the bulk of their energy to discussions of district or state policy. Still others sought opportunities to train other professionals by leading workshops or assuming leadership roles within the Collaborative. Through acquiring knowledge of professional community, of educational policy, and of their discipline, each teacher reformed his or her own notions of function and obligation according to his or her own interests and context. Effective empowerment strategies, we conclude, must afford teachers opportunities for this *situational construction* [or reconstruction] of professional role and responsibility. Again, this challenge is fundamentally knowledge-based.

This perspective on teacher empowerment shifts reformers' attention from efforts to heighten workplace control and participation as the major reform to consideration of professionalization in teaching through a comprehensive view of teachers' professional lives. Collaborative participants show the important ways in which the self-esteem and sense of efficacy that motivate classroom practice also extend beyond the classroom to the broader community and policy system in which teachers work. Our research has led us to realize that, as far as professionally empowered teachers are concerned, the walls of the classroom are an illusion. The meaningful focus of teacher development may include the classroom, but also necessarily transcends it. We ought no longer to confuse where teachers work with how they work; knowledge gained outside the classroom informs (and is informed by) knowledge teachers gain within the classroom. Both sources of knowledge are essential to teacher empowerment.

As teachers extend themselves professionally, they develop a network that extends their own understanding of their role. Meeting people who are influential within their own discipline, in industry, in local, state, or national policy enhances teachers' sense of connectedness and their beliefs that what they do has import beyond the boundaries of the classroom or school. Teachers we interviewed demonstrated that once they have this knowledge, they become active participants in the many arenas that comprise their professional domain. It has not been necessary for school, district, and state-level administrators to give authority to these teachers, so much as it has been necessary to allow them to take it, or, more precisely, share it. Allowing teachers authority in the decisions that are most relevant to their practice requires blurring boundaries between practitioners and policymakers, not simply shifting them.

A system built upon such conditions depends in large part on teachers taking initiative to pursue the kinds of knowledge we associate with professional empowerment in this chapter. We found teachers eager to engage in development opportunities precisely because the knowledge they stood to gain was professionally relevant. As teachers assume greater responsibility for their individual and collective growth, power relationships and traditional ways of thinking about the roles of teachers and administrators will necessarily change as well.

Empowerment does involve altered power arrangements, but it denotes power and occupational self-direction quite differently from the ways in which reformers or policymakers usually consider them. Empowerment depends upon teachers' enhanced sense of efficacy and competence in the various domains of their profession, which include the classroom as well as policy arenas. This broader view anticipates teachers' development of professionally relevant knowledge as necessary to genuine teacher empowerment. Without such knowledge and capacity, institutional strategies dependent primarily on changes in authority and participation to empower teachers—new roles and responsibilities—may comprise an empty warrant.

ACKNOWLEDGMENTS. We acknowledge support from the Center for Policy Research in Education (CPRE) and from the Education Development Center (EDC) in Newton, Massachusetts, through a grant from the Ford Foundation. We are greatly indebted to the teachers and project administrators who participated in the study. They gave freely of their time and thoughts about teacher empowerment, hoping that their participation in the study would help to inform policymakers about teachers' realities and the factors that empower teachers. Judith Warren Little and Diane Sharkan, both of the University of California, Berkeley, collaborated in the study and conducted many of the interviews. Our Stanford colleagues, Nina Bascia and Carol Colbeck, provided thoughtful review and comment. None of these helpful people, of course, is responsible for shortcomings of the study.

Notes

1. See Lorraine McDonnell, *The Dilemma of Teacher Policy* (Santa Monica: Rand Corporation, 1989) for a comprehensive analysis of the issues and tensions central to teacher policy at the state level. The new group of "Wave Two" reformers are represented by such reports as *A Nation Prepared: Teachers for the 21st Century* (New York: Carnegie Forum on Education and the Economy, 1986), *Tomorrow's Teachers* (East Lansing, MI: Holmes Group, 1986), *What Next? More Leverage for Teachers?* (Denver: Education Commission of the States, 1987); *Time for Results: The Governors' 1991 Report on Education* (Washington, D.C.: National Governors' Association Center for Policy and Research, 1987).

2. See Samuel B. Bacharach and Joseph B. Shedd, "Power and Empowerment: The Constraining Myth and Emerging Structures of Teacher Unionism in an Age of Reform," in *The Politics of Reforming School Administration*, ed. Jane Hannaway and Robert Crowson, the 1988 Yearbook of the Politics of Education Association (New York: Falmer Press, 1988), pp. 139-160.

3. For example, Rosabeth Moss Kanter, *Men and Women of the Corporation* (New York: Basic Books, 1977) provides the key elaboration of the concept of empowerment in her discussion of women in large-scale organizations. See also Richard H. Hall's discussion in chapter 10 of *Dimensions of Work* (Beverly Hills: Sage Publications, 1986).

4. Sara Lawrence Lightfoot, "On Goodness in Schools: Themes of Empowerment," *Peabody Journal of Education* 63 (Spring 1986): 9.

5. Floretta Dukes McKenzie, "Implications and Rewards of Teacher Empowerment," in *Preparing Schools for the 1990s: An Essay Collection* (New York: Metropolitan Life, 1989), pp. 1-6.

6. See Richard F. Elmore and Associates, *Restructuring Schools: The Next Generation of Educational Reform* (San Francisco: Jossey-Bass, 1990).

7. This research was sponsored by the Center for Policy Research in Education (CPRE) and is part of its "New Roles and Responsibilities" research program.

8. Choya Wilson conducted this literature review and analysis.

9. See, for example, Gene I. Maeroff, *The Empowerment of Teachers* (New York: Teachers College Press, 1988); Sharon C. Conley and Samuel B. Bacharach, "From School-Site Management to Participatory School-Site Management," *Phi Delta Kappan* 71, no. 7 (March 1990): 539-544; William A. Clune and Paula A. White, *School-Based Management* (New Brunswick, NJ: Center for Policy Research in Education, Rutgers University, September 1988); Jane L. David, "Restructuring in Progress: Lessons from Pioneering Districts," in Richard F. Elmore and Associates, *Restructuring Schools* (San Francisco: Jossey-Bass, 1990).

10. Philip W. Jackson's *Life in Classrooms* (New York: Holt, Rinehart and Winston, 1968) and Dan Lortie's *Schoolteacher: A Sociological Study* (Chicago: University of Chicago Press, 1975) are the classic statements of teachers' isolation and lack of community among teachers.

11. "Marsha McGregory" is a pseudonym, as are all of the individual and school names that follow. The notations in parentheses following quotations or respondents (e.g., BAO12) identify respondent transcripts from which comments were drawn.

12. See Anthony Ralston, "The Really New College Mathematics," in *The Secondary School Mathematics Curriculum*, ed. Christopher R. Hirsch and Marilyn Zweng (Reston, VA: National Council of Teachers of Mathematics, 1985).

CHAPTER IV

Challenges to an Alternative Route for Teacher Education

GARY NATRIELLO AND KAREN ZUMWALT

The contexts in which individuals are prepared to become teachers have received a great deal of attention in recent years[1] in part because of growing discontent with current arrangements for the preparation of teachers and in part because of the renewed interest in making teaching more professional. Among the most widely promoted and widely attacked designs for reforming teacher education have been alternative programs for teacher certification.[2] Although there is considerable variation among alternate route programs,[3] these programs are typically linked to new arrangements for the certification of teachers, and usually involve new arrangements for the education of teachers—arrangements which generally shift the context for the preparation of teachers from colleges and universities to local schools and school districts.

Alternative route programs across the nation have raised a number of issues for educators and the public alike. In this chapter, through an examination of the New Jersey Provisional Teacher Program, we focus on four challenges facing alternate route programs if they are to meet their proponents' promises and address their critics' reservations.

An important challenge for alternate route programs is to maintain and, indeed enhance, the quality of individuals entering teaching. Many alternate route programs were begun in an attempt to attract competent professionals from other sectors and recent liberal arts graduates into classroom teaching. In New Jersey and elsewhere policymakers acted in response to the growing perception of declining quality among those entering teaching.[4]

Gary Natriello, whose field is sociology of education, is Associate Professor of Education at Teachers College, Columbia University. Karen Zumwalt, Professor of Education at Teachers College, Columbia University, is in the field of curriculum and teaching.

A second issue concerns the staffing needs of certain schools. The policymakers who proposed the alternate route program pointed to the need for developing a way to staff urban schools that would be more effective than granting emergency certification to unprepared teachers. Urban schools in New Jersey and elsewhere have experienced shortages of teachers in key areas as beginning and experienced teachers have sought jobs in the suburbs. A challenge for alternate route programs is to recruit and retain individuals with an interest in teaching in urban schools. Part of this challenge lies in recruiting more members of minority groups to enter teaching. At a time when the student population is becoming increasingly minority,[5] the proportion of minority group members in the teaching force is declining.[6]

A third challenge for alternate route programs is to contribute to efforts to make teaching more professional. Critics of alternate route programs have contended that they diminish the professional status of teachers by allowing individuals not prepared in college-based programs into the field.[7] Alternate routes are viewed by some as undermining the attempts to professionalize teaching because they minimize the need for a specialized knowledge base and controlled entry, the hallmarks of established professions. In contrast, proponents argue that alternate route programs could enhance the professionalism of teachers by emphasizing individual teacher selection as a mechanism to upgrade the existing teaching force.[8]

A fourth challenge for alternate route programs is to retain individuals in teaching. Proponents of alternate route programs sometimes argue that they are needed because many graduates of college-based programs never enter teaching and many of those who do leave after several years.[9] Critics of alternate route programs have suggested that alternate route teachers who have not made a commitment to the field and have not devoted significant time to preparing to enter the field may be more likely to leave teaching than individuals prepared in college-based programs.[10]

The New Jersey Teacher Education Study

In this chapter, we will be considering each of these issues in the context of one alternate route program, the New Jersey Provisional Teacher Program. This program, developed by the New Jersey State Department of Education, has been in operation since the 1985-86 school year. Prospective elementary and secondary teachers who have not completed a college-based teacher education program may enter the Provisional Teacher Program if they have completed a bachelor's degree with a thirty-credit academic major, received a passing score on the National Teacher Examination (NTE) test in their teaching subject or, for elementary teachers, the NTE general knowledge test, and have an offer of employment from a public or private school in New Jersey.

Alternate route teachers[11] in New Jersey must attend 200 hours of instruction offered at a regional training center established by the State Department of Education and operated under the direction of a dean or director of teacher education from a New Jersey college or university. Eighty hours of instruction are completed prior to the beginning of the school year, or for those hired immediately prior to the start of school, during the first thirty days of teaching. The remaining 120 hours of instruction are completed during the remainder of the school year. The content of the instruction focuses on a set of generic topics under the broad categories of the curriculum, the student, and the classroom and school setting.

A school district hiring an alternate route teacher must sign a contract agreeing to provide a support team consisting of at least the principal and a fully certified teacher in the same field and to arrange a twenty-day period during which the new teacher will have only limited teaching responsibilities and more intensive supervisory support. During this first phase, the alternate route teacher is to work with a fully certified teacher on the support team. During a second phase of ten weeks' duration, the alternate route teacher is observed at least once a week. During a third phase of twenty weeks, the alternate route teacher is observed at least once a month and evaluated twice. At the end of the first and second phases the principal completes an evaluation report indicating whether the candidate may continue on to the next phase. Those not recommended for the next phase may be asked to leave the program or to repeat a phase. Once a candidate has completed 200 hours of instruction at the regional training center and the third phase of supervised teaching, he or she must obtain the principal's recommendation for certification.

In using the New Jersey Provisional Program to explore how an alternate route program is meeting the four challenges, we are drawing upon data taken from a series of surveys conducted between the spring of 1987 and the spring of 1990. During this time, we periodically contacted teachers prepared through college-based programs and teachers prepared through the Provisional Teacher Program.

In the spring of 1987, we administered an initial survey to all individuals completing New Jersey college-based teacher preparation programs in the fields of secondary English and secondary mathematics and to a 40 percent sample of the individuals completing college-based teacher preparation programs in the field of elementary education. Included in this college-based sample were 121 elementary teachers, 36 secondary English teachers, and 30 secondary mathematics teachers. In the summer and fall of 1987, we administered an initial survey to all the individuals entering the Provisional Teacher Program in all fields. For comparative purposes, in the current analyses we included the 75 elementary teachers, 24 secondary English teachers, and 30 secondary mathematics teachers.

Individuals in all six groups were surveyed again in the spring of 1988 and the spring of 1989. In addition, teachers in the three college-prepared groups were asked to complete a brief tracking survey in the fall of 1987, and teachers in all six groups were asked to complete such brief tracking surveys in the fall of 1988 and the spring of 1990. Group response rates were 87 percent or higher for the initial survey. And of those initially surveyed, over 80 percent were retained over the three years of the study.

The data utilized in this chapter focus on the recruitment, placement, and retention of alternate route and college-prepared teachers. Future analyses of data on these teachers' experiences in teacher education institutions and student teaching, in regional training centers and phase one teaching, and during the first few years of teaching will undoubtedly add to our understanding of different contexts for teacher education. The initial data analysis here of items related to the recruitment, placement, and retention of new teachers provides suggestive patterns of how the New Jersey alternate route program is meeting the challenges of enhancing the quality of the teacher pool, staffing urban public schools, professionalizing teaching, and retaining teachers.

We turn now to a discussion of our findings in terms of each of the four challenges mentioned at the beginning of the chapter.

Enhancing the Quality of the Teacher Pool

In New Jersey and elsewhere, alternate route programs were begun in an attempt to attract competent professionals from other sectors into the classroom. An initial question for any alternate route program is the degree to which it can attract individuals from other professional sectors. Examining our data from the cohort of individuals entering teaching in New Jersey in 1987, we find that the Provisional Teacher Program did attract older people. The average age of the beginning alternate route teachers was thirty years, whereas the average age of the newly graduated college students was twenty-five. The program also had some success in attracting individuals from other sectors. About one-half of the elementary and English teachers and about two-thirds of the mathematics teachers who entered teaching through the Provisional Teacher Program came from sectors other than education. Although they came from a range of other sectors, the largest number in all three fields came from administration, management, or sales positions, with engineering running a strong second among mathematics teachers.

Interestingly, about one-third of the alternate route teachers had previously held teaching positions at the school level and subject they were teaching and 21 to 37 percent had experience as substitute teachers. Hence, the Provisional Teaching Program, not only attracted prospective teachers from other sectors, but also enabled noncertified teachers in public, private, and parochial schools to obtain the credentials to permit employment in the generally better paying public sector.

Another question often asked is whether alternate route programs can attract underrepresented individuals, such as males and members of minority groups, into teaching. The Provisional Teacher Program was more successful than the college programs in recruiting males and members of minority groups, especially Blacks, into teaching. Males comprised from 3 percent to 17 percent of the college-prepared groups and 24 percent to 62 percent of the alternate route teacher groups. Whereas about 11 percent of the college-prepared sample were members of minority groups, about 30 percent of the alternate route teachers were minorities.

Attracting individuals from new sectors and groups to teaching is assumed to enhance the pool of talent from which teachers may be drawn. However, direct measures of talent or ability must also be considered. In examining the college-prepared and alternate route teachers along a number of traditional indicators of performance or ability, we found neither group to be consistently superior. For example, in the case of grades, in all three fields, the grade point averages (GPA) of college-based teachers exceeded those of the alternate route teachers. The GPAs for college-based elementary, English, and mathematics teachers were 3.18, 3.37, and 3.35, respectively; the corresponding averages for the alternate route teachers were 2.89, 3.12 and 3.00.

However, the alternate route teachers attended more selective colleges in achieving these grades. On the six-point Carnegie scale of college selectivity, with "1" representing the most selective institutions and "6" representing the least selective, college-based elementary, English, and mathematics teachers attended colleges with mean selectivity ratings of 3.73, 3.59, and 3.84; the corresponding figures for alternate route teachers were 2.93, 2.53, and 2.95. Although alternate route teachers generally attended more selective colleges, the variation in selectivity ratings among colleges attended by alternate route teachers was greater than among the colleges attended by the college-based teachers. Among other things, this reflects the fact that New Jersey colleges offering teacher education programs are more similar in their degree of selectivity than the broad range of out-of-state colleges.

Completion of a major in the teaching field has long been deemed an important quality for prospective teachers since it signals preparation in the subject to be taught.[12] College-prepared elementary teachers were most likely to have majored in education (69 percent) whereas alternate route elementary teachers were most likely to have majored in the humanities (38.9 percent). Beginning with the 1988-1989 school year, all elementary teachers in New Jersey must have a major in an area other than education so this difference has disappeared. Among secondary teachers, college-prepared teachers were more likely to have majored in the actual subject they were teaching than the alternate route teachers. Among English teachers 89.7 percent of those from college-based programs majored in English, while 82.6 percent of alternate route teachers majored in English. The differences are more substantial in the case of mathematics teachers, where 83.3 percent of college-prepared teachers, but only 40 percent of alternate route teachers majored in mathematics.[13]

The advantage of college-based secondary teachers in terms of majoring in their teaching discipline, however, was not reflected in the test scores of individuals in the two programs. For teachers in all three fields, the NTE scores of alternate route teachers exceeded those for teachers prepared in college-based programs. College-based elementary teachers averaged 659.39 on the general knowledge test of the NTE, while alternate route teachers averaged 664.12, an advantage of .34 standard deviation units favoring the alternate route teachers. College-based English teachers averaged 599.31 on the English subject area test of the NTE, while alternate route teachers averaged 626.81, an advantage of .39 standard deviation units in favor of the alternate route teachers. College-based mathematics teachers averaged 620.40 on the mathematics subject area test of the NTE, while alternate route teachers averaged 648.33, an alternate route advantage of .32 standard deviation units.

There were also differences in terms of the socioeconomic background of individuals entering teaching through the two routes. Higher socioeconomic background is generally associated with a stronger general educational background. Using common indicators of socioeconomic background such as parents' education and occupation, we found that alternate route teachers were more likely, with some exceptions, to come from families with higher educational and occupational status. In contrast to earlier findings,[14] entering secondary teachers in both college and alternate route programs, especially English teachers, had parents of higher educational and occupational backgrounds than elementary school teachers. In terms of parents' education, only a majority of the English teachers and of the alternate route mathematics teachers had at least one parent who completed four years of college. In terms of occupation, only a majority of the alternate route English teachers had fathers holding professional jobs.

The Provisional Teacher Program was clearly able to attract individuals from sectors and groups historically less likely to enter teaching (males, minorities, students from selective colleges and higher status families). It was also able to attract individuals who scored higher on the NTE. However, these new entrants to the teaching field had lower grade point averages and were less likely to have majored in the subject they found themselves teaching.

Although the quality picture is mixed, the reality of the potential dynamic of the hiring process suggests a more positive interpretation of the contribution of the Provisional Teacher Program. Since the program has expanded the pool of those who might be hired as teachers, it adds in effect another queue to the hiring process and thus reduces the necessity for those involved in the hiring process to reach as far down in the original queue of college-prepared teachers. This may be particularly significant in areas where fewer college-prepared individuals present themselves as candidates for employment, most notably urban school districts. Of course, this potential benefit of the Provisional Teacher Program assumes that the alternate route teachers are willing to take jobs in urban schools, an assumption that we examine next, and that they are prepared well enough to survive the rigors of the first few years of teaching, an assumption that we examine later in considering retention. Ultimately, judgments of quality of teaching, in the long and short term, need to be ascertained to determine whether these background characteristics do indeed enhance the quality of the teaching pool.

Staffing Urban Public Schools

The preferences and actual placements of individuals in both programs reveal that the Provisional Teacher Program does seem to be fulfilling some of its promise as a source of teachers for difficult-to-staff urban public schools. By the third year, however, some of the differences disappear.

These differences in patterns of early teaching experiences first appear in the preferences expressed by teachers during student teaching and phase one teaching. The majority of prospective teachers grew up in the suburbs, and that is where they would like to teach. Alternate route teachers expressed greater preference for teaching in urban areas than college-prepared teachers, a pattern that may reflect both initial interest and job placement. Alternate route teachers may be simply adjusting their stated preferences to their current teaching opportunities since it was in urban districts that alternate route teachers were most likely to find jobs. Nevertheless, among alternate route teachers, 26 percent of elementary teachers, 17.4 percent of English teachers, and 20.6 percent of mathematics teachers expressed a preference for teaching in urban areas; the corresponding figures for college-prepared teachers were 8.3 percent, 5.6 percent, and 0 percent.

In addition to preferences about job location, college-prepared and alternate route teachers in our study were also asked to express their preferences for the types of children they would like to teach. Choices included "students with emotional needs," "nice kids from average homes," "creative and intellectually demanding students," "underprivileged children from difficult homes," and "children of limited ability or slow learners." The type of children preferred by most of the teachers in each group were "nice" and/or "creative" children, with the exception of the alternate route elementary teachers, 35 percent of whom preferred to teach underprivileged children. Between 13 percent and 20 percent of the teachers in the other groups preferred to teach underprivileged children, except for college-prepared mathematics teachers, none of whom preferred to teach underprivileged children. Children with emotional needs were the preference of the smallest numbers of teachers in each group. Among the college-prepared teachers, from 7.6 percent to 11.1 percent expressed a preference for working with slow learners, whereas from 0 percent to 3.4 percent of the alternate route teachers expressed such a preference.

In addition to preferences, a number of aspects of the teaching positions of college-prepared and alternate route teachers during the three years of the study are relevant to determining the promise of alternate route programs for providing teachers for urban public schools. The alternate route teachers were more likely to take teaching positions in public schools in urban areas. While most college-prepared and alternate route teachers did student teaching and phase one teaching in public schools, more alternate route teachers were teaching in public schools by the second year. However, the differences converged over time so that by the spring of 1990, when the individuals in our sample were completing their third full year of teaching, about three-fourths of both groups were teaching in public schools.

Alternate route teachers were more likely than college-prepared teachers to be teaching in low socioeconomic status (SES) districts throughout the three years of the study. This is particularly true for elementary teachers where those in the alternate route are about twice as likely to be working in low SES districts during this time. In the spring of 1990 about one-third of college-prepared elementary and English teachers and slightly less than one-half of college-prepared mathematics teachers were in low SES districts. During this same period over three-fourths of alternate route elementary teachers, somewhat less than one-half of alternate route English teachers, and somewhat more than one-half of alternate route mathematics teachers were teaching in low SES districts.

Although the percentages of teachers teaching gifted students converges by the third year, during the first two years, alternate route English teachers and college-prepared mathematics teachers were more likely to be teaching gifted students. Similarly, the percentages of teachers teaching remedial students converge by the third year except that by then college-prepared mathematics teachers were more likely to teach remedial students. During the first two years, alternate route mathematics teachers were more likely to teach remedial students than their college-prepared counterparts who were more likely to be teaching gifted students. Obviously, there were differences in the teaching positions for which alternate route English and mathematics teachers were being sought, with English teachers staffing fewer and mathematics teachers staffing more basic skills courses. Why college-prepared and alternate route mathematics teachers' placements in regards to gifted and remedial students indicate opposite patterns over time is something worth pursuing. Perhaps the differences reflect some combination of job availability, personal preference, differential hiring and retention, or judgments about who was better able to teach the remedial students.

Finally, there are some differences in teaching positions taken by grade level. Alternate route English and elementary teachers are more likely to be teaching the middle school grades than their college-prepared counterparts who are more likely to be teaching in high school and the primary grades, respectively.

Overall, by the third year of teaching, although many differences in teaching placements disappear, alternate route teachers are more likely to be teaching in low SES districts and in the harder-to-staff middle school grades. These staffing patterns undoubtedly reflect the preferences of individual teachers, the availability of jobs, and the hiring preferences of school districts. Although the substantially greater proportions of alternate route teachers in low SES school districts during the third year of full-time teaching support the notion that alternate route programs will contribute to the staffing of urban public schools, at this point we do not know whether this pattern will be sustained when the alternate route teachers acquire more experience or when more jobs become available in higher SES suburban school districts.

The Professionalization of Teaching

Recent reform efforts in education have directed attention to the professionalization of teaching in hopes of improving the status and working conditions of teaching so as to attract and retain the best teachers. Some proponents of professionalization stress reforming teaching by incorporating the features of other professions such as rigorous entry requirements, supervised induction, autonomous performance, peer-defined standards of practice, and increased responsibility with increased competence.[15] Others, such as the Holmes Group, speak about the development of systematic knowledge which is codified, transmitted, and transformed through professional education and individual and collegial reflective practice.[16] Alternate routes are seen by critics as undermining the efforts to upgrade teaching by providing an easy entry with a minimum of preparation and socialization to the culture of teaching. In contrast, proponents of the alternate route view it as enhancing the status of teaching by emphasizing individual teacher selection. In both cases, it is assumed that having teachers with more professional attitudes and competencies will enhance the profession and improve the education received by students.

While future analyses of qualitative data on these teachers' first years in teaching will be more illuminating, our survey data on recruitment, placement, and retention shed some light on the interaction of alternate route programs and the professionalization of teaching. In this section, we look at whether college-prepared teachers and alternate route teachers were attracted to teaching for the same or different reasons, how their expectations compared to the reality of teaching, their self-reported evaluations, the factors that would encourage them to remain in teaching, their reaction to reform proposals, and their future career plans. Basically, we are exploring whether their attitudes and their teaching experiences indicate any different orientations toward the profession.

The attractions teaching holds for individuals entering the field have a bearing on the future of the profession because they suggest the future demands of the teaching force. If alternate route teachers enter teaching for radically different reasons than college-prepared teachers, we might anticipate new forces emerging to shape the future of the profession.

Our analysis reveals that, for the most part, alternate route teachers and college-prepared teachers were attracted to teaching for the same reasons. However, the financial rewards of teaching were more of an allure to alternate route teachers than to their college-prepared counterparts. Since other aspects of teaching were similarly attractive to individuals in the two programs, the greater saliency of the financial rewards may just indicate the fact that alternate route teachers, who had all graduated from college at the time of the first survey, may be more dependent on earning a living than the college-prepared teachers who were completing student teaching and their bachelors degrees.

Attractions to teacher education noted by individuals in the two routes were also examined. In rating factors that influenced their decision to enter a particular teacher education program, the college-prepared teachers attributed more importance to specific qualities of the program than the alternate route teachers. The most important factor for the college-prepared students in selecting their program was the quality of the student teaching experience. For alternate route teachers, the most salient feature of the alternate route program was their ability to teach immediately; specific internal characteristics of the program were less important. The Provisional Teacher Program was viewed as the easiest, cheapest, and quickest way to enter teaching, hardly the perceived attributes of a professional preparation program. Thus, independent of the actual quality of the program, individuals in the Provisional Teacher Program had not been attracted to the program by characteristics generally associated with quality professional preparation.

Individuals in both the college-based programs and the Provisional Teacher Program came to teaching with certain expectations—expectations that were soon confronted by the realities of teaching. Aspects of the teaching job viewed as better or worse than originally expected by the individuals in the six groups were examined. For college-prepared students, the aspects of teaching that were worse than original expectations had to do with labor market conditions and the difficulty of finding a suitable teaching position. For alternate route teachers, the aspects of teaching seen as worse than expected involved the conditions of teaching, i.e., resources, the number of students with special needs, the calibre of colleagues, the responses of students. These aspects of their teaching positions were disappointing to alternate route teachers. They suggest a dissatisfaction with the conditions of teaching, or at least a greater gap between expectations and reality than experienced by the college-prepared teachers, all of whom had confronted the realities of teaching to some extent in their required sophomore and junior year practicums as well as their semester of student teaching.

Other key factors for which beginning teachers held expectations were the quantity and quality of administrative support and supervision. At the end of the second year of teaching, alternate route teachers and college-prepared elementary teachers were more likely than the college-prepared secondary group to state that administrative support was better than expected. This feeling may be related to the prescribed support teams for alternate route teachers which, at the time of the study were not in place for college-prepared teachers. At the end of the first year, however, alternate route teachers were more likely than college-prepared teachers to report that the amount and quality of supervision were worse than expected. By the end of the second year, these differences regarding supervision converged. The first year data, however, may be particularly important because this is the year the alternate route teachers were to receive intensive supervision at their schools while attending regional training centers.

Some indication of how well these beginning teachers met the expectations of those who hired them can be seen in their self-reported evaluations. At the end of the second year of teaching, they were asked whether they had received excellent, good, satisfactory, or unsatisfactory evaluations at the end of their first year of teaching. Alternate route mathematics teachers self-reported the lowest formal evaluations of their teaching followed by alternate route elementary teachers. Approximately 47 percent of the alternate route mathematics teachers and 21.4 percent of the alternate route elementary teachers reported that they had received only satisfactory ratings compared to 0 percent to 9.5 percent of the other groups.

While the alternate route mathematics teachers received relatively fewer excellent/good ratings, it should be noted that very few teachers in the sample reported they had received unsatisfactory ratings. They did note other factors that might influence their decisions to remain in teaching. Overall, college-prepared teachers were more likely than alternate route teachers to identify factors that encouraged them to remain in teaching; alternate route mathematics teachers were the least likely to mention factors which would influence them to remain in teaching.

There were a number of reform incentives viewed as attractive to alternate route and college-prepared teachers. The most powerful incentive for all teachers to remain in teaching was a "substantial salary increase." In addition, over 50 percent of all teachers indicated that three factors relevant to the professionalization of teaching would be extremely or very significant in keeping them in teaching: opportunities for professional development (60 to 77.2 percent); opportunities for advancement such as career ladders and master teacher status (50 to 68.2 percent) and greater teacher autonomy in curricular and teaching decisions (53.3 to 61.9 percent). Mandated continuing education requirements for teachers were the single incentive which differentiated the responses of college-prepared and alternate route teachers. In contrast to college-prepared teachers, alternate route teachers were more likely to report that added requirements would not be a significant factor in their decision to remain in teaching.

Finally, we considered issues regarding the likelihood that college-prepared and alternate route teachers would remain in teaching.

Eighty percent or more of college-prepared and alternate route teachers reported that they expected to be teaching a third year. As for long-range plans, college-prepared elementary teachers (81.7 percent) were the most likely to have long-range plans to remain in schools; 65 to 73.8 percent of those in the other groups had such plans as well. Alternate route math teachers were the only group to depart from the general trend; only 40 percent of these individuals had long-range career goals to remain employed in school systems. A relatively large proportion (40 percent) of them expressed an interest in employment in higher education.

In summary, there are some differences between college-prepared and alternate route teachers in terms of these issues related to the professionalization of teaching, such as their differential attraction to teacher education programs and the different nature of their dashed expectations. These differences are worth pursuing in later analysis. But the most striking differences are not those between college-prepared and alternate route teachers in general, but between alternate route mathematics teachers and the other five groups. These differences suggest that viewing alternate route programs generically may be misleading and that treating alternate route programs as either a threat or a boon to teacher professionalism may be overestimating their effects.

Retaining Teachers

The issue of retention of individuals in teaching is central to any consideration of the potential of alternate route programs to contribute to the preparation of the teaching force. If few remain in the field, the preparation, good or bad, may be irrelevant.

Regardless of the base one uses to compute retention rates, the pattern essentially remains the same over the three years of our study. About 85 percent of the elementary teachers remain in teaching. But differences exist among the secondary teachers. About three-quarters of the alternate route English teachers stayed in teaching through the third year compared to about two-thirds of the college-prepared English teachers.[17] The differential is reversed and even more substantial in the case of mathematics teachers; about 80-90 percent of the college-prepared mathematics teachers remained in teaching compared to about 60 percent of the alternate route mathematics teachers.

Once again, we see that subject-matter and grade-level differences are important in considering the consequences of alternate route programs. The different experiences of the alternate route English and mathematics teachers in our study of the New Jersey program would be overlooked in a simple comparison between college-prepared and alternate route teachers. These differences are worthy of more detailed examination.

Disaggregating the Effects of Alternate Route Programs: The Experiences of Alternate Route English and Mathematics Teachers

Although the demand for mathematics teachers in New Jersey during the period of the study was substantially greater than the demand for English teachers, the alternate route English teachers apparently had a more positive beginning teaching experience. The alternate route mathematics teachers found more aspects of teaching worse than expected, received lower evaluations of their teaching, were less likely to stay in teaching, and were the least likely to report that they would advise a son or daughter to enter teaching. In contrast, the alternate route English teachers found more aspects of teaching better than expected, were more likely to stay in teaching than their college counterparts, were more likely to intend to remain in K-12 education than the alternate route mathematics teachers, and were the most likely of all groups to report that they would advise a son or daughter to enter teaching.

While a fuller explanation of these differing experiences awaits a more complete analysis of our survey data together with case studies of selected individuals, the alternate route mathematics and English teachers differ on several characteristics which may provide insight into the set of interrelated circumstances creating different realities for them.

First, alternate route mathematics teachers were more likely to have first considered teaching as a career at a later point in life than alternate route English teachers. Over half of the alternate route mathematics teachers first considered becoming teachers after completing college, whereas only about one-third of alternate route English teachers first considered teaching this late in their lives. In fact, about one-third of the alternate route English teachers had thought about teaching as a career before entering college compared to 13.3 percent of the alternate route mathematics teachers. Having considered teaching as an option for a longer time may indicate a different kind of commitment to teaching and different reactions to the inevitable challenges of the beginning years.

Second, alternate route mathematics teachers were more likely to be males (62 percent) than alternate route English teachers (45 percent). Indeed, they were more likely to be males than any of the other five groups of teachers studied. The lower satisfaction and lower retention rate of this predominantly male group of teachers may simply mirror the broader problem of attracting and retaining males in the teaching field.

Third, the alternate route English teachers came from the highest socioeconomic backgrounds of any of the six groups of teachers in the study. How this demographic factor might interact with real and perceived differences in the experiences of beginning teachers will be explored in future data analyses.

Fourth, the alternate route mathematics teachers, drawn from a number of related fields in science and engineering, were the least likely of any of the six groups in the study to have majored in the subject they are teaching. In addition, they were less likely to say that teaching the subject matter was an attraction of teaching than were the alternate route English teachers, most of whom majored in English.

Fifth, the alternate route mathematics teachers were the group least likely to report that they would have entered a college-based program if the alternate route had not been available. While 28 percent of the alternate route mathematics teachers would have entered a college teacher education program, 40.9 percent of the alternate route English teachers would have done so. The alternate route was the only mode of entry acceptable to a greater proportion of alternate route mathematics teachers, perhaps indicating greater reluctance to sacrifice time and money to enter teaching.

Sixth, the alternate route mathematics teachers were the least likely of the three groups of alternate route teachers to have had previous teaching experience. The alternate route English teachers were more likely to have held teaching jobs or to have been substitutes than the mathematics teachers. Thus, teaching was a new experience for a greater proportion of the alternate route mathematics teachers.

Seventh, the alternate route mathematics teachers obtained initial teaching positions that exposed them to fewer gifted and more remedial students than the alternate route English teachers. Moreover, the alternate route mathematics teachers were more likely to begin teaching in schools in communities of low socioeconomic status. Although these differences converge over time, initial experiences may be particularly critical. Many of the alternate route mathematics teachers have already left teaching by the time the patterns begin to converge.

Eighth, the alternate route mathematics teachers were more likely to have been disappointed by their interactions with students than the alternate route English teachers. Sixty percent of the alternate route mathematics teachers reported that the responses of the students they taught were worse than expected compared to only about one-fourth of the alternate route English teachers.

Ninth, the alternate route mathematics teachers expressed greater disappointment with their control over their work than the alternate route English teachers. While 60 percent of the alternate route English teachers noted that control over their work was better than expected, only one third of the alternate route mathematics teachers reported that it was better than expected. While some of this difference may be related to differences in how realistic initial expectations were, some is undoubtedly related to curricular differences. English and mathematics are conceived quite differently as school subjects, and teachers have correspondingly different degrees of freedom in the classroom.

Tenth, the alternate route mathematics teachers were less likely to find working with children a compelling reason to remain in teaching. Although working with children was the factor most often mentioned by all six groups of teachers as influencing them to remain in teaching, 60 percent of the alternate route English teachers cited this factor as compared to only 47 percent of the alternate route mathematics teachers.

Hence, we see that as groups the alternate route mathematics and English teachers have different background characteristics, different attitudes, and different experiences during the beginning years of teaching. These within-program differences are as important to study as the differences between teachers prepared in college-based programs and alternate route programs.

Conclusions

At the outset we posed four challenges facing alternate route programs for the preparation of teachers. Our examination of the New Jersey Provisional Teacher Program contributes to an understanding of the potential of alternate route programs to meet these challenges.

In terms of maintaining and enhancing the quality of individuals entering teaching, the New Jersey program suggests that alternate route programs are able at least to maintain the quality of those currently entering teaching and have the potential to enhance that quality. Although the New Jersey alternate route teachers had lower grade point averages than their college-based counterparts, they came from more selective colleges and also scored higher on NTE tests despite being less likely to have majored in the teaching area. This last finding may have as much to do with the limited number of selective colleges in New Jersey as it does with the ability of the Provisional Teacher Program to attract students from selective out-of-state institutions. It should be noted that the measures of quality examined here are measures of characteristics upon entering teaching, not measures of the quality of teaching.

In terms of staffing urban schools, the New Jersey Provisional Teacher Program did encourage the entry into teaching of individuals who were more likely to be teaching in low SES urban districts and in the harder-to-staff middle grades throughout the three years of our study. However, in view of the exit of substantial numbers of alternate route mathematics teachers from positions in urban schools with remedial students, and in view of the tendency of the alternate route and college-based teaching placements to converge over time, it is not clear whether the remaining advantage of alternate route teachers in staffing urban schools can be maintained over a longer period of time as positions become available in higher SES suburban school districts. Nonetheless, the Provisional Teacher Program in New Jersey did contribute substantial numbers of teachers to urban schools.

There seemed to be few meaningful differences in issues related to professionalism between college-based and alternate route teachers overall. The one group that stands apart from the others in terms of having responses least consistent with a professional model of teaching is the alternate route mathematics teachers, suggesting effects on professionalism of not just the Provisional Teacher Program, but of a complex set of recruitment, preparation, and hiring processes.

In terms of retention, once again, there are no consistent advantages for college-prepared or alternate route teachers. The most striking difference is the higher retention rate for college-prepared mathematics teachers in contrast to their alternate route counterparts and the markedly lower proportion of alternate route mathematics teachers expressing a long-range interest in remaining in teaching.

In the case of New Jersey, data on the recruitment, placement, and retention of alternate route mathematics and English teachers indicate that varying contexts justify considering separately the policy implications of establishing alternate routes to teaching in different subject areas. Much can be learned from viewing alternate route programs in different teaching fields as a variety of context-specific, naturally occurring experiments rather than extolling or dismissing alternate routes in general.

ACKNOWLEDGMENT. The study upon which this chapter is based was funded by the National Center for Research on Teacher Education (OERI); Teachers College, Columbia University; and Michigan State University.

NOTES

1. Holmes Group, *Tomorrow's Teachers: A Report of the Holmes Group* (East Lansing, MI: Holmes Group, 1986); Carnegie Forum on Education and the Economy, *A Nation Prepared: Teachers for the Twenty-first Century*, Report of the Task Force on Teaching as a Profession (New York: Carnegie Corporation of New York, 1986); John I. Goodlad, Roger Soder, and Kenneth A. Sorotnik, eds., *Places Where Teachers Are Taught* (San Francisco: Jossey-Bass, 1990).

2. Nancy E. Adelman, *An Exploratory Study of Teacher Alternative Certification and Retraining Programs* (Washington, DC: Policy Study Associates, 1986); Neil B. Carey, Brian S. Mittman, and Linda Darling-Hammond, *Recruiting Mathematics and Science Teachers through Nontraditional Programs* (Santa Monica, CA: Rand Corporation, 1988); C. Emily Feistritzer, *Alternative Teacher Certification: A State-by-State Analysis* (Washington, DC: National Center for Education Information, 1990); Frank W. Lutz and Jerry B. Hutton, "Alternative Teacher Certification: Its Policy Implications for Classroom and Personnel Practice," *Educational Evaluation and Policy Analysis* 11, no. 3 (1989): 237-254; Robert A. Roth, "Alternate and Alternative Certification: Purposes, Assumptions, and Implications," *Action in Teacher Education* 8, no. 2 (1986): 1-6.

3. Karen Zumwalt, "Alternate Routes to Teaching: Three Alternative Approaches," *Journal of Teacher Education* 42, no. 2 (March-April 1991): 83-92.

4. Barnett Berry, "Why Bright College Students Won't Teach," *Urban Review* 18 (1986): 269-281; Donna H. Kerr, "Teaching Competence and Teacher Education in the United States," *Teachers College Record* 84 (1983): 525-552; Gary Natriello, "The Policy Context and Program Design of the New Jersey Provisional Teacher Program" (Paper presented at the Annual Meeting of the American Educational Research Association, San Francisco, 1989); W. Timothy Weaver, "In Search of Quality: The Need for Talent in Teaching," *Phi Delta Kappan* 61 (1979): 29-32, 46.

5. Gary Natriello, Edward L. McDill, and Aaron M. Pallas, *Schooling Disadvantaged Students: Racing against Catastrophe* (New York: Teachers College Press, 1990).

6. Jacqueline J. Irvine, "An Analysis of the Problem of the Disappearing Black Educator," *Elementary School Journal* 88, no. 5 (1988): 503-514.

7. Peter S. Hlebowitch and Joan Coady, "Retrenchment in Teacher Preparation: New Jersey's Alternative Credential," *Educational Horizons* 66, no. 3 (Spring 1988): 133-134.

8. Saul Cooperman, Arnold Webb, and Leo F. Klagholz, *An Alternative Route to Teacher Selection and Professional Quality Assurance: An Analysis of Initial Certification* (Trenton, NJ: New Jersey State Department of Education, September 1983).

9. Nick Penning, "The Alternate Route to Teaching," *School Administrator* 74, no. 4 (April 1990): 34, 36.

10. Steven R. Banks and Edward Necco, "Alternative Certification, Educational Training and Job Longevity," *Action in Teacher Education* 9, no. 1 (Spring 1987): 67-73.

11. Although these teachers are officially called provisional teachers in New Jersey, we will refer to them as alternate route teachers to avoid confusion with the term "provisional teachers," which in other states refers to teachers who have completed preparation for initial certification but have not met the experience and degree requirements for permanent certification. In actuality, in New Jersey these teachers are often referred to informally and in the press as alternate route teachers.

12. James D. Koerner, *The Miseducation of American Teachers* (Boston: Houghton-Mifflin, 1963).

13. An interesting correlate to the fact that alternate route teachers are less likely to have majored in the subject that they are teaching is the fact that during their phase one student teaching and their first year of teaching, alternate route teachers are less likely to be teaching in their certification area than college-prepared student teachers. After the first year, college-prepared teachers and alternate route teachers are just as likely to report teaching in their prime certification area. The fact that alternate route teachers are less likely to teach in their prime certification area during phase one and their first year may reflect the way districts are hiring phase one alternative route teachers—as fill-ins for teachers on leave or when additional sections need to be created. Because of the generic nature of alternate route certification and the ability of prospective teachers to pass tests and qualify for certification in several areas, districts may have more flexibility in hiring them. They are more likely initially to teach a patchwork of courses than the college-prepared teacher who must be placed in a subject- or grade-relevant student teaching position and then seeks a job in his or her certification area.

14. Michael Sedlak and Steven Schlossman, "Who Will Teach? Historical Perspectives on the Changing Appeal of Teaching as a Profession," in *Review of Research in Education*, vol. 14, edited by Ernst Z. Rothkopf (Washington, DC: American Educational Research Association, 1987).

15. Linda Darling-Hammond, *Beyond the Commission Reports: The Coming Crisis in Teaching* (Santa Monica, CA: Rand Corporation, 1984).

16. Holmes Group, *Tomorrow's Teachers*.

17. This pattern, of course, may reflect differences in the difficulty of obtaining a job, a possibility supported by the fact that one-quarter of the college-prepared teachers still in teaching in the third year were in substitute positions.

CHAPTER V

A Teachers' Union Revisits Its Association Roots

ROBERT M. MC CLURE

There are two major national organizations of teachers in the United States today—the National Education Association (NEA) and the American Federation of Teachers (AFT). In addition to its national headquarters in Washington, each organization has active state and local affiliates. The NEA was established in 1870 and the AFT in 1916. The two organizations initially had quite distinct purposes and, accordingly, quite different internal structures. Emphases in the NEA and the AFT have changed over time as each organization has broadened the scope of its activities in its efforts to serve its membership as well as the cause of education generally. As one who has been associated with NEA for four decades, I am in this chapter tracing some of the developments in that organization that reflect changes in its role as a professional organization of educators. An account of similar developments in the AFT may be found in an article by Marilyn Rauth in the *Phi Delta Kappan* of June 1990.[1]

During the last few decades the National Education Association has been variously identified as a teachers' *association* and a teachers' *union*. As a member of NEA in my early teaching career in the mid-1950s, I was a member of an association. In the 1960s, 1970s, and 1980s, as a member of the NEA staff, I was a member of a union. I am currently associated with the same organization, and I predict that in the 1990s the organizational designation will be a combination of the two, perhaps *professional union*.

Is this labeling indicative of something more than a fad? Does this self-perception of the nation's largest teacher organization relate to the current efforts to renew schools? Does it embrace new ways of thinking about how teachers can play a role in getting schools right

---

Robert M. McClure is the Director of the Mastery In Learning Consortium, National Center for Innovation, National Education Association.

for the students presently in them? I will make the case here that there is such a relationship and that this change of perception will impact positively on the improvement of American schools.

The Changing Role of a Professional Association of Teachers

Teachers in the 1990s are more involved with change in their schools than at any time in the recent past. The relatively short period from the beginnings of the national effort to improve schools to the present has seen a marked rise in such involvement. In 1983, early in the current reform movement, the teachers (and, most likely, their unions) were seen as the cause of the nation's educational ills. Three years later, with the reports of the Carnegie Task Force on Teaching as a Profession[2] and of the National Governors' Association,[3] a different view emerged; teachers were viewed as the solution to the schools' problems, and their organizations were seen as important to the success of the movement to improve schools. In this "second wave" of reform, a more balanced relationship evolved between top-down leadership and the leadership coming from individual practitioners and school faculties.

In this shifting environment, leaders of the National Education Association launched a new set of directions for the organization and changed its relationship to the school reform movement. What follows is a brief description of the contexts and dynamics that shaped those directions.

CONTROLLING TEACHERS AND TEACHING

The bureaucratic model of supervision is well entrenched in American education.[4] In the early part of this century, teachers in the United States were largely young, transient, poorly paid, and only slightly better educated than their students. In a previous era, the profession had been predominantly a male occupation. Beginning with the mid-nineteenth century, many men shifted to other occupations where compensation was better than in the classroom. In those days, conditions that existed for women—lower salaries than their male counterparts (an even greater discrepancy than today), the requirement to leave teaching at the time of marriage, and absence from the political arena—established a low status for teaching.

In 1923, the NEA reported that 36 percent of rural teachers in the nation had less than two years of teaching experience, while 64 percent had more than two years of teaching experience.[5] Similar reports from the U.S. Office of Education noted the transient nature of teachers: "[T]he high rate of transiency among teachers in the public school systems in the past has been detrimental not only to educational planning but unquestionably it has also been of significance in lowering the professional status of teachers in the public mind."[6]

In 1920, half of all teachers in the United States had less than four years of teaching experience; twenty years later the figure had climbed to ten years of experience. In 1940, a NEA *Research Bulletin* stated, "Teaching has not yet become a life-career service, but the tendency is definitely in that direction."[7]

To correct this absence of a stable, career-oriented teaching force, a system of bureaucratic control was created with decision making vested outside the classroom. Certainly, this system was not directed at creating a professional cadre of teachers. Rather, the system promoted "teacher proofing" of the schools through teacher guides, highly specific courses of study, behavioral objectives, standardized tests, and other "directive" controls. Supervision was focused on the teacher and was:

largely a matter of evaluating personalities, determining cleverness or lack of it in discipline, and checking on the details of classroom procedure. Such supervision emphasized uniformity and demanded strict adherence to detailed courses of study that had been designed to inculcate certain knowledge and common skills. There were two fundamental criteria: Could the teacher control the class? Were administrative edicts being strictly followed?[8]

THE BEGINNING OF TEACHER EMPOWERMENT

Because of several societal conditions that occurred in postwar America, chiefly the baby boom and the GI Bill, the building of a career-oriented teaching force was finally becoming a reality. As those who saw teaching as a true career grew in number, so did frustration with the bureaucratic model of supervision that was so prevalent. This frustration was manifested nationwide. As the ferment was developing in the 1950s and 1960s, two widespread calls were sounded for significant upgrading of the nation's schools. In the 1950s, James Conant,[9] with the support of President Eisenhower and other major figures, had a great impact on the course of secondary education. And in the 1960s, the launching of the Russian Sputnik also launched another reform movement in education, this time with the support of President Johnson and massive federal funds.

During this era, the National Education Association was a significantly different organization from what it is today. Membership totalled 750,000 with aspirations for even greater numbers. "A million or more by '64" was the NEA theme as the Sputnik-inspired reform got underway.

Through the 1960s, the NEA was an umbrella organization housing under one roof the great majority of professional associations that were giving substantive drive to American education. These associations included several subject-matter groups (music, mathematics, social studies, physical education, science, vocational education) as well as the educational researchers, teacher educators, media specialists, curriculum supervisors, elementary and secondary principals, and the superintendents.

Also in residence with some twenty-six of these organizations was the Educational Policies Commission (EPC). In 1938, the Commission had produced the influential report, *The Purposes of Education in American Democracy*.[10] In 1918, EPC's predecessor, the Commission on the Reorganization of Secondary Education, had produced the *Cardinal Principles of Education*[11] which shaped American secondary education in the early twentieth century. There was thus a rich history upon which NEA leaders could reflect and from which they could draw lessons for the future.

In the late 1950s and early 1960s, rank and file teachers were less interested in the history of their organization; they were more concerned that their organization lead in securing a better compensated career and the resources necessary for doing a better job in their classrooms. The process chosen by their organization to respond to these dual purposes was collective bargaining.

The setting in which teacher collective bargaining was to be defined and implemented was not propitious:

In the late 1950s and early 1960s, before collective bargaining, school boards were not necessarily unwilling to listen to the proposals of teacher organizations. The organizational spokesperson often would be allowed to appear at school board meetings and make the view of staff known with regard to salaries, sick leave, class size, and other matters. The problem was that there rarely was any perceptible relationship between the action ultimately taken by the school board and the proposals made by the teacher organization. This process was derisively characterized as "collective begging."[12]

With more activists entering teaching, with the American Federation of Teachers actively engaged in bargaining and widely publicized strikes, with NEA membership growing markedly, and with a more activist leadership in NEA, unionism and collective bargaining took hold.

In 1959, Wisconsin was the first state to provide teachers with legal access to collective bargaining. During the next decade, thirty-four other states followed suit. Robert Chanin, the NEA's legal counsel and a primary shaper of this revolution, recalls:

What occurred in those relatively few years was total restructuring of the historical power relationship between teachers and school boards. In its place was a process of proposal and counterproposal, of action and reaction, of give and take—resulting finally in deal or no deal, in mutual agreement or stalemate. This process assumed a parity of legal standing between the parties and a rough parity of bargaining power. Bilateral determination of terms and conditions of employment through collective bargaining meant that neither party had the ability to impose its will on the other. Agreement was the objective, but if agreement was not achieved, there were mechanisms for resolving disagreement—mediation, fact-finding, arbitration, and the strike.[13]

By the 1970s, what was later termed "teacher empowerment" was well underway. The thrust became an outright attack on unilateral decision making, the foundation of the bureaucratic model of supervision. At first, early successes occurred in the economic arena. Later, attempts were made to move the bargaining process into professional concerns outside the usual parameters defined by labor law. Here the bureaucracy stiffened and argued, successfully for a while, that professional, curricular, and pedagogical concerns were not fit subjects for the bargaining table.

Events outside the world of these arguments, however, were progressing rapidly. The early 1980s produced a new set of conditions that shaped American education and caused the NEA to ponder how to behave in this new world. What began in the early 1980s with a U.S. government report, *A Nation at Risk*,[14] was turning into a full-fledged national cottage industry: almost every state legislature, think tank, and trade organization issued a more or less detailed plan for fundamental reform of the public schools.

In 1984, Mary Hatwood Futrell became president of the NEA. Along with a majority of NEA leaders, she began to take cognizance of these events and to realize their potential impact on the organization. Talk ensued of the NEA becoming a new kind of union, a "professional union," one in which the usual definition of "conditions of work" would be greatly expanded. These leaders were responding to several stimuli:

- a restive membership, concerned that other powerful forces were determined to change the schools into new institutions without input from the faculties who taught in them;
- the fruition of several civil rights movements—not only for women and minorities but for parents and students as well—in which the Association had been a key actor;
- a growing body of knowledge about teaching and learning which was frustrating to people in the schools because they had so little access to it;
- an aging membership, most of whom were unwilling to turn away from collective bargaining but wanted also to build on a bargaining base to focus more directly on teaching and learning ("We have achieved the power that we fought for, now let's use it for the right purposes");
- a public increasingly concerned about school quality and equating decline in quality with perceived excesses of unionism;
- national and state political leaders who were convincing legislatures and the public that teachers (and their organizations) were the cause of the problems in the schools;
- a grave concern that negative accusations leveled at some trade unions might rub off on the NEA—the steel workers, for example, and their "responsibility" (in the eyes of the public) for the demise of their industry;
- a growing body of positive experience in business and in a few schools with site-based decision making, employee/teacher empowerment, and other efforts to increase worker productivity, commitment, and satisfaction.

A UNION GOES TO SCHOOL

During Ms. Futrell's first term in office, the NEA initiated the Mastery In Learning (MIL) Project. MIL was an effort to initiate faculty-led school restructuring programs, to bring to those faculties current research and other kinds of knowledge and to help them to apply this knowledge in their decision making, to learn from their experiences, and to use that knowledge to help others. It was the Association's first foray into field-based work in school improvement since the reform movement of the 1960s.

The NEA's support of the Mastery In Learning Project—first uneasy and then more forthcoming—reveals something of the ambivalence characterizing the union's reticence to move into a leadership role in school improvement. Initially, the Mastery In Learning Project was seen exclusively as an opportunity to demonstrate to the public and policymakers that the Association cared about improving schools. Later, as Futrell's leadership became more focused on the national urgency to improve schools, the Mastery In Learning Project and its staff became more closely aligned with NEA's mainline programs.

The dialogue and debate that accompanied this transition of support for MIL reveals the dichotomy of thought within NEA. The prevailing position was that *the* purpose of the organization is to represent members and protect their interests. In this context, it is argued that Association programs designed to improve educational opportunities for students absorb members' dues intended to support advocacy for teachers. Programs to improve professional practice and students' educational opportunities are seen, from this perspective, as the sole responsibility of management. According to a strict view of unionism, the danger is that such actions are in conflict with the union's goals of protecting its members.

In the Association's early involvement with school renewal, the emphasis was on site-based decision making. As Chanin asked in 1989, "Can a process such as site-based decision making that is premised on a sharing of common interest, mutual trust, and consensus building find happiness in a system of labor relations that is inherently adversarial in nature?" After rejecting arguments for either a simple "yes" or "no" answer to his question, he suggested what has become a part of the Association's stance: "The task, as I see it, is to determine how the potential advantages of site-based decision making can be realized within the framework of the current adversarial system of labor relations."[15]

Chanin's rationale would not permit two tracks of action, one for local school decision making and a separate, unrelated one for districtwide collective bargaining. Rather, the conditions by which faculties would be involved with school improvement would be established by the contract—not the products of the action, but the processes through which action would occur.

Early on, leaders of the Mastery In Learning Project determined that site-based decision making had to be only one part of a total school improvement agenda; it alone could not carry the burden of school renewal. The culture that then dominated those working in schools would have made it impossible for them to recreate a new educational institution for the future. In particular, four characteristics of this culture suggested that site-based decision making by itself was not enough:

1. Principals and teachers relied heavily on textbook manuals, mandates from outside the school, directives from supervisors, and advice from others in similar roles. They accepted the status quo and doubted that challenges to it would have much impact.

2. Most of the practitioners in the MIL network knew about or had experienced previous efforts to improve schools and believed much of that work had been misguided and harmful. They believed it was their responsibility to resist efforts that would, once again, damage educational quality.

3. Most staff members did not describe themselves as risk takers. They saw their school systems as closed organizations uninterested in input from "low-level" staff, as organizations that punished those who took risks.

4. School staffs accepted, almost without question, the technologies that control schooling: behavioral objectives, textbooks, and standardized tests.[16]

In short, if these faculties had been given the responsibility to change their school but had not been provided with the intellectual and human resources necessary to do that job properly, the outcome would likely have been "more of the same—done better."

In its network of twenty-six schools, the Mastery In Learning Project initiated three related efforts, each informed by a body of knowledge about effective school renewal practices. The first was to install site-based decision making in participating schools through agreements with the local representatives of the teachers and the school district administration.[17] The second was to change the cultures of these schools by helping them to become "centers of inquiry."[18] And the third was to help the twelve hundred teachers in these schools not only to use research and other knowledge, but to become partners in the creation of new understandings about teaching and learning.[19] Fuller description of these three processes and the results derived may be found elsewhere.[20]

Learnings from this work and other NEA school improvement initiatives have shaped a new way of thinking about the Association's role regarding professional issues. In several lighthouse districts, collectively bargained contracts have changed dramatically since 1985. Case studies[21] from these precursors of the future reveal that bargaining and site-based decision making, coupled with significant professional development opportunities, can improve schools *and* strengthen the union. According to a Rand study, *Teacher Unions and Educational Reform*, these are the "enabling conditions that unions must attain before they can move on to questions of professional autonomy and full participation."[22]

Several of NEA's state affiliates, often the most conservative segment of the organization, are increasing their programs in school improvement and beginning to redefine their roles. For example, it is not uncommon for these affiliates to have staff members with the title "instructional advocate" or "director of school restructuring."

The NEA has recognized that the current reform movement represents an opportunity, not a threat. It has increased its financial investment in programs for school restructuring, worked with its local affiliates to create pilot projects, launched a major campaign to help the public understand the importance of taking significant and unusual steps to improve education, and is coordinating all its programs so as to have a greater collective impact on the school improvement movement.

Perhaps most significant is the creation in 1990 of the NEA's National Center for Innovation. The Center's program is one of the most ambitious and comprehensive efforts in the country for the transformation of schools. These efforts range in scope from the school program level, to the school site (the second generation of the MIL work), to initiatives in entire school districts to better understand and support school restructuring, as well as programs in teacher education to build the kinds of programs that prepare prospective teachers for schools of the future.

The Effect on School Improvement

This joining of teacher organization resources and commitment to the cause of school improvement is important for many reasons. First, both of the major teacher unions (the National Education Association and the American Federation of Teachers) are superb at organizing, training, and helping people to act collectively. Such skills (and an appreciation of them) are scarce among those providing leadership to the national effort to improve schools and can significantly help the movement maintain its momentum. Secondly, these organizations have strong political action programs which, when employed in the name of school improvement, will do much to set the tone and develop the resources necessary for true educational renewal. Third, teacher organization leaders and staffs have a variety of competencies that can serve the effort well. These include skills related to research, finance, lobbying, public relations, and teacher compensation, as well as those seen to be more directly related to school improvement such as curriculum and instruction, teacher evaluation, teacher preparation, in-service professional development, and student assessment. And fourth, both major teacher organizations are trusted by their members. Given that many practicing teachers have negative views about attempts to reform schools, it is important that their organization help them see the seriousness of the current effort to improve education. Hopefully, that advocacy within the membership will stress the need for reforms to be deep, substantive, and lasting.

To maintain this trust and to expand their influence in the school renewal movement, teacher organizations will need to serve both as unions and as professional associations. The two functions will be balanced. If they are to be successful in performing both roles, their work must embrace the values their members have believed in for some time: high academic standards, equity, and a standing for the profession commensurate with its importance to the society.

Notes

1. Marilyn Rauth, "Exploring Heresy in Collective Bargaining and School Restructuring," *Phi Delta Kappan* 71 (June 1990): 781-784, 788-790.

2. Carnegie Forum on Education and the Economy, Task Force on Teaching as a Profession, *A Nation Prepared: Teachers for the 21st Century* (New York: Carnegie Forum on Education and the Economy, 1986).

3. National Governors' Association, *Time for Results: The Governors' 1991 Report on Education* (Washington, DC: National Governors' Association, 1986).

4. The material in this section is drawn from Gary D. Watts and Robert M. McClure, "Expanding the Contract to Revolutionize School Renewal," *Phi Delta Kappan* 71, no. 10 (1990): 765-774.

5. National Education Association, "What Are the Weak Spots in Our Public School System?" *Research Bulletin* 1, no. 4 (1923): 266.

6. Edward S. Evenden, Guy C. Gamble, and Harold G. Blue, *National Survey of the Education of Teachers*, Bulletin no. 10 (Washington, DC: U.S. Department of the Interior, Office of Education, 1933), p. 32.

7. National Education Association, "The Status of the Teaching Profession," *Research Bulletin* 18, no. 1 (1940): p. 59.

8. National Education Association, "Teacher Personnel Practices, 1950-51: Appointment and Termination of Service," *Research Bulletin* 30, no. 1 (1952): 12-13.

9. James Bryant Conant, *The American High School Today: A First Report to Interested Citizens* (New York: McGraw-Hill, 1959).

10. Educational Policies Commission, National Education Association, *The Purposes of Education in American Democracy* (Washington, DC: National Education Association, 1938).

11. Commission on the Reorganization of Secondary Education, National Education Association, *Cardinal Principles of Secondary Education* (Washington, DC: United States Department of the Interior, Bureau of Education, 1918).

12. Robert Chanin, "Is Collective Bargaining Compatible with Site-Based Decision Making?" (Speech delivered at the NEA National Conference, Denver, Colorado, April 8, 1989), p. 3.

13. Ibid., p. 5.

14. National Commission on Excellence in Education, *A Nation at Risk* (Washington, DC: U.S. Government Printing Office, 1983).

15. Chanin, "Is Collective Bargaining Compatible with Site-Based Decision Making?" p. 9.

16. Robert M. McClure, "The Evolution of Shared Leadership," *Educational Leadership* 46, no. 3 (1988): 60-62.

17. Maxine M. Bentzen, *Changing Schools: The Magic Feather Principle* (New York: McGraw-Hill, 1974).

18. Robert J. Schaeffer, *The School as a Center of Inquiry* (New York: Harper & Row, 1967).

19. Charles L. Thompson, "Knowledge, Power, Professionalism, and Human Agency," in *Teachers and Research in Action*, edited by Carol Livingston and Shari Castle (Washington, DC: National Education Association, 1989).

20. For a description of the NEA Mastery In Learning Project, see Robert M. McClure, "Individual Growth and Institutional Renewal," in *Staff Development for Education in the 90s*, edited by Ann Lieberman and Lynne Miller (New York: Teachers College Press, 1991), pp. 221-241, and Peter A. Barrett, *Doubts and Certainties: Working Together to Restructure Schools* (Washington, DC: National Education Association, 1991).

21. Watts and McClure, "Expanding the Contract to Revolutionize School Renewal."

22. Lorraine M. McDonnell and Anthony Pascal, *Teacher Unions and Educational Reform* (Washington, DC: Center for the Study of the Teaching Profession, RAND Corporation, 1988), p. ix.

Section Two
THE CHANGING SCHOOL CONTEXT

CHAPTER VI

*Challenging the Limits of School
Restructuring and Reform*

TERRY A. ASTUTO AND DAVID L. CLARK

From whom or what are at-risk children at risk? How did a consensus develop that allows us to accept as ordinary the ineffectiveness of American schools for large segments of our children and youth? At what point did we decide that schools and school systems which serve poor children should be judged as doing a good job if they perform at a level above average for this condition of disadvantage, although their level of performance is far below the average for children from affluent homes?

Why are we struggling to implement systems of site-based management in our schools while ignoring such technical adjustments as keeping schools open twelve months a year? Why do we insist that intersector attention to the developmental needs of children and youth cannot be made available within school buildings? Why should young Americans be without health care, adequate nutrition, and psychological and general welfare services? In what sort of reform movement do we find ourselves?

We have reached a time when radical educational reform is needed for our public educational system to serve the needs of our children and youth and the only radical reform being proposed is abandonment of the system. We are caught in a nest of assumptions that are limiting our options so severely that genuine reform seems to be beyond our grasp. In *The Predictable Failure of Educational Reform*, Sarason argues

---

Terry A. Astuto is Associate Professor of Education, Curry School of Education, University of Virginia, Charlottesville, VA. David L. Clark is Professor of Education, School of Education, University of North Carolina, Chapel Hill, NC.

that we are overlooking the obvious in thinking about reform because "we all have been socialized most effectively to accept the power relationships characteristic of our schools as right, natural, and proper, outcomes to the contrary notwithstanding."[1]

Our intent is to extend Sarason's argument. The limitations of our imagination about school reform involve relatively unchallenged assumptions about the structural, educational, personal, and contextual domains of schools and schooling. The aphoristic status of these assumptions needs to be challenged so that they become matters for discussion rather than for assumptive action.

What Is Blocking Educational Reform?

If most people accept the necessity of fundamental reform in American education, if examples of such reform can be described as possible and in fact are already operating in some schools and some classrooms, if the reforms can be argued as quite reasonable and attainable even though fundamental, there must be powerful factors precluding the introduction of these reforms in most schools and school systems. We believe these prohibiters lie in a set of assumptions about schools and schooling that are erroneous and pernicious. These assumptions cross domains of concern to policymakers, educators, reformers, and the general citizenry and include *structural, educational, personal,* and *contextual* premises. They are built upon a consensual validation of what is true, right, and possible that lacks empirical and face validity and traps us within a narrow band of reform proposals based on what we know how to do rather than what needs to be done.

WHAT WE KNOW ABOUT THE STRUCTURE OF SCHOOLS

The most common characteristic of the common school is the distribution of power and authority from those in elected or appointed positions as board members through designated leadership positions established by the board to the classroom teacher and, finally, to the student. Most of us believe that:

- *Schools and school systems are, of necessity, organized as bureaucracies with authority and power vested in a set of designated hierarchical positions.*

If you think that this assertion is not treated as a truism, try a simple proposal. Suggest to a school board or district administrative staff, or state education agency that a staff of professional teachers ought to be granted the privilege of organizing its school in an appropriate fashion. If the teachers think they would be better off without a full-time administrator, they can choose that route. If they want a full-time administrator, they can choose one; democratic election would be a good way to do it. Then listen to the rebuttals. Who would be held accountable for the results in such a school? Who would provide the leadership for high standards of performance and needed change? There would be chaos from day one. The teachers would choose a "soft" principal who would not hold them to standards of high performance. This just could not work in most schools because it would not provide a reasonable guarantee of coordination and control.

Schools run by teachers as either professional or democratic organizations would not guarantee a successful environment for students. Neither does a bureaucratic organization. The point is that the necessity of bureaucracy with its inherent domination of workers on-the-line by designated bosses is a matter of choice not mandate. Substantial evidence supports the efficacy of democratic organizations. The choice of organizational type includes several options ranging from radical forms to pure forms to an eclectic invention of alternative forms. Contemporary discussions of site-based management have faltered because of the belief that it has to be adopted within the constraints of standard bureaucratic structure. Nonsense! Teachers can be allowed control over major decisions, not simply participation in the decision-making process. They ought to choose their colleagues and their leaders. And they ought to be expected to assume the same posture toward freedom and involvement in relation to their students and to the parents who are concerned vitally with the effectiveness of the school.

- *The buck has to stop with someone if an organization is to be effective.*

People should assume responsibility for excellence in organizational performance. In ordinary bureaucratic settings the locus of that responsibility is assigned to the designated leader. The superintendent is held responsible for the effectiveness of the district; the principal for the effectiveness of the school; the teacher for effectiveness in the classroom. Of course, that turns out to be a fiction. If a school district is in trouble, there are a thousand legitimate excuses that can be used by all the operatives in the system. Perhaps the chief school administrator is prevented from moving ahead by a politically infested board of education or by twenty-two principals who were appointed before the chief administrator came on the scene, or by a truculent teacher's union that is interested only in gaining economic advantage for teachers. The principal could be a star, but is constrained by a heavy-handed central office that is insensitive to the needs of the school. Or the individual teachers are very effective professionals, but they are impeded by an ineffective, domineering principal or an unresponsive central office staff.

The buck does not stop in complex human organizations. Everyone has to be responsible for effectiveness. The arbitrary assignment of authority and power to designated individuals creates an environment of buck-passing not buck-stopping. In the most responsible (and responsive) organizations those employees closest to the point of effective action control the process of production. In education that is the teacher and the student.

- *Educational improvement will be achieved by well thought out goals (consensus about where we need to go), an effective plan for getting there, and monitoring of achievement along the way.*

Not since the earliest days of the efficiency movement in educational management has this set of assumptions been so powerful. From the Charlottesville Summit in 1989, through the National Assessment of Educational Progress, to the state-based report cards on school system performance, to the recent proposal by Educate America for a national test for all high school seniors, this country is placing its confidence in educational reform on mechanistic devices planned and administered by individuals far removed from the school site. These centralized devices for change require a simplicity in the task to which they are applied that is uncharacteristic of and probably inimical to American education. Consensus on goals is easy to obtain nationally so long as the goals are not defined operationally or consequentially. No one wants to debate the utility of preventing school dropouts. The consensus becomes ambiguous, however, when arbitrary performance on standardized tests is argued as the measure of educational accomplishment. Would you prefer to force students out of school by imposing standards they are unable to meet at a particular grade level or by retaining them in school while they fail to meet grade-level standards for graduation? Or would you solve the problem by establishing a tracking system that allows the student to stay in school but traps him or her in a curriculum that closes off the possibility of future options for employment or education?

Centralized planning and goal setting postpone the identification of the trade-offs that will occur in policy and practice, isolate the design for improvement from the site of improvement, and create a sense of uninvolvement on the part of those who will bear responsibility for implementation.

The structural issues raised by centralized planning built upon assessment of outcomes quickly overlap with educational program assumptions. Educate America's news release in support of a national test noted that "[the test] would focus on the ends of learning, not the means. What is taught in school and how it is taught would continue to be determined by local school boards and individual states."[2] Of course, that is not true. A national test is a control device within a centralized plan for national school improvement. By its very nature it will be insensitive to local variability in needs and to student experiences, abilities, and aspirations. A national test will influence directly what local schools teach and how they teach it. That is its purpose; that is its failing. Centralized planning falls apart because it is, by its nature, insensitive to the units and people who will have to implement the improvement. In bureaucratic terms, it separates the design of production from its execution. This is the most extreme case of the division of labor. Giroux argues that this division of conception and execution produces "a management model [that] is demeaning to teachers and students alike. If we are to take the issue of schooling seriously, schools should be the one site where democratic social relations become a part of one's lived experiences."[3]

WHAT WE KNOW ABOUT EDUCATIONAL PROCESSES

The impact of aphorisms on the educational process is influenced not only by derivative implications from the foregoing structural assumptions, but by a similar set of assumptions asserted specifically about curricular decisions.

- *The best way to organize for instruction in secondary schools is around subject-matter specializations offered to students in segmented periods of instruction by individual teachers certified in the subject area.*

The strength of some beliefs needs to be demonstrated only by their prevalence in practice. Visit a high school in the Bronx or in a remote, rural district in Wyoming and you will find high school students sitting with a teacher for a forty-five to fifty minute period in English before they move on to history or physics or whatever. The fact that many educators view this structure as inimical to effective instruction is beside the point. Attempt to propose that teachers and students should be grouped together at the secondary level in a small cohort (say six teachers with varying substantive expertise and ninety students) for their high school years and you will not be taken seriously. But the matter is of the utmost seriousness to millions of adolescents. Their most pressing need is to connect to an adult who cares, who gets to know them, who works with them in a group of individuals with whom they can relate.

Schools have become caught in a pattern of instructional delivery so powerful that it seems invulnerable. Affluent school districts, for example, hire tutors to work with students in English classes on written composition because the "regular" teacher is processing 125 to 150 students a day through the class schedule. The trap set by the scheduling of instruction is not even on the agenda of reform in education; alternatives are ruled out by arguments of complexity, inefficiency, and impracticality. Why does it seem so reasonable to persist in this dysfunctional practice? Probably because it fits the mechanical model of bureaucratic organization on which we have decided to build our schools.

- *Students (and teachers) need prolonged periods of respite from their labors—the traditional summer vacation.*

When school boards are found advocating the year-round school, it is normally because they are short of school facilities. The discussion is not whether students should be in school all year but rather whether vacations can be scheduled to optimize the use of school facilities during the summer months. There is no dearth of evidence on the disadvantages of continuing the practice of a ten-week summer vacation for students. The decrement in learning over this vacation period has been documented thoroughly. The decrement is sharper for students who are learning at a below-average level during the school year and is sharpest of all for students who come from home and community backgrounds that provide limited academic stimuli. School dropout decisions are more frequently made by students during this time period than at any other time in the school year.

The extended summer vacation period is a depressant to school change and student productivity. Hundreds of thousands of teachers are not on vacation during the summer. They are taking on any jobs they can find to support themselves during the break. Professionals are not part-time. Teachers need the opportunity and responsibility of thinking about and working on their professional tasks full time.

As poverty sweeps through the youth of this country, students are not being favored by being sent into dangerous environments from which many never return. If nothing but learning opportunities for American youth relative to those for youth in other countries is considered, eliminating the extended vacation period deserves serious consideration as an effective reform strategy in education, although it is not even on the agenda.

- *Students need to be held to standards of performance at specific grade levels and at graduation.*

This belief has now been reified in goals adopted by the National Governors' Association. The concept has embedded within it three problematic practices in the organization of instruction: (1) the utility of grade levels as a way to group students for instruction; (2) retention as a tool for enforcing arbitrary levels of achievement; and (3) tracking students into curricula of varying levels of difficulty as a method of accounting for students at particular grade levels who are unable to meet the arbitrary grade-level standards. Repeated systematic inquiry about these educational devices leads to the conclusion that they are all dysfunctional. The majority of students who are retained learn less, not more, than they would have had they been promoted to the next grade. Tracking gives up on student learning capacity by restricting learning opportunities before they have a chance to occur. Oakes, for example, comments on the anomaly that Shakespeare is not a part of the curriculum for students in low-track classes although "Shakespeare wrote plays for audiences far less literate than most 9th, 10th, and 11th grade low-track American high school students."[4] The very notion of creating grades with arbitrary, but uniform, curricula and tests based on the age of students is absurd when examined against the variable developmental progress of children and youth, violating even such obvious differences as the gender-related maturational advantage of girls.

One thing is certain. The practices derived from these beliefs have contributed directly to the conversion of the American public school into a sorting machine dominated by the economic status of the student's family. If we were serious about maximum achievement opportunities within American public schools, we would be forced to find alternatives to organizing students by age-based grade levels, emphasizing performance on standardized tests as a measure of progress and achievement in school, and enforcing arbitrary standards of achievement for students within and at the end of their school experience. We would have to abandon the most popular policy tools now in use at national and state levels in the reform of American education.

WHAT WE KNOW ABOUT PEOPLE IN ORGANIZATIONS

Contemporary American schools seem to be built upon and operating on assumptions about human nature described a quarter century ago by Douglas McGregor as Theory X views of human behavior.[5] When translated into the school context (with apologies to McGregor) these views would sound like this:

- *The average school teacher and student have an inherent dislike of teaching, studying, preparing, doing homework and will avoid such work if possible.*
- *Most teachers and students must be coerced, controlled, directed, and threatened with punishment to get them to put forth adequate effort to achieve the national goals of education.*
- *The average teacher and student prefer to be directed rather than making their own decisions, want to avoid responsibility rather than taking on more responsibility, have little ambition, and are more interested in security than risk taking.*

This set of assumptions does more than justify a bureaucratic form for school organization. State and national policies, rules, and regulations reflect the same beliefs. Mandated performance standards assume that, without them, lax behavior and the avoidance of responsibility will result, indeed, have resulted. Restricting participation by students in school activities unless they maintain a specified grade-point average; establishing arbitrary test scores that must be attained at specified grade levels; utilizing a national test to ferret out low performers; assuming that local testing or classroom testing is an inadequate method for evaluating students; retaining students in grades as a punishment for inadequate year-long performance; emphasizing the importance of teacher evaluation—all these fit the mind set of the individual who knows that people need to be prodded to performance. Oddly enough, individuals who hold that belief do not think *they* need such prodding. In fact, they see themselves as individuals who seek self-actualization by working hard, assuming responsibility, going the extra mile. And they probably believe this to be true of their children, their best friends, their closest colleagues. But the further human beings get away from themselves, the more uninspired and slovenly they become.

As McGregor argued in his classic treatise, this belief system is nonsensical and without foundation in the accumulated research evidence on human behavior or human development. The overwhelming majority of people seek self-actualization and success. They work to achieve and take pride both in their accomplishments and in the process of work itself. They struggle to be recognized as "good" at their job. They seek autonomy and the responsibility for making their own work-related decisions. They choose to be adults in behavior and in fact.

When you find a person exhibiting unnatural behavior, you need to look for the cause outside the individual. Of course, there are people who dislike their jobs, who have given up on work and the possibility of achievement. Something caused that response. In most instances the cause is what is argued to be the cure, i.e., a pattern of failure, rejection, coercion, control, direction, threat, and lack of trust. The repetition of the pattern will not enhance performance; it will reinforce the maladaptive behavior that produced the problem in the first place.

People are the only route to increased productivity available to organizations. They are the key to improvement, the natural resource of the workplace. Intelligence, creativity, and ambition are widely, not narrowly, diffused among the population. Administrators and policymakers who "know best" undoubtedly do not. All of us ultimately rely on others to achieve our ends. The more powerful and authoritative our position and status, the more that becomes the case.

Sarason argues this point by contending that reform has failed in the past because we have assumed erroneously that "schools exist only or primarily for children."[6] Schools must be considered as the living space for both children and teachers. If they are unsatisfactory for the latter, they cannot be satisfactory for the former. Teachers are the key to the success of educational reform, not the cause of the current difficulties. In arguing for a reconsideration of the power relationship in schools and constant attention to staff development, Sarason noted:

Teaching is regarded as something you can do (and do well!) day in and day out, month in and month out, year in and year out without any decrease in motivation or change in style, satisfaction, patience, sensitivity, and sense of challenge. . . . It should make no difference if the teacher does not experience any collegiality, has no role in decision making, . . . and regards him or herself as a member of the educational proletariat.[7]

That will not do. Teachers, not administrators, are the key to educational excellence. There are millions more of them and they are closer to the action. A pattern of reform that diminishes their role in the educational process, limits their flexibility and autonomy, and ignores their need for self-development and recognition has no chance of succeeding with students. Schools will eventually have to become free and supportive environments for students and teachers—that above all!

WHAT WE KNOW ABOUT CONTEXTUAL ELEMENTS OF EDUCATION

The constant interaction between schools and the local, state, and national communities in which they exist gives rise to economic, political, and social assumptions that ultimately influence the limits of reform that have been considered practicable.

- *The United States already spends more on education than other nations and faces a fiscal crisis that eliminates the possibility of increasing that level of expenditure. In any case, the problems of education cannot be solved by throwing money at them.*

The first of these assertions is not supported by fact. The United States spends less per pupil than many other countries. In terms of percent of governmental expenditures for education, the United States is below average. The second assumption is in the eye of the beholder. Economists assume different positions in defining the country's fiscal crisis. Some are deeply concerned about the national debt; others see it as a reasonable percentage of our gross national product. In either case, the debt crisis could be solved by generating more revenue. If President Bush's lips asserted that the United States required a healthy tax increase, an increase that would place us in an average position in relation to tax rates in other Western countries, the fiscal crisis would not be an *a priori* justification for holding the line on educational costs. The debate would then have to switch to the issue of whether increased dollars would solve some or all of our educational ills.

This brings us to the third of the economic assumptions, one that gained aphoristic standing during the Reagan administration. President Reagan tapped into a populist belief that the federal government could not solve social ills through federal expenditures (in fact, he contended that federal increases in educational expenditures worsened the condition of education) and that the difficulties of education were not linked directly to underfunding. The argument that you cannot solve problems by throwing money at them has become a shibboleth of those who would either prefer to spend money elsewhere on their own problem or simply cut governmental expenditures overall.

The broad effect of these assumptions has been to eliminate the discussion of educational alternatives that would sharply increase expenditures. When the President of the American Federation of Teachers suggested that the route to progress in fighting urban school failures might be to turn over ninety students to eight teachers for three years, the first calculation in most persons' minds was the cost of modifying the student-teacher ratio. Keeping schools open for children and youth from six in the morning until midnight, twelve months a year is viewed as financially not feasible. Providing free meals at school three times a day or free medical and dental services in the school building is ruled out before the merits of the proposals are debated.

The economics of schooling have limited the consideration of reform proposals to such a narrow band of policy alternatives that pessimism about the outcomes of reform seems justified. "Throwing money at problems" is an important option to reintroduce to educational reform. From 1980-1988, President Reagan demonstrated that excess funds, risk capital, and slack time and resources have an amazing impact on problem solving. United States military capacity was enhanced markedly during that time frame by massive increased support. Increased expenditures of substantial magnitude have to be reinstated as a policy option to be debated as problems with the existing educational system are identified.

- *Schools should concentrate on schooling. Our educational system has drifted away from a focus on the basics. Schools are for teaching and learning, not for rendering social services.*

The debate over the scope of the school's responsibility for services to children took a sharp turn toward a narrow construction of the school's role during the past decade—just at the time when the needs of children in a variety of life's domains increased markedly. Throughout the years of the Reagan administration, the emphasis on reform was not simply that schools should "tend to their knitting" but that return to the basics meant an emphasis on the 3Rs, on "hard" subjects in high school, on increased subject-area requirements for graduation. The assessment tool of choice to figure out how the schools were performing their defined task was the standardized achievement test—an old idea whose time had come. This narrowed focus affected the curriculum itself (e.g., de-emphasizing music, art, physical education, vocational education), but had an even more dramatic effect on noncurricular services (e.g., health, nutrition, counseling, dental care). The possibility of the school becoming the center for youth development services provided on an intersector basis has not even surfaced in the current school reform proposals.

There are markedly different ways to think about schools. One of the obvious advantages of school buildings is that they are everywhere. In big towns and small, in every corner of the city you can find a school building. Their limitation is that they are not used for much. Sarason tries to jolt his readers into thinking about the peculiarities of our assumptions about schooling by picturing a school as being observed by a visitor from space. In a search for regularities, his space person discovers that "for five consecutive days the school is one of the most densely populated settings; for two consecutive days it is devoid of humanoids. What . . . should I make of that?"[8] What should one make of a public service building that is closed for three months a year and is in disuse almost half of the time that it is purportedly open? If this is a society in which public services are needed by all children and are needed desperately by an increasing proportion of children, why should the most accessible building be designated as a place in which the rendering of such services is inappropriate? Is it difficult to imagine schooling being successful in a building that houses youth services? Is it not reasonable to imagine, on the contrary, that children would view the school building as a more congenial environment for learning if it also provided facilities that enhanced the youngster's life as a human being?

- *However hard they try, schools can effect only marginal gains in the education of students. Social and economic (by implication ethnic and familial) characteristics of the student's background are more influential in predicting educational achievement than within-school modifications or innovations.*

If this belief did not begin with the Coleman Report of the 1960s, an existing belief was affirmed by the apparent findings of that national study.[9] The instructionally effective schools movement of the late 1970s and the early 1980s attempted to counter that finding with shaky research evidence.[10] The movement, however, provided a more solid political platform by arguing that if one child from a "disadvantaged" background or one classroom of such children or one school with such pupil characteristics could achieve average success, the contention that social class determines success in American schools is demonstrably incorrect.

Despite all the rhetoric of the past fifteen years, most people, and most policymakers, believe that the key determinant of school success is family or social or ethnic background. The often asserted public school position that "all children can learn" is belied by the fact that American public schools are an efficient sorting machine that reproduces adults in roughly the same social class where they began as five-year-olds entering school.

The issue is not whether schools do, in fact, make a sufficient difference in the lives of children so that most of them can share in the success of this society as adults; they obviously do not do so. The issue is why they do not do so, since they obviously could. If the overwhelming proportion of children from a particular social or ethnic group are failing to achieve in an extant organization, the problem lies in the organization, not the people. The goal should not be for the people to fit the organization. The goal should be for the organization to fit the people. Current schools do not fit poor children, bilingual children, minority children.

The assumption of who or what must be adjusted to fit is embedded in the most developed of the state-level achievement testing systems. Connecticut is proud of the fact that it makes adjustments for school districts and schools that serve large numbers of poor and minority youngsters when comparing those schools with others in more affluent areas. The outcome of this adjustment is to support the assumption that our schools are all right, some just have less able children with whom to deal. Critical theorists would surely point out the coincidence that the schools with more able youngsters are located in communities with affluent, influential, and well-educated parents. These testing systems are a contemporary device to hold criticism of schools within bounds and to contain the schools that work least well for poor children and youth within those communities.

Foundations for Unauthentic Reform

These widely held assumptions are nested in such inextricable patterns that it is nearly impossible to discuss them singly. They reinforce one another so that one unfounded assumption is used unconsciously to support a second unlikely proposition. An individual defending a practice which is as dysfunctional as a secondary school organized in segments of instruction taught by certified specialists in each subject area can call upon arguments drawn from (1) *structural considerations* (i.e., efficiency, accountability, expertness, division of labor); (2) *assumptions about people* (i.e., assignment of limited, specific responsibilities to teachers and students, narrow span of responsibility, precise monitoring of performance); and (c) *contextual elements* (i.e., cost reduction, focus on basic subjects, ease of creating tracks or levels within subjects for students of varying abilities).

The frustrating feature of this pattern of assumptions is that it generates its own set of incremental reforms that have no chance of effecting major change in schools or schooling or, more importantly, no chance of helping poor children and youth to save themselves. This incrementalism is a peculiar form of neoorthodoxy that reinforces the weaknesses of our educational system by doing something new that we know how to do rather than dealing with what needs to be done.

SITE-BASED MANAGEMENT

No one assumes that bureaucracy has no costs. Most reformers believe that teachers ought to be involved in decisions that affect their lives. Research on organizations over the past thirty years affirms the desirability of participatory decision making. Critics of education point to the low status of most teachers in the school organization and the utility of enhancing their professional prestige and autonomy.

If you know there are problems in autocratic, tightly controlled bureaucratic systems but you also "know" that bureaucracy is inevitable, that clients want unitary control, and that most people in organizations are untrustworthy, you have to invent a neoorthodox response that fits the challenge. Site-based management as it is devised and practiced in most school districts fits the bill:

- *In most forms it simply transfers bureaucratic authority from one level to another, i.e., from the central office to the principal's office.*
- *Teacher involvement in decision making is constrained to nonessential decisions. In almost no instances do teachers choose their colleagues or their principal. Their decisions have to "fit" system directives or they are overruled. If the teachers feel the requirements for standardized testing are impeding rather than facilitating instruction, they have simply exceeded the bounds of their newfound authority.*
- *Students are seldom involved in the new management structure. When they are involved, their scope of decision making is almost always held in tight check.*
- *When parents and other citizens are given newfound power and authority in decision making, the new school-level structure looks like a mini-school system, i.e., a local citizens' group is appointed or elected*

as if it were the old school board. In fact, the most revolutionary site-based management systems are best described as decentralization—the formation of a smaller bureaucracy.

The basic structural deficiencies of bureaucracy are left unchallenged by our current examples of site-based management. The impossibility of converting a bureaucracy into a free organization will not be confronted in the foreseeable future unless we challenge the assumption that bureaucracy is inevitable.

TESTING AND ASSESSMENT

A full range of reforms rely on testing outcomes as the tool for school improvement. The genesis of this peculiar approach to school improvement lies in a lack of confidence in people to perform except under conditions of control. Add to this the confidence in competition as a spur to productivity, and investments in local, state, and national testing schemes are the result. Nothing about this movement suggests that it will affect positively either the process or outcomes of education. All these schemes conflict with the purposes of site-based management while being argued to make it possible, i.e., you can run your school the way you want to; we just want to check on the results, not the techniques.

Such an assertion is a political slogan, not a real-world consideration. Those caught in such a system are foolish not to align their content closely to the outcome measure. This removes the local unit from any control over the substance of instruction. What is left are techniques of instruction. They need to fit the form of the questions being asked. And, of course, they will. Testing leads to conformity. Site-based management suggests variability. The two together should amount to incremental change in a system that needs basic overhaul.

Testing advocates assure critics that they are well on their way to the development of authentic tests that will reflect what children and youth really know. That promise has been made before. The scientism of the 1950s promised that social and behavioral researchers would produce theoretical structures and empirical knowledge that would lead to a science of administration, a science of human behavior.

The current fascination with outcomes and outcome measurement is reminiscent of the emphasis in American business and industry on outcomes measurement that W. Edward Deming faced in the post-World War II years. He finally took his basic message to Japan. Focus on process not outcomes; outcomes will take care of themselves. The human and fiscal resources that any organization has available to devote to improvement are limited; use them up on people and the restructuring of the core tasks to be performed. Product improvement will never occur by counting rejects and blaming employees. The key to improvement is staff development, invention, improvement in design, improvement in working conditions—not comparison, competition, condemnation, and coercion.[11]

Keys to Authentic Reform

Escaping the trap of the nested set of traditional assumptions about school structures, educational processes, people in the workplace, and the contextual elements of education frees the imagination to consider different ways of supporting learning communities for students and teachers. The keys to authentic reform are rooted in competing assumptions about schooling and organizing that have always challenged the dominant orthodoxy, but now have cumulated to the point where they represent clear alternatives supported by organizational theory, research, and experience.

SCHOOL STRUCTURES THAT SUPPORT LEARNING COMMUNITIES

Imagine an educational experience for adolescents and young adults that is built on principles of shared leadership, individual and community responsibility, and human growth and development. Professional teachers work together in teams with a heterogeneous community of learners for an extended period, at least the four years that currently comprise most secondary schools. These teachers work with specialists (e.g., health care professionals, counselors, social workers, paraprofessionals, school administrators) whose skills can be focused on individual student needs. Individual professionals are expected to assume leadership responsibilities for individual students and the entire learning community. Coordination is grounded in pedagogy and curriculum. Control results from negotiated norms of individual freedom, interpersonal respect, and mutual responsibility. The thrust of the professional's work is the effective delivery of instruction, the growth and development of each student, and ongoing improvement of practice. School administrators serve as educational representatives to the larger community—communicating school purposes and expectations, creating linkages with social service agencies, seeking out needed resources (human, technical, and financial), and responding to the routine informational and professional needs of the learning community.

School structures supportive of learning communities of teachers and students are based on beliefs about freedom in the workplace:

- *Schools and school systems are, of necessity, organized as teaching and learning work units with authority and power vested in the professional staff.*
- *The buck never stops if an organization is to be effective; diffused responsibility directs everyone's attention to the effectiveness of the whole.*
- *Educational improvement is achieved by responsiveness and responsibility to individual students, expectations for human growth and development, and professional agreements about actions targeted to individual student growth.*

EDUCATIONAL PROCESSES THAT SUPPORT LEARNING COMMUNITIES

Imagine an educational experience for adolescents and young adults built on principles of critical thinking and problem solving, individual responsibility for learning, the complexity of the knowledge explosion, and the lifelong needs of adults. The school day is organized according to the rhythm of teaching and learning, not arbitrary time and content segments. Young adults work individually and in groups with teachers to acquire relevant information, hone the tools of learning (including basic skills development), think critically about relevant issues and problems, and engage in active inquiry. Segmented impersonal classes, conducted behind classroom doors, are replaced with active engagement in learning activities with appropriate blocks of time, a wide range of resources, and student involvement in the selection and assessment of learning-related products. The multidisciplinary teaching team maps the range of content over a four-year period in the humanities, sciences, social sciences, and fine and performing arts. Subject and discipline specialists work with teachers to generate ideas about the knowledge bits necessary for entry into a productive, independent adult life. Timing and sequencing are based on principles of individual growth and development, cultural and gender-related learning needs and preferences, and cognitive strengths and abilities. Pedagogical decisions are focused on stretching each individual student to mastery levels of competency.

Educational processes supportive of learning communities of teachers and students are based on beliefs grounded in human growth and development, such as:

- *The best way to organize for instruction in secondary schools is around principles of student learning and pedagogy provided by multidisciplinary teams of education specialists.*
- *Students (and teachers) need and want prolonged opportunities for study and learning.*
- *Teachers and students need to develop standards of performance for themselves that are challenging and relevant to productive adult lives.*

PEOPLE AS THE SOURCE OF PRODUCTIVITY IN LEARNING COMMUNITIES

Imagine an educational experience for adolescents and young adults built on the belief that people are the key to school effectiveness. Teachers build on student strengths and talents. Instead of using measures of failure as a prod for increased achievement, evidence of student success is the building block of further success. Professional colleagues recognize that individual talents are complemented by the talents of others. Collaboration replaces competition; collegiality replaces isolation; the possibility of success replaces the probability of failure.

Again with apologies to Douglas McGregor, schools would be built on assumptions about human nature described as Theory Y:

- *The average school teacher and student like teaching, studying, preparing, doing homework.*
- *Most teachers and students routinely demonstrate personal initiative and put forth high levels of effort to further learning and human growth and development.*
- *The average teacher and student prefer the freedom and autonomy to make their own decisions, want to assume responsibility, take initiative, and are interested in improvement, innovation, and risk taking.*

LEARNING COMMUNITIES RELEVANT TO SOCIETAL CONTEXTS

Imagine an educational experience for adolescents and young adults that recognizes and is responsive to the economic and social contexts in which schools exist. Community centers for young adults replace traditional high schools. Teaching and learning occur in these centers, but the educational enterprise is sensitive to the range of needs and problems confronting today's youth. These centers exist for young adults for whatever assistance they need, to respond when they are sick or hungry or homeless or depressed or frightened or lonely. The full range of community health, protection, and social services converges on these sites so that the services are where the needs are.

Political, public, and professional support for youth centers are based on beliefs about investments in the future and the promises of a democratic society:

- *The United States is among the wealthiest nations in the world. The future of the society demands a significant investment in our youth.*
- *The school house needs to be replaced by community youth centers because the needs and problems of youth are multiple and interactive.*
- *Education professionals, policymakers, and the general public can no longer tolerate beliefs about the inevitability of below par school performance of poor children and other historically underserved populations. Schooling for all children must deliver on the promise of a productive life in a just and equitable society for all citizens.*

Authentic reform is practical, comprehensive, and integral to the conditions blocking school improvement. Contemporary school structures are not working for teachers and students, especially students historically underserved by the educational system. Undoubtedly, they also act as depressants in other ways for all children and youth—gifted children who are unchallenged by them, middle-class children who are provided with more meaningful opportunities for growth outside of school. Almost everyone believes that reform is necessary, but the options for choice under consideration are based on beliefs and assumptions about school structures, teaching, and learning that are incompatible with contemporary conditions. Those assumptions need to be challenged to free the imagination to pursue the kind of radical reformation that pays more than lip service to the critical role of schools in fostering an educated citizenry prepared to live in a democratic and just society.

Notes

1. Seymour B. Sarason, *The Predictable Failure of Educational Reform* (San Francisco: Jossey-Bass, 1990), p. 7.

2. Robin Gallagher, "Orange High Principal Slams Test Idea," *Chapel Hill Newspaper*, 1 February 1991, p. 1.

3. Henry A. Giroux, *Teachers as Intellectuals* (Granby, MA: Bergin and Garvey, 1988), p. 9.

4. Jeannie Oakes, "Making the Best of Schools," *Network Newsnotes* (National Network of Principals' Centers), November 1990, p. 12.

5. Douglas McGregor, *The Human Side of Enterprise* (New York: McGraw-Hill, 1985), pp. 33-34.

6. Sarason, *The Predictable Failure of Educational Reform*, p. xiii.

7. Ibid, p. 140.

8. Ibid, p. 174.

9. James S. Coleman, *Equality of Educational Opportunity* (Washington, DC: U.S. Government Printing Office, 1966).

10. David L. Clark, Linda S. Lotto, Terry A. Astuto, "Effective Schools and School Improvement: A Comparative Analysis of Two Lines of Inquiry," *Educational Administration Quarterly* 20, no. 3 (Summer 1984): 41-68.

11. W. Edward Deming, *Out of the Crisis* (Cambridge, MA: Center for Advanced Engineering Study, Massachusetts Institute of Technology, 1986).

CHAPTER VII

How Teachers Perceive Teaching: Change over Two Decades, 1964-1984

MARILYN M. COHN

The year 1983 launched the most significant and sustained effort to renew our nation's schools. It began with the publication of *A Nation at Risk*,[1] which in dramatic and compelling language called upon Americans to stem "a rising tide of mediocrity" by making sweeping changes in education. Today, reform pressures continue unabated, as a plethora of new proposals, projects, partnerships, and policies aim at altering the context in which teachers work.

The year 1983 also marked the beginning of our own particular line of inquiry on the changing context of teaching. The study upon which this chapter is based was conducted in 1984-1985. Its overarching purpose was twofold: (1) to identify continuities and changes in teacher attitudes and orientations toward their work and work rewards from 1964 to 1984, a period of dynamic social change in our nation's history, and (2) to understand how macro societal changes manifested themselves in the microcosm of the classroom. Thus our study was built on the premise that there were significant changes in the context of teaching which predate the current reform efforts and that an understanding of these changes, from the viewpoint of teachers, could inform future endeavors.

Our research took as its point of departure Lortie's *Schoolteacher*, a seminal sociological study of the occupation of teaching.[2] Lortie's work, based on survey data collected from Dade County (Florida) public school teachers in 1964 and interview data from teachers in suburban Boston, described the ethos of the occupation, that is, "the pattern of orientations and sentiments which is peculiar to teachers and which distinguishes them from members of other occupations."[3]

Since 1964, however, a multitude of extraordinary social, political, and economic forces have wrought far-reaching changes in the work

---

Marilyn M. Cohn is Adjunct Associate Professor of Education and Director of Teacher Education at Washington University, St. Louis.

and life-styles of most Americans. The Viet Nam war, the civil rights movement, the women's movement and the opening of opportunities for women in occupations previously closed to them, the changing family structure and the increase in the number of families with two working parents, immigration, the widespread use of drugs, and the increasing pervasiveness and power of the media have all had their effects on almost every facet of our society, including the schools. Further, in dealing with issues of equity the schools have been the special focus of desegregation programs through busing, mainstreaming of students with special problems into regular classrooms, and bilingual education. Finally, in the face of challenges to provide excellence as well as equity, schools have also been pressured to go "back to basics" and to be "accountable" for student outcomes particularly in the form of test scores. This concept of accountability has been promulgated by new types of state legislative policy on educational standards and corresponding mandates from central offices of local school districts.[4]

In 1984-85, we visited the Dade County public schools in search of understanding what effect, if any, the changing context had on the "ethos" of the occupation.[5] We asked teachers some of the same questions Lortie had posed two decades before and some new questions designed to capture their views of what it meant to be a teacher in the 1980s and beyond. Our work was guided by three related assumptions: (1) schools in general and teaching in particular were in crisis; (2) the crisis had something to do with the extraordinary societal and school changes that had occurred over the past two decades; and (3) too many school critiques and proposals for reform, past and current, were based on the views of "outside" experts rather than teachers, who are the "inside" experts on schooling and teaching. In recognition of the value of reaching a relatively large sample and of conversing with individuals in depth, we constructed both a survey schedule and an interview schedule for Dade County public school teachers. For our survey, we drew a 40 percent random sample of teachers from each of the 250 schools in the system. A total of 2,718 teachers (64 percent of the sample) responded to the survey. From the 40 percent sample we drew a random stratified sample of 100 teachers who were to be interviewed at length.[6]

The data base accumulated in Dade County is a large one that offers insights into many issues that are important to teachers and to those seeking to improve working conditions for teachers. In this chapter, however, I focus only on the subject of the decline in teacher satisfaction over the twenty-year period, examine two related changes that appear to be major contributors to that problem, and conclude with some implications for the current efforts to improve schools and redefine the roles of teachers. I begin with a limited number of our comparative findings from our surveys and then look for explanations for these results in our analyses of interviews.

Teachers' Perceptions of Their Work: The Survey Results

Eighteen questions in Lortie's survey were replicated in our 1984 study. Thus we were able to compare demographics and attitudes of the 1964 sample with the sample of 1984. With respect to demographics, the 1984 sample was older, more experienced, and had more formal education.[7] In addition, the ethnic composition was different because the percentage of African Americans had increased from 17 to 25 percent and a totally new Hispanic segment made up 16 percent of the sample in 1984. I focus first on changes in attitudes as revealed by responses to six questions contained in both the 1964 and the 1984 surveys.

DECLINE IN JOB SATISFACTION

The first question involved teachers' feelings about job and workplace, and the results showed a pattern of decline in satisfaction in both domains. Neither decline was precipitous, but the decline in satisfaction with their workplace was larger. These trends are consistent with those reported in a national sample of teachers.[8]

A second question involved the types of extrinsic rewards teachers received from their work. Teachers reported a decline in "respect I receive from others" and "opportunity to wield some influence," but, most significantly, twice as many teachers in 1984 as in 1964 (over a quarter of the respondents) indicated that they received no extrinsic rewards. Taken together, the responses to these two questions revealed a teaching force in Dade County that over the twenty-year period had grown less satisfied with the job of teaching and the school as a workplace, and had also perceived a serious decline in the external reward system.

DESCRIPTIONS OF THE WORK OF TEACHING

The remaining four questions focused on specifics of classroom work. On the question of the kinds of students Dade County teachers prefer to teach, there was a major shift. In 1964, the modal response was "creative and intellectually demanding students who call for special effort," but in 1984 the modal response was "nice kids from average homes, who are respectful and hard-working."

On the issue of the most important school goals for younger and older students, there were important differences over twenty years that revealed a narrowing and lowering of expectations. For elementary students, there was a shift from "efficient use" of the three R's to the acquisition of those skills. For secondary students, there was a move toward "efficient use" of the three R's and away from helping adolescents become (1) problem solvers, (2) persons who can work and live with others, and (3) emotionally stable individuals who can handle life's realities. (The distinction here between "acquisition" and "efficient use" is between knowledge of the three R's and application of that knowledge. The survey items read as follows: (1) The basic tools for acquiring and communicating knowledge—the three R's, and (2) efficient *use* of the three R's—the basic tools for acquiring and accumulating knowledge.)

The question that asked teachers to describe their teaching orientation yielded responses consistent with the goal statements above in that the percentage who chose "I'm pretty much the 'no-nonsense, get-the-learning-of-the-subject-matter-done' kind of teacher" nearly tripled.

Finally, on the question which focused on the indicator that a good teacher is most likely to use in judging personal effectiveness, there were some striking differences. Teachers in the 1964 sample indicated that good teachers were more likely to rely on self-assessment whereas teachers in the 1984 sample maintained that good teachers were more likely to rely on one of several forms of external evaluation.

In short, the last four questions reveal considerable change over twenty years in the way teachers describe their work. They see the work of teaching today in terms of a heavier emphasis on the acquisition and use of basic skills gained through a no-nonsense approach, the results of which are increasingly monitored and measured by external sources. In striving to achieve these ends, teachers have come to prefer "nice, respectful, hard-working kids." While few would argue with a no-nonsense approach to teaching the basic skills, few would also maintain that this is the essence of teaching or the image they had in mind when they chose teaching as a career. Most teachers in our study, as well as in the Lortie study, reported choosing teaching because of (1) the opportunity to interact with young people who generally exude energy, creativity, honesty, and good humor; (2) the excitement of "reaching" students and seeing "light bulbs" go on; and (3) the opportunity to influence students' attitudes toward thinking and learning, toward becoming good citizens, and toward realizing their full potential. The nature of teaching today comes through in our survey results as decidedly less intellectually stimulating and varied; less joyful, emotional, and human; less autonomous and professional. In the rest of this chapter, I argue that the decline in teacher satisfaction and in the receipt of extrinsic rewards revealed in responses to the first two survey questions is related, at least in part, to the shift in the nature of the work indicated in the latter four survey questions. To develop this argument, to explore why the work of teachers changed in this direction over the twenty-year period, and to convey the effects of this change on teachers, in their own words, I move to the analysis of responses obtained in our interviews.

Explaining the Decline in Job Satisfaction: Recurring Themes in Interviews

Every one of the seventy-three teachers interviewed maintained that multiple and major changes in the society had impacted on their daily classroom life. Moreover, there was remarkable agreement that the most potent and pervasive of these forces were related to (1) changes in the attitudes of students and parents and (2) changes in the attitudes and demands of their administrators.[9] As teachers talked about these shifts, they gave vivid voice to their perception of new realities that had altered the nature of their work and triggered their growing sense of dissatisfaction. It is important to note that the changes teachers report in interviews are their perceptions and therefore cannot be considered realities. While we became convinced that their perceptions were generally well-founded, we could not corroborate their statements with our own observations.

ATTITUDES OF STUDENTS AND PARENTS TOWARD EDUCATION

Teachers in our interview sample shared a strongly held conviction that both students and parents are less cooperative than they were in the past. Although there is a generalized tendency to recall the past in more glowing terms than may be deserved, and although Lortie's sample in 1964 also cited students and parents as sources of discontent,[10] both the number and nature of the teacher complaints in 1984 suggested a serious escalation of the problem. The situation spanned elementary and secondary schools and communities that were poor, middle-class, and affluent, although it often revealed itself in differing ways, depending on the community context. Moreover, the expressed frustration came not only from veterans but also from beginning teachers. Novices compared the attitudes of students and parents today with those of their own families or those of their peers. First, let's listen to how teachers talked about students.

Students as less motivated and more difficult to teach. While secondary teachers expressed the sentiment more strongly than elementary teachers, almost every interviewee indicated in one way or another that students today are more difficult to teach than those of the past. The frustrations of elementary teachers regarding students were often inseparable from complaints about the parents. It appears that teachers believe young children should not be held primarily responsible for their behavior at school. Still elementary teachers expressed surprise and sometimes even shock at the types of attitudes and children they encountered in the classroom. The following statements capture variations on the theme:

I had thought that the parents would be more cooperative, that the kids would be more motivated than they are at such a young age—I guess it has to do with the background of the parents, the incentives that the parents give the kids to go to school and want to learn. . . . A lot of the parents don't have education above elementary school, and therefore can't help the kids. That becomes a problem. I guess the kids feel, why do it if mom doesn't really push me at home and teachers have no control over me at 3:00 (14, F, W, Elem/M, 3rd).[11]

I would say that the children that I see coming now—I just don't remember coming in contact with children who were bruised with cigarette marks, children that come in crying and are from broken homes. If my teacher had to deal with it, I never realized it. . . . I must have been in a very sheltered environment. Now there are just so many things that children are having to deal with, and it's emotionally draining on the teachers. It's not just academics, but to see children who are hungry and a little girl almost faints and you ask her why and she doesn't want to tell you and you take her out in the hallway, and she hasn't eaten since Friday and it's Monday. That kind of thing (09, F, W, Elem/H, Kindergarten).

Still others complained that some children have lost respect for teachers as well as an interest in school and have resorted on occasion to threatening teachers. One elementary teacher spoke of students threatening to sue her if she touched them and another talked of almost quitting after a small boy yelled, "I'm going to break your ass" (61, F, W, Elem/H, Kindergarten).

At the secondary level, the difficulty revealed itself primarily in terms of a lack of motivation and interest toward academic achievement. Teachers told us that some of their unmotivated students would do almost nothing while others would do the bare minimum to pass. When they did put forth some effort, the motivating factor appeared to be grades as opposed to the desire to learn. The following statements from three veteran high school teachers in different fields and settings convey the general sentiment:

Children now do the work for grades. They won't work unless they know you are going to check it. The children in the 50's and 60's would work. They didn't worry about your checking their work. They worked just for the sake of learning, so they could understand how to do these problems. The difference now is the ones who come to me don't give a tear about learning how to do the problem, they simply want the grades. . . . I really don't know what it is, but I'll find so many children who will tell me, I just want to make a D. . . . It's hard to believe that children in a high school geometry class will come in with no paper, no pencil, no books. "Where's your book?" "I forgot it." Now how can you justify that, . . . remembering to come to class and not thinking about the book? (28, F, B, Sr/M, Math/German).

When I decided to become a teacher I think the students then wanted to learn more so than now. Now they don't care about learning. I feel like the kids now come to school because they have to, they are underage and they have to come, most of them. . . . When I first started teaching [19 years ago] all the kids were gung ho, they wanted phys. ed. They enjoyed it, and we had a good time. Then as the years went on, I could see that the kids did not want to dress, they did not want to do anything. They just wanted to come out and sit and talk under a tree (67, F, B, Sr/M, Phys. Ed/Math).

The kids would rather go out and buy a ghetto blaster, they range anywhere from $79.00 to $200.00, depending on the size, rather than buy themselves an instrument for the school band. . . . Also they will get on the bus and go to this mall which has a theater in it, but they won't get on the bus and buy the supplies, like maybe a mouthpiece or a reed. They just don't think that way. . . . I think that those who hold teachers responsible for test scores and mediocrity in the schools really need to come in and try teaching themselves. It's very difficult, if the kid is not motivated to learn. You can be a motivating teacher, but there are some kids who just want to get by. They don't see the need and value of education (54, M, B, Sr/L, Fine Arts/Music).

The fact that so many of the students they faced didn't "see the need and value of education" was simply shocking to many of the middle-class, achieving teachers we interviewed. What was even more perplexing was that their offers of additional assistance were often rebuffed. One of the teachers who had always offered special help before and after school, and even on weekends, became increasingly discouraged and frustrated:

I've almost given up. This last nine weeks I've closed my doors in the mornings. If they want to come, they can come after school. And I've closed them in the mornings because I've found that just a few of them take the opportunity, and the ones who really need it, don't.... I even invited three kids over this weekend. I said, "Come over to the house Saturday, we'll sit at the table and we'll work. Here's my phone number, call me, we'll get together. I'll make it my business to be there. You need the help." I got no phone call, and I stayed home all day. And that behavior is not like it used to be. When my kids needed help, they came. I have never in my 16 years of teaching failed a kid that really worked and learned. I have 23 kids failing this year in Algebra, out of 96. That's terrible. They don't care. They see me in summer school and they still don't care (01, F, W, Jr/M, Gen. Math.).

Some of the most enthusiastic and upbeat teachers we interviewed maintained, however, that teachers cannot give up on these students.[12] To the contrary, they believed it was their responsibility to make them care, and to repeatedly give them a reason for coming to school. One such enthusiastic teacher spoke for his counterparts with this statement:

With these kinds of kids, you have to work a lot harder. You have to put your nose to the grindstone. You have to be constantly there, after them, trying to show them why they have to do it. It's funny, but these kids don't know why. Why do I have to do anything? They would rather be out working in the supermarket, stacking boxes and making a couple of bucks to buy themselves a big radio or something (22, M, H, Sr/M, Phys. Ed./Dr. Ed.).

The students' increased desire for material possessions was, in fact, one of the larger societal factors teachers cited when they tried to account for the changing attitude of students. Others mentioned television, claiming that some students almost "demand" to be entertained or they tune the teacher out. Still others described students who increasingly tuned themselves out with cocaine as opposed to the marijuana of yesteryear. The growth and urbanization of our society with its accompanying anonymity, and the efforts at integration in the schools through busing were also "blamed," but, according to the teachers in our sample, the most powerful and influential societal change on the motivation of students is what might be broadly labeled as the "changing family structure." Almost every teacher spoke at length about how divorce, multiple relationships, working parents, and single-parent homes had made life more difficult for students. One secondary teacher who had recently returned to teaching after her own divorce spoke about the emotional effect on her children:

When kids are worried about the finances and hostility and feelings, they are not always tuned into school. I don't know this for a fact but you can see it. I've seen it with my daughter. She gained a lot of weight, she doesn't study. She is social. They like to talk. They need to talk. . . . Lack of being with grandparents, the lack of affection, the anger. They're dealing with anger of parents and shuffling back and forth. Absolutely, that affects people. If your family is wrong, you're not going to sit there and dedicate yourself to education. You can't concentrate. . . . "What's going to happen to me?" Very traumatic (10, F, W, Sr/M, Eng.).

Interestingly, adolescents not only want to talk about their problems with their peers, but also with some of their teachers. One teacher explained:

In many instances, in this day and age, you've got to be the mother, you've got to be a social worker, you've got to be a friend. I have some who come in and sit at the end of the school day who would simply want to talk, not about math, not about any course, they simply want to sit and talk. And they will sit for as long as I'm here. In fact, I will say sometimes, I'm not rushing, but I've got to go. Then, of course, the next day, if they pass by and see me in the room, they'll come in and talk to me again. . . . They simply want someone to listen. . . . You've got to be a psychologist (28, F, B, Sr/M, Math./Geom.).

At the elementary level, teachers often discussed changing family structure in terms of the working mother. They expressed concerns with the fact that young children may be "dumped" at school at 7:30A.M. and not picked up until 6:00P.M. In addition to the long hours, there were questions raised as to the quality of the before- and after-school programs. One kindergarten teacher felt that the efforts she put forth all day in behalf of students' self-esteem were nullified after school.

The after-school program is housed in the kindergarten so I'm very familiar with it. When I am sitting in my office I can hear the whole thing because the supervisors are screaming and yelling. Sometimes the supervisors are university kids who are majoring in education, and it's a way to pick up money from 3:30 on, but their techniques are nil. They scream and yell at these kids, and here you've gone through a whole day of trying to be positive and then somebody yells at them for two and a half hours (61, F, W, Elem/H, Kindergarten).

Thus, although teachers were frustrated with the fact that students are more difficult to teach, they also recognized that many children were having their own difficulties, particularly due to family circumstances beyond their control. Teachers in our sample often expressed great empathy for children who they felt were victims of the changing family structure, but they never absolved parents of their responsibility in terms of support for schools and teachers. To the contrary, teachers maintained that parents—single, poor, working, or otherwise—must play a crucial supporting role in their child's education.

Parents as unsupportive. Although there were a few suburban teachers who spoke of highly supportive parent groups, most of the teachers in our sample, unfortunately, would give parents a failing grade in the subject of support and would go as far as to blame parents as a group for the general decrease in motivation among students. While almost all teachers want more parental support, it was clear from their statements that "support" is a complex concept that involves just the right amount and mix of interest and involvement.[13]

The most frequent complaint was of too little support: parents who did not look at report cards, who did not attend school meetings or performances of their children, who did not supervise homework. Among the many critics of parents who stressed the changing attitudes was an elementary teacher who grew up in a poor neighborhood and is now teaching in the same elementary school she attended. Speaking of her own school days, she recalled:

Parents were involved. There wasn't a day you didn't turn around that your mother wasn't trying to find out what you were doing. You didn't do anything wrong because if you did, you knew what would happen (58, F, B, Elem/L, Kindergarten).

Today, however, in the same neighborhood, she described parents who send their children to school without being toilet trained but with marijuana in their pockets, parents who are never home, parents who are "on the streets, . . . prostitutes, out mixing with other men, partying." Her explanation: "Their values have changed. They just don't care. They don't know what respect, what a role model is."

While the common stereotype of parents in poor neighborhoods is one of lack of involvement in the schools, an equally familiar stereotype is that of parents in affluent neighborhoods as highly involved. Our data suggest that teachers working in *all* types of neighborhoods condemn parents for lack of interest. The following comment on parental attendance at school meetings is a case in point:

You have to get the people more involved in schools. We had parents' night at school. It's embarrassing because nobody comes. We have a pretty good neighborhood out there, a lot of money, upper middle class, and we cover a pretty good range. . . . And they go through all kinds of methods to bring the parents in. We even try to find the right time when the average parent gets home from work, to try to find the right day. Because you are not going to compete with Monday night football. It's crazy. Isn't that silly? You figure your kid, your son or your daughter, is more important than listening to Howard Cosell on Monday night football. But it's true, they just don't come. We don't get the parents out. This year we had maybe 50, if that many, out of 2,800 students (02, M, H, Sr/H, Phys. Ed.).

As another dimension of too little interest and involvement, teachers also faulted parents for their reactions to teacher telephone calls regarding problems at school. Traditionally, a call home has served as an escalated step on the discipline ladder, and one that teachers generally could depend upon for home follow-up. Instead, many teachers reported that today they can expect to encounter lack of interest, resignation, or belligerence. A veteran who has experienced all these reactions, contrasted this behavior with times past:

Years ago, when I first began teaching, if a student did something wrong, if you ever had to contact the parent, the parent would be furious with the student. I would say in 90 percent of the cases, the student would be in trouble at home. In many situations today, I have called parents, and some parents have told me that they're not interested, you handle it anyway you can. You have different reactions from parents today. Many of the parents are completely cooperative and will talk to the students or punish them or have some kind of action in which they will follow through, but you also have other reactions. Sometimes, some of the parents will throw up their hands and say I don't know what to do with this person. I never heard that 25 or 28 years ago. I think the role of the parent has changed, and this has made it a lot different for the teacher or the school who wants to contact the home. Some parents are belligerent. Immediately, if you talk about their child being in trouble, they want to blame you, and this was unheard of 28 years ago (23, M, W, Jr/H, Lang. Arts/Eng.).

At the other end of the scale, there were teachers who described as "unsupportive" parents who, in certain negative ways, exhibited too much interest and involvement in school affairs. For example, teachers reported that some parents would cover up or make excuses for students, lie for students, and try to get them out of work. Other teachers reported that wealthy parents could exert enormous power with administrators and with the school board. We heard that parents could get grades changed, classes and programs changed, and policies changed. One such teacher in response to the question "Who has the power in this school?" responded: "Dare I say the parents?" She explained:

I really feel that they are telling us what to do . . . more and more. And I think that is what is aggravating me more than anything else. . . . If the youngster comes home with a bad paper, it is the teacher's fault. . . . Then there is the matter of the placement of students in classes. I don't think I'm exaggerating that 150 schedules were rearranged, purely because parents wanted it that way. . . . There are students in the honors program, for example, who have no business being there, but mother actually takes the sheet of paper and writes down, I want my daughter to be in the honors program, and that is it (25, F, W, Sr/L, Lang. Arts/Eng.).

One of the most troubling ways in which too much parental interest and involvement has manifested itself recently, however, has been through the threat of lawsuits. The vast majority of our interviewees were convinced that parents at all socioeconomic levels are much more inclined to threaten to sue teachers for such things as negligence, child abuse, or sexual harassment. Accordingly, they felt increasingly vulnerable and compelled to take special precautions. Elementary teachers reported being more cautious in the writing of observations for cumulative records, putting children on their laps, and helping kindergartners zip up their pants. Secondary teachers reported they increasingly made it a practice not to be alone in a classroom with a student.

Impact on job satisfaction of teachers. At one level, it can be argued that the strong and generally negative sentiments expressed by teachers regarding changing attitudes among their clientele is little more than "ritual complaint" or "blaming the victim." In response to public criticism of the schools and to statistics showing that American students are less achieving than they used to be or less successful than the students of other countries, teachers are perhaps saying, "It's not our fault; we simply have less to work with." As a matter of fact, a number of teachers voiced their strongest criticisms of parents when asked to comment on the line in *A Nation at Risk* that claims there has been "a rising tide of mediocrity" in schools. As one teacher countered defensively:

There are an awful lot of mediocre parents too. I don't think the whole blame falls on the teachers or the schools. I think the mediocrity is due to a bunch of lazy, uncaring parents (50, F, W, Sr/L., Arts/Eng.).

While a defensiveness that includes a counterattack may be a factor in teacher sentiments on the changing attitudes of parents and students, I am convinced it is not the whole story. Instead, I give considerable credence to the teachers' view for a number of reasons. First, the perceptions of changing attitudes were voiced by all teachers in our interview sample, the most enthusiastic, the most disillusioned, and all points in between. While the enthusiastic teachers appeared to have more insights and strategies to deal effectively with what was perceived to be the lack of motivation and cooperation from students and parents, they nonetheless acknowledged the change and labeled it as problematic.[14] Second, our sample's views on changing attitudes, particularly in the parent realm, are substantiated by another recent interview study of eighty-five urban and suburban teachers in five districts in the San Francisco Bay Area.[15] Third, the various factors that teachers cite as giving rise to the changing attitudes are well documented by statistics as well as by scholars who focus on societal trends and changes.[16] Moreover, because the teaching force in Dade County, as in many other parts of the country, was older and more experienced in 1984 than the counterpart of 1964,[17] many of our interviewees were veterans with fifteen to thirty years in the classroom. Their careers had, therefore, spanned the period of tremendous change in the school population, whether from abrupt forces coming from outside their own school boundaries in the form of busing or immigration, or from more gradual forces within their school boundaries in terms of changing family or community structure or the growth and influence of drugs and the media in the society. Such teachers had long-established pedagogical approaches that had, in their view, been successful with a different population. The new population, however, did not respond as positively or as compliantly. Thus, these veterans found themselves working harder, but with less success in the classroom, less cooperation from parents, and less respect from the public at large. Their present frustration and failure loomed in stark contrast to a vivid recollection of past satisfaction and success.

Therefore, as we listened to the teachers through the interview process and reflected upon what we heard, we began to see the changing attitude of students and parents as a real and potent force that could account, at least in part, for the decline, as expressed in the surveys, in satisfaction with their job and workplace as well as in their extrinsic rewards. If, as teachers described in concrete images, students are much more difficult to reach and teach than they were in the past, and if, as teachers have consistently reported, the chief reward of teaching depends upon "the times I know I have 'reached' a student or group of students and they have learned,"[18] then satisfaction must inevitably be on the decline. Further, if, as teachers steadfastly maintained, parents are either less involved and less responsive or alternately involved to the point of interfering or threatening, then teachers must also surely feel less supported and less respected. Finally, if students are more difficult to reach because they are less interested, hard-working, and respectful, and more personally troubled, and if these problems are believed to be related in some ways to the changing family structure, then teachers' increased preference for students who are "nice kids" from "average homes" and who are "respectful and hard-working" is also more than understandable. For some, in fact, the ability to realize such a preference may be the sole source of their survival in the profession.

ADMINISTRATIVE ATTITUDES AND DEMANDS

A second major interview theme that sheds light on the survey results is that teachers also perceived a changed attitude toward them from school and district administration. From the particulars that teachers cited, the general change they experienced was feeling less "professional." Some scholars, however, have maintained that teaching has never fully warranted the label of "profession,"[19] and have instead described it as an "occupation,"[20] or a "moral craft,"[21] or at the most a "semi-profession."[22] Still, there have been others—particularly teachers—who have consistently and steadfastly insisted that teaching deserved professional status. The rationale that teachers have typically offered is the relatively high level of authority and autonomy that has traditionally characterized their classroom decision making. The comments from the vast majority of teachers in our sample, however, suggest that in recent years their role has changed because their autonomy and authority in decision making has diminished significantly. The examples they offered were in four key areas: keeping of students' records, teacher planning, curriculum and instruction, and teacher evaluation.

Keeping track of teachers and students through paperwork. When teachers were asked what bothers them most about teaching, the most frequent response was "paperwork." Teachers reported a tremendous increase in the amount and type of paperwork expected, and while they clearly disliked the more secretarial nature of the role, their real concern had to do with the time the record keeping took from instruction. The following statements reflect the sentiment:

A tremendous amount of paperwork. The paperwork is just overwhelming. Not the paperwork having to do with teaching *per se*, but all the rest—there is just so much time spent and wasted, some of it with tremendous amounts of paperwork. It's unreal (40, F, W, Elem/H, 2nd).

The more paperwork you give a teacher to do, especially classroom teachers, means that they have less time to teach. Going back to English, because it's the one area I know the best because my wife teaches it.... She keeps a folder on each kid and a sheet on each kid and all these things.... She spends more time on paperwork than on what she's supposed to be doing. Mountains and mountains of it! And every time there's something in the paper that says our kids are not graduating with a good enough education, we just get a few more forms to fill out (22, M, H, Sr/M, Phys. Ed./Dr. Ed.).

As the last comment indicates, some teachers recognized that the administration assumed that the route to school improvement lay in keeping track of both students and teachers through paperwork. The increased paperwork connected to student activity took two different forms. One time-consuming activity involved keeping track of student whereabouts. For example, when students were absent, teachers were expected to call home to find out if students were really sick or simply cutting. Teachers described with considerable irritation the difficulties of locating parents and the records they had to keep to document the attempts. As one teacher put it:

When I have a good day, I don't have a lot of paperwork crossing my desk that's garbage.... For example, I can see taking roll as legitimate, but trying to chase down why this kid or that kid wasn't there, is he cutting, or is he really sick? I shouldn't have to worry about that. Either a kid is in my classroom or he's not in my classroom. Why should I have to call parents and check? If Attendance wants to do that, great. . . . But there again am I there to teach the children? What are you paid to do, keep records or teach? I personally would rather spend my time getting the material across to the students than sitting at the desk filling out forms (47, F, W, Sr/H, Gen. Sci.).

A second type of increased monitoring of student activity involved testing and keeping records on acquisition of basic skills. Particularly in elementary classrooms, teachers were expected to use new basal reading and mathematics series in which they teach, test, and reteach for mastery of discrete skills with great frequency. Charts had to be kept on the progress of each child in each skill area. For many elementary teachers, the time-consuming nature of this record-keeping has been painful. One such teacher told us:

I think there's more, much more stress in teaching today. . . . I feel tremendous stress from the system itself in terms of paperwork, the charting, the checking, getting audited, our school seems to get audited a lot. . . . I could not possibly do all my checking and my charting and grading within the school day or the hour planning time. It's not possible and I really resent, you know, then you look in the paper, and they say Johnny can't read, and I'm working 24 hours a day, and at a certain point, you say forget it (20, F, W, Elem/H, 2nd).

But the whole concept of teacher planning has also taken on a negative association because of additional paperwork—in this instance, for monitoring the behavior of teachers as opposed to that of students. In recent years, teachers have been told they must produce lesson plans according to a certain format, turn them in for review by a certain time, and plan certain types of assignments with certain degrees of frequency. The time required to meet these expectations and the amount of control exercised by those outside the classroom were galling to many teachers, especially highly experienced ones. One thirty-year veteran English teacher expressed her frustrations in these terms:

I have never gone into a classroom, I shouldn't say never because I slip now and then, but, over the years, I have always had lesson plans. You have to know what you are going to teach. I mean you can't, even after thirty years, I would never go into a class and just teach off the top of my head. I mean I have to know where I'm going and what I'm doing. But does it have to be spelled out? The student will be able to do Objective #10, Objective #11, and Dade County Objective #6. There are some schools that are doing that. Fortunately we are not doing that here. We can still spell it out pretty much in our own terms. . . . But for accountability we have to turn in plans every Friday. There are times you can't get the plans in on Friday and rather than give up marking a set of papers to return to the students, I would rather wait until Monday to do my plans, and get the papers done first, but I don't have a choice. We have to have folders for every student which I have always done because how else do you know how the student is progressing? But now they tell us what we have to put into the folders, and we have to have grade books that are arranged just the way they want them. We have to spell out in the grade book what every mark stands for, every plus stands for, is it green, is it red, is it orange? I mean it is getting to be a game. I can see where new teachers would become awfully frustrated with the whole thing (25, F, W, Sr/L, Lang. Arts/Eng.).

Clearly this teacher, along with many of her peers, found the new regulations for record keeping and lesson plans demeaning as well as time-consuming. She reported feeling "hurt" by such policies because they were an assault on her authority, her autonomy, her "professionalism." In her words, "The same accountability they want from the kids, they want from us. Maybe that is what hurts."

Loss of control in curriculum, instruction, and teacher evaluation. As teachers talked of the pressures of paperwork and the resulting loss of autonomy and authority, they also referred to loss of control in other domains having little or nothing to do with paperwork. In the area of curriculum and instruction, for example, teachers reported that, of late, the central office administration was making too many decisions that belong to the classroom teachers. Elementary teachers, in particular, expressed deep frustration with a sometimes overwhelming emphasis on the basic skills and a heavy-handed prescriptiveness that regulated what they taught, when and how it was to be taught, and the materials to be used. Most teachers appeared to believe in broad guidelines and objectives coming from the district, but they felt strongly that daily decisions on instructional matters should fall within the purview of the teacher. The following comment by an elementary teacher captures the widespread dissatisfaction with the current specificity mandated from above.

I believe that we have to have some kind of guidelines, but we have taken the word guidelines and made them into specifications. A guideline is one thing, but we don't need "On Tuesday do this, on Wednesday do this, and Friday, don't forget to give a test." And it keeps getting worse and worse. I think that on the first teacher workday last year, they handed me about four books of guidelines (26, F, W, Elem/L, 4th).

Teacher evaluation was yet another area in which there was a perceived loss of autonomy. While teachers have never exercised complete control over evaluation procedures, they felt that recent attempts to use external systems and observers to assess their performance were decreasing their capacity to monitor themselves as professionals do. One such effort was the Teacher Assessment and Development System (TADS), the purpose of which was to identify instructional weaknesses and then provide remediation. TADS was developed by the Management Academy of the Division of Staff Development in the Dade County Public Schools. It was comprised of specific performance indicators in the following categories: preparation and planning, knowledge of subject matter, classroom management, techniques of instruction, teacher-student relations, assessment techniques, and professional responsibilities. The process used consisted of an observation during a single class period made by an administrator, using a prescribed list of eighty-one criteria. Although the teachers' union had considerable input into the instrument, there was little agreement as to its value. While some teachers thought the process was helpful, others argued strongly against it on the basis that it was too detailed and too structured with too little opportunity for on-the-spot decision making by teachers. The idea of being assessed separately on so many specific items during a single class period seemed problematic to a number of teachers. One of them expressed his concerns this way:

I think it is impossible. I think that you have to guess at some of them. And the worst thing is if you miss on one item, you are marked substandard and fail the evaluation. . . . If one student puts his head down and sleeps—perhaps the best thing I can do is let him do that in that particular situation—but if one student does that, we are off task. I am rated down, and I do not get the rating. I'll be written up, and unless I can defend my actions, which sometimes might be hard to do, I will be in trouble (23, M, W, Jr/H, Lang. Arts/Eng.).

This teacher was particularly frustrated by the fact that once a teacher started a lesson within this evaluation framework, he was expected to follow through even though he might not think it was working as planned or he might see a more promising direction to pursue. In his view, this new rating system neither respected the teachers' conception of the teaching-learning process nor afforded teachers the control they need to exercise in order to perform well. Instead, as he put it, teachers increasingly felt that unless they could "defend" their actions, they would be "in trouble."

In addition to TADS, there were two merit pay plans implemented in Dade County public schools during the period we were conducting interviews. One was a state-designed program which assessed individuals for merit pay increases. One component of the assessment was classroom observation by two individuals—one an administrator in the "home school" and another from a different school. Teachers in our sample who participated were uniformly negative about the observations. One of the "losers" had this to say:

I've been observed for the past two years with TADS and I got excellent recommendations from my principal.... for this master teacher program.... I thought the observations went extremely well.... I didn't think I could have done any better if I had known what they were looking for. It was one of those good days, everything went off like clock-work. When I received my scores, I was in the 50th percentile (11, F, W, Elem/H, Primary).

For this teacher the criteria were simply a mystery. To complicate the matter, she is by self-report a "star," a person whom her principal both praises and relies upon as a leader. The mixed messages were very troubling to her. For another teacher, a "winner" who was rated in the 99th percentile, there was no mystery or mixed message, only a sense of cynicism. In his words:

I put on a performance.... It was a big spectacle.... I knew it would impress.... What is that as far as education? ... Teaching is a long-term thing with an average of things and any one day, and any one time and all those objectives, a person is a person, and how they teach and what they teach that day means nothing (65, M, W, Jr/H, Sci.Bio.).

To counteract teacher frustration and cynicism over observations of single lessons using external criteria and personnel, the Dade County public schools developed a merit program which offered pay raises to the entire staff of schools that had been designated meritorious on the basis of schoolwide achievement through collaboration of all the personnel in the building.[23] While teachers expressed a little more faith in the school merit plan than the individual one, there were objections to both.[24] What teachers argued for instead was some approach to evaluation of performance which respected both the complexity and professional nature of their work.

Impact on job satisfaction of teachers. The stories that Dade County teachers told us regarding new policies and procedures in the areas of keeping students' records, teacher planning, curriculum and instruction, and teacher evaluation all gave credence and meaning to their conviction that the role of the classroom teacher had evolved into a different and less professional one. At the same time, these interview accounts illuminated the survey results which portrayed significant changes over two decades in the goals teachers held for their students, the orientation they took toward their work, the students they preferred to teach, and the means by which they judged their success. As we listened to the different and more prescriptive demands imposed from above, we could see them as directly connected to the district's attempt to hold teachers accountable for student acquisition and use of the basic skills. This press toward accountability for the basics in turn led teachers to narrow their focus, lower their expectations, and take a "no-nonsense" approach that would, hopefully, yield the desired outcomes. Since the outcome measures increasingly took the form of progress charts, audits, test scores, and observations monitored by external sources, teachers began to rely more on the judgment of others than on their self-assessment in evaluating personal effectiveness. And, of course, when the daily curricular diet consisted of drill and practice of discrete skills, teachers found it preferable to have as students "nice kids" who would be "respectful" and "hard-working" as opposed to students who would question the purpose or value of such a curriculum, or students who would either be bored or have difficulty with achieving the results desired.

With increased insight as to how and why the teacher's role and work have shifted over two decades comes increased understanding of the decline of satisfaction in job and workplace as well as the decline in extrinsic rewards. Teachers found the increase in paperwork for the purposes of monitoring students and teachers alike and the decrease of authority and autonomy in decisions regarding curriculum, instruction, and evaluation both demeaning and debilitating. They also found the pressure to concentrate on limited cognitive goals to the exclusion of broader intellectual, social, and emotional aims for students both frustrating and unfulfilling. Under such circumstances, teaching as a career ultimately became less satisfying and less extrinsically rewarding.

Implications of Changing Contexts for Efforts to Reform Schools

The portrayal that teachers gave in interviews to the changes in the attitudes of their clients and of their administrators was typically one of separate but equally disturbing phenomena. In exploring these changes to increase our understanding of differences in teacher attitudes and descriptions of work over two decades, I have maintained that separation. I conclude by considering the relationship between these two contextual changes and the implication of this relationship for current and future efforts to improve schools and teaching.

A "CONSTRUCTED" CHANGE IN CONTEXT IN RESPONSE TO A "NATURAL" CHANGE

As teachers spoke, it became apparent that the attitudinal changes they described in students and parents were, at least in part, explanations for the lack of success they were experiencing in terms of student learning. As detailed above, teachers in our study were convinced that changes in the larger society and in the smaller family unit had produced students who were more difficult to teach. As the difficulties began to manifest themselves in lower performance and test scores, the state of Florida, like other states, intervened through legislation designed to make teachers more accountable for the quality and results of schooling. In Florida, which was one of the leaders of the "legislated learning" approach to school reform,[25] law after law was passed from 1976 to 1984 to regulate teacher behavior to the end of ensuring improved student outcomes.[26] Florida mandated basic skills objectives, types of textbooks and instructional materials, and performance standards on competency tests for all students. Legislators also designed laws to raise teacher performance through teacher testing and merit pay incentives. The Dade County Public Schools responded by devising systems and selecting textbooks that matched the mandated basic skills curriculum and by implementing more prescriptive lesson planning, more records on students, and performance-based evaluation procedures for teachers. As teachers immediately experienced it, the result was a loss of time in the pursuit of monitoring students and their own efforts through paperwork and a loss of control over curricular, instructional, and evaluative decisions. The long-range result was a loss of professionalism and status.

But to make matters even worse, teachers viewed the substance of the decision making at the district and state level as fundamentally wrong-headed and ineffective because it was exclusively cognitive at a time when societal and familial changes dictated more attention to students' emotional and social needs. Teachers felt the new accountability procedures consumed them with secretarial tasks when they needed to spend more time "reaching kids." The procedures focused the attention of teachers on coverage of skill packages at the expense of developing interpersonal relationships with students and pursuing broader intellectual as well as social and emotional goals. According to Lortie, teachers hold goals for students that go beyond the prescribed curriculum. Moreover, he maintains that teachers have long understood that effective teaching has two components: the "ultimate instructional results" and the "proximate relational conditions," although they do not use this vocabulary.[27] The first are the outcomes as expressed in curricular objectives; the second are the means which contribute to achievement of the outcomes. From the teacher's vantage point, the means or conditions for effective teaching "consist of interpersonal transactions and states which teachers realize with their students."[28] Our interviewees believed that attention to the establishment of interpersonal relationships as means to cognitive ends was particularly critical with their students. For example, when our sample was asked to specify the knowledge, skills, and attitudes it took to be an effective teacher, the largest cluster of responses (40 percent) referred to interpersonal relationships with students.[29] Moreover, the prevailing position was that the interpersonal relationships with today's students must aim at developing each individual's self-esteem. Without self-esteem, the academic outcomes were perceived to be largely unattainable. The following statements capture this sentiment:

There's a tremendous amount of self-esteem that has to be developed along with just teaching. This is what I'm constantly working with. I'm working with youngsters who are almost always from divorce situations. They have culture shock, this one is from Nicaragua, this one is from South America. They're all of a sudden put together, and you have to build some kind of bridge where we can all work together very successfully (46, F, W, Jr/M, Soc. Stud.).

I'm teaching children, I'm not teaching reading, writing, math. That's secondary. I really think that if you can't reach them, you can't teach them anything (57, F, W, Elem/M, Kindergarten).

I don't know if all teachers feel the way I do, but I feel that you can't accomplish anything if they don't feel good about themselves, or if they don't feel they can do it.... I think you have to deal with the whole student, and you have to work and talk.... You can't just have such a structured situation that there's no time for personal things.... If a kid has a problem, he can't learn (55, F, W, Sr/L, Spec. Ed./L.D.).

But most teachers saw the heavy emphasis on acquisition of basic skills through completion of prescribed materials, externally monitored and frequently tested, as leaving little room for dealing with personal problems or building self-esteem. One teacher put it this way:

Just recently a little girl came up to me whose mother has had a series of lovers. She doesn't have a father that lives at home. She wanted my attention. I knew she deserved it, and I had to say "I'm sorry, Shantara. I can't talk to you now. I have to do charts and then after that I have to work on clusters. After that I have to do the skill pack." I just felt at a loss, and it made me very depressed and angry as well (19, F, W, Elem/H, 3rd).

Clearly, state mandates and district policies related to basic skills were never intended for teachers to feel unable to respond to students' personal needs, but the evaluative pressures teachers experienced within the system led the more frustrated and disillusioned ones to do just that.

At the risk of oversimplifying a complex situation, it seems that what might be termed a "natural" problematic change in the context of teaching, that of a differing clientele, gave rise to a "constructed" change in which authorities outside the classroom specified how teachers were to handle the problem. The "constructed" change not only failed to solve the problems of the "natural" change; it created a new context and role for teachers which led to greater problems, including dissatisfaction with job and workplace and a decline in rewards. In some instances, the demoralization brought about by the "constructed" change was so overwhelming that some teachers who were perceived to be talented and effective left the classroom while others who remained became dysfunctional. Teachers in both categories reported telling their own children, as well as others, not to become teachers, thereby indirectly threatening the viability of the entire educational enterprise.[30]

IMPLICATIONS FOR THE FUTURE

Within the last few years, there has been some recognition that the form of "legislated learning" that occurred in Dade County and elsewhere was flawed on a number of dimensions, some of which are identified in a recent reassessment of the Rand Change Agent Study.[31] First, it was formulated without input from teachers and, as such, failed to respect some of the "micro realities" of classroom teaching. One reality is that working with today's students requires more, not less, attention to interpersonal relationships as means for achieving cognitive outcomes. Another reality is that teachers today, like teachers two decades ago, hold a much broader array of purposes for their students than the acquisition and application of basic skills. Yet another reality is that successful teaching involves the exercise of professional insight, creativity, and judgment. Policies and methods of implementation that disregard such realities are doomed to failure.

A second flaw was that the approach was uniformly applied to all schools, classrooms, students, and teachers. Just as local factors should affect national policy, different schools and different teachers should have the flexibility to shape policy to fit their circumstances. Some thirty-year veterans may need instruction in writing behavioral objectives, but those who do probably need much more than regulation of lesson planning to improve their teaching. In our sample, the more enthusiastic and confident teachers explained how they ignored or subverted policies that appeared absurd, but, too often, others told how these policies had demoralized and immobilized them.[32]

In many school districts around the country, there are still basic skills accountability programs designed without teacher guidance and implemented uniformly through a large bureaucracy. Our findings suggest that such districts need to listen to their classroom teachers to determine if the flaws identified in the Dade County accountability efforts and federal efforts studied by Rand are actually undermining rather than fostering the achievement of desired outcomes. At the same time, our findings also suggest that listening to teachers is a necessary but insufficient condition for addressing the complexities and challenges stemming from the changing attitudes of students and parents. In Dade County, it is clear that state legislators, policymakers, and district bureaucrats were too far removed to see or hear the realities of teachers; however, it is equally clear that teachers tended to be so immersed in their day-to-day human interactions that they found it difficult to see the legitimate concerns of those responsible for educational outcomes at the state and district level, let alone create their own solutions. Lortie would argue that the outlooks of presentism, conservatism, and individualism that characterize teacher orientations toward their work are almost occupational barriers which can prevent them from questioning the status quo, attending to the macro perspectives, and generating radical alternatives.[33] Thus, perhaps, the most important finding of our Dade County study regarding reform is the importance of creating forums for dialogue and consensus which can ultimately bring together both the micro realities of teachers and schools and the macro perspectives of district and state policymakers and the general public.

In some parts of the country, including Dade County, there are promising movements in this direction. These experiments, in many instances, are designed to counteract the problems of too little variability and too little teacher input. They feature "school-based management," in which principals, working under a broad framework of district goals, formulate visions for their particular schools in cooperation with an "empowered" teaching staff who work collegially with one another to shape and share in decision making.[34] These efforts appear to be steps in the right direction toward constructing a new context of teaching in which variability and micro realities are acknowledged alongside some of the macro issues. Still, such new configurations may also be unwittingly generating additional and unanticipated challenges. My own experience in two recent projects involving school-based management, teacher empowerment, and collegial decision making suggests that in constructing these new contexts there are multiple realities to consider as well as the link between micro realities and macro perspectives.

Collegial endeavors in education cannot easily occur without all the various constituencies in direct and open communication. Depending on the particular arrangement, this may mean that teachers must be able to speak honestly to each other as well as to principals, superintendents, and board members without fear of reprisal. It may mean that principals and superintendents must be able to share power and learn to operate within new parameters with teachers, parents, students, and community members. As the base is expanded horizontally as well as vertically and new roles and responsibilites are created, there are many more voices and views to be heard. With increased participation by all the key actors in the schooling process comes new potential for a shared conception of the problems and possibilities of reaching today's young people and their parents. But with increased participation also comes the probability of genuine differences and disagreements. If we hope to confront the social forces that have found their way into classrooms by constructing new contexts which actively involve all the stakeholders, we must recognize the complex and time-consuming tasks that lie ahead. In place of mandating and legislating uniform solutions, we must first pause to develop a process that permits the multiple realities of all constituencies to be heard and considered. More importantly, however, this process must eventually encourage the participants to reach consensus on the broad goals to pursue and then enable teachers to exercise their creative and professional judgment in achieving those ends. With such a process there can be no guarantees of desired outcomes, but without such a process there can be no hope for an increase in teacher satisfaction and no chance for meaningful change.

ACKNOWLEDGMENTS. This chapter is based on a study by a research team whose assistance is acknowledged here. I am particularly indebted to Eugene F. Provenzo, Jr., whose vision brought this study into being. His strong working relationship with the Dade County Public Schools and the United Teachers of Dade enabled the team to collect a comprehensive data base. Team members Robert B. Kottkamp, Gary N. McCloskey, O.S.A., and Eugene F. Provenzo contributed to the data analysis. Robert B. Kottkamp, Louis M. Smith, and Lauren Sosniak made helpful comments on an earlier draft. Finally, I deeply appreciate the financial support of the National Institute of Education and the help of the many teachers who provided the voices and views that made this work possible.

NOTES

1. National Commission on Excellence in Education, *A Nation at Risk: The Imperative for Educational Reform* (Washington, DC: U.S. Department of Education, 1983).

2. Dan C. Lortie, *Schoolteacher: A Sociological Study* (Chicago: University of Chicago Press, 1975).

3. Ibid., p. viii.

4. Gary N. McCloskey, Eugene F. Provenzo, Jr., Marilyn M. Cohn, and Robert Kottkamp, *A Profession at Risk: Legislated Learning as a Disincentive to Teaching* (Washington, DC: Office of Educational Research and Improvement, U.S. Department of Education, 1987); Arthur E. Wise, *Legislated Learning: The Bureaucratization of the American Classroom* (Berkeley, CA: University of California Press, 1979); idem, "The Two Conflicting Trends in School Reform: Legislated Learning Revisited," *Phi Delta Kappan* 69 (1988): 328-333.

5. Lortie contended in 1964 that Dade County was a "better-than-average site" for ascertaining the attitudes of teachers with varying regional and cultural orientations. His rationale was based in part on the fact that the large district contained rural, urban, and suburban school settings and in part on the fact that Miami was populated by people born and raised in all sections of the United States. We invoked the same rationale in 1984.

6. Stratification was accomplished by assigning each school to a three-by-three matrix consisting of three levels of socioeconomic status and three levels of grade range (elementary, junior high, and senior high). Of the seventy-three teachers who were eventually interviewed, fifty-three were women and twenty were men. Thirty were elementary teachers, seventeen were middle school or junior high school teachers, and twenty-six taught in senior high schools. Forty-nine were white, fifteen were black, and nine were Hispanic.

7. See Robert B. Kottkamp, Eugene F. Provenzo, Jr., and Marilyn M. Cohn, "Stability and Change in a Profession: Two Decades of Teacher Attitudes, 1964-1984," *Phi Delta Kappan* 67, no. 8 (April 1986): 559-567. The findings reported in this section of the chapter are taken from this source.

8. Metropolitan Life Insurance Company, *The Metropolitan Life Survey of the American Teacher* (New York: Metropolitan Life Insurance Company, 1984).

9. Marilyn M. Cohn, Robert B. Kottkamp, Gary N. McCloskey, and Eugene F. Provenzo, Jr., "Teachers' Perspectives on the Problems of Their Profession: Implications for Policymakers and Practitioners" (Unpublished paper, Washington University, St. Louis, MO, 1987).

10. Lortie, *Schoolteacher*, pp. 176-177.

11. Each quotation from the interviews is identified by a numeral assigned to each interviewee and by a designation for sex (Female, Male), for ethnicity (Black, Hispanic, White), for school grade level (Elementary, Junior High, Senior High), for the school's socioeconomic level (Low, Medium, High), and for the interviewee's teaching area or grade level.

12. In other papers we have identified teachers who remained "enthusiastic" about teaching despite increased frustration, and teachers who became "disillusioned" and almost dysfunctional because of increased frustrations. See Marilyn M. Cohn and Robert B. Kottkamp, "A Teacher Is Not a Teacher Is Not a Teacher" (Paper presented at the Annual Meeting of the American Educational Research Association, Boston, 1990) and Marilyn M. Cohn, Eugene Provenzo, Jr., and Robert Kottkamp, "Toward an Understanding of Enthusiastic Teachers: Insights from Interviews" (Paper presented at the Annual Meeting of the American Educational Research Association, San Francisco, 1986).

13. Annette Lareau, "Perspectives on Parents: A View from the Classroom" (Paper presented at the Annual Meeting of the American Educational Research Association, San Francisco, 1986).

14. Cohn, Provenzo, and Kottkamp, "Toward an Understanding of Enthusiastic Teachers."

15. Lareau, "Perspectives on Parents."

16. A. J. Cherlin, *Marriage, Divorce, Remarriage* (Cambridge, MA: Harvard University Press, 1981); James S. Coleman, "Families and Schools," *Educational Researcher* 16, no. 6 (1987): 32-38.

17. Kottkamp, Provenzo, and Cohn, "Stability and Change in a Profession"; Lareau, "Perspectives on Parents."

18. Kottkamp, Provenzo, and Cohn, "Stability and Change in a Profession."

19. Wayne Hoy and Cecil Miskel, *Educational Administration: Theory, Research, and Practice* (New York: Random House, 1987).

20. Lortie, *Schoolteacher*.

21. Alan R. Tom, *Teaching as a Moral Craft* (New York: Longman, 1983).

22. Amitai Etzioni, *Modern Organizations* (Englewood Cliffs, NJ: Prentice-Hall, 1964).

23. Eugene F. Provenzo, Jr., Gary N. McCloskey, Marilyn M. Cohn, Robert B. Kottkamp, and Norman Proller, "A Comparison of Individual and School Level Approaches to Merit Pay: A Case Study of the Dade County Public Schools" (Unpublished paper, University of Miami, 1987).

24. Marilyn M. Cohn, Robert B. Kottkamp, and Eugene F. Provenzo, Jr., "Merit Pay: Why Teachers Reject a Business Approach to Educational Problems" (Paper presented at the Annual Meeting of the American Educational Research Association, Washington, DC, 1987).

25. Wise, *Legislated Learning.*

26. McCloskey et al., *A Profession at Risk.*

27. Lortie, *Schoolteacher,* p. 117.

28. Ibid.

29. Marilyn M. Cohn and Robert B. Kottkamp, "The Interrelationship of Research, Theory, and Practice in Teaching and Teacher Education" (Paper presented at the Annual Meeting of the American Educational Research Association, San Francisco, 1989).

30. Cohn and Kottkamp, "A Teacher Is Not a Teacher Is Not a Teacher."

31. Milbrey W. McLaughlin, "The Rand Change Agent Study Revisited: Macro Perspectives and Micro Realities," *Educational Researcher* 19, no. 9 (1990): 11-16.

32. Cohn and Kottkamp, "A Teacher Is Not a Teacher Is Not a Teacher."

33. Lortie, *Schoolteacher.*

34. Marilyn M. Cohn and Mary E. Finch, "Teacher Leadership and Collaboration: Key Concepts and Issues in School Change" (Paper presented at the Annual Meeting of the American Educational Research Association, Washington, DC, 1987); Marilyn M. Cohn and Victor Lenz, "A Systemic Approach to School Improvement: An Inside/Outside Look at the Vertical Team Concept as a Vehicle for Change" (Paper presented at the Annual Meeting of the American Educational Research Association, Boston, 1990); Ann Lieberman, ed., *Building Professional Cultures in Schools* (New York: Teachers College Press, 1989).

CHAPTER VIII

Restructuring and the Problem of Teachers' Work

Karen Seashore Louis

Studies of worker productivity, human resources in organizations, and the nature of professionalism in nonschool settings provide educators and policymakers with concrete, robust evidence that working conditions should have a powerful impact on what teachers do in the classroom. Drawing on this body of theory and research, the Center for the Study of Effective Secondary Schools at the University of Wisconsin studied high school teachers' work life. The objective was to identify characteristics of the schools and their environments that facilitated or undermined teachers' commitment to and excitement about their work.

The first phase of the study, directed by Mary Haywood Metz, examined eight high schools in communities with varied social class compositions. The schools were "ordinary" in the sense that they had not engaged in major projects to change the conditions of teachers' or students' work. All but one were comprehensive public schools that drew students from the surrounding neighborhoods. Based on interviews with teachers and observations of the schools, Metz identified the social class of the community and students as a dominant influence on teachers' immediate circumstances and their subjective experiences of work. Standardized expectations about how schooling should be conducted, which were shared among teachers, administrators, and community members, were reflected in the schedules and curriculum. This institutionalized vision of what constituted "real school" made it difficult for the staff to adapt to the very different skills, interests, and life situations of students—or to see much need to do so. In schools serving lower socioeconomic communities, the mismatch between "real school" and what was needed to engage teachers and students was greatest.[1]

Karen Seashore Louis is Professor of Educational Policy and Administration, College of Education, University of Minnesota.

The second phase of the study is reported here. It builds on Metz's study by examining the quality of teachers' work in eight high schools, using a framework derived from a broad examination of the writings on reform in education and the research on the "quality of work life" that has been conducted primarily in nonschool settings. The purpose of the study was to see whether organizational characteristics might seem more significant for the quality of teachers' work life in schools that exhibited more significant structural variation than was present in the Metz study.

The Problem of Teachers' Work

Over the past fifteen years many reports have highlighted the deteriorating status of working conditions for teachers in typical high schools. Teachers have little influence over their work because school bureaucracies prescribe limited zones for teacher autonomy in the classroom, while administrators and boards make school policy. Long hours, with little relief and refreshment through personal development, contribute to spiraling demoralization. Since the early 1980s we have been further inundated with well-publicized recommendations from a variety of commissions about how to improve teaching and teachers. The following argument emerged: current conditions of teachers' work make professional behavior virtually impossible. This logic has figured prominently in such reports as *A Nation at Risk*, which viewed teachers as part of the problem, *A Nation Prepared*, and *Tomorrow's Teachers*.[2]

The reform literature suggests a wide variety of alternative structures, programs, and activities that could directly support or improve teachers' working conditions. Recommended innovations range from career ladders and merit pay to more teacher control over curriculum, policy, and resources, to improved professional development, to more opportunities for teachers to interact professionally, to extended roles for teachers in running schools. However, there is little consensus about what reforms are "the best" and there are contentious debates about whether reforming teachers' work will necessarily have any impact on student achievement, despite the accumulation of evidence linking the two.[3]

Two key assumptions supported the study summarized in this chapter. First, we assumed that working conditions and career opportunities affect the degree to which teachers are actively engaged with teaching and strive to create exciting learning environments in their classrooms. Thus, the improvement of staff working conditions is a subset of the broader objective of creating "effective schools" that increase student engagement, learning opportunities, and achievement. Second, we assumed that the structure of schools can be altered to improve the attractiveness of the profession and the probability that teachers will remain engaged over a long-term career. However, there is not necessarily a single preferred method for restructuring to achieve these ends in all schools. Rather than selecting particular structures to study, we chose first to try to understand general qualities of work most likely to increase teacher engagement. Beginning with a theory of quality of work life (QWL), we would then investigate how particular structures might contribute to high-quality work environments.

WHAT MAKES TEACHERS' WORK ENGAGING?

Many themes common to the school reform literature are consistent with the conceptual frameworks used to study work life in other organizational and professional contexts, ranging from factory work to nursing to law. The social science research on work life offers a more detailed definition of quality of work life than does the educational reform literature, and suggests more specifically what *kinds of restructuring might promote working conditions that tangibly contribute to the establishment of a more professional work life and career for teachers.* Hence, there is a "nuts and bolts" quality to the QWL literature that is absent in many of the current professionalization proposals.[4] A review of the quality of work life indicators in this organizational literature identified seven criteria that are consistent with issues expressed in the educational reform literature:[5]

1. *Respect from relevant adults.* "Relevant adults" include teaching peers, administrators in the school and district, parents, and the community at large. Many observers of the current educational scene in the United States and in other developed countries point out that lack of respect from parents and administrators, along with public discussions of poorly prepared and underperforming teachers, has contributed to the demoralization of the teaching force and the reluctance of current students to consider teaching as a career.[6]

2. *Participation in decision making.* Having influence over decisions that affect the way in which the school operates and how the work is carried out augments the teachers' sense of control over their work setting.[7] A considerable body of research suggests that perceived satisfaction and engagement increase when workers—professional or

otherwise—are given genuine opportunities to make decisions about how to organize and carry out their work. In most cases, there is also a measurable increase in performance, but occasionally improvements are limited to reductions in sick days, turnover, and other indirect factors affecting performance.[8]

3. *Frequent and stimulating professional interaction.* Collaborative work with peers increases teachers' sense of affiliation with the school, and their sense of mutual support and responsibility for the effectiveness of instruction.[9] As a number of researchers have indicated, it is the "sense of community" that changes.[10] In addition, collaboration is associated with increased commitment to carry out more substantial (and difficult) innovations that affect instruction.

4. *Frequent, accurate feedback, leading to a higher sense of efficacy.* One frustrating aspect of teachers' work is uncertainty about the best way to teach and about one's impact on students.[11] Although teachers often indicate that they can tell whether they have succeeded with students, they have few mechanisms for determining their relative impact, or even the effects of their own work over the long run. In educational settings, the mechanisms permitting teachers to obtain frequent and accurate feedback about their performance and the specific effects of their performance on student learning may contribute most directly to teachers' belief that they are able to have a long-term effect on students—an important factor motivating teacher effort.[12]

5. *Use of skills and knowledge.* Teaching is very challenging, and most *new* teachers believe that they are given full opportunity to stretch and use a broad range of their talents. However, the opportunity to experiment, and to acquire new skills and knowledge (self-development) over a full career may be particularly critical in retaining teacher involvement with work and preventing a sense of dull routine.[13] This may not only be a matter of traditional in-service and additional formal training that focuses on the elaboration of teaching roles in the classroom, but also on the opportunity to perform other roles in the school such as counselor, project leader, curriculum developer, or mentor.[14]

6. *Resources to carry out the job.* A pleasant, orderly working environment is necessary to maintain minimal commitment.[15] The absence of disruptive student behavior is a particularly important aspect. In addition, the QWL literature repeatedly makes the point that it is unreasonable to ask people to work under the loaves-and-fishes principle: schools do not need luxury, but they must have sufficient and adaptable resources to support teacher experimentation.

7. *Goal congruence.* Teachers must feel a connection between their personal goals and values, and those of the school as a whole. Where values and goals are not congruent, alienation is likely to result. This is not as difficult a proposition as it may initially sound. Teachers overwhelmingly espouse cognitive achievement and personal and social development for students as the proper focus of the school program. It is when administrator and/or teacher behavior undermines these goals that lack of congruence most often occurs.[16]

The Study of Teachers' Working Conditions

In looking for schools to participate in the study, we tried to maximize variety in the community context, in the socioeconomic and racial mixture of students, and in the kinds of alternative structures that were being used in the schools. Eight schools were selected to participate in the study.[17]

The research in each school involved two staff members spending a total of between ten and eleven days (and evenings) observing meetings and public spaces, sitting in on sixteen classes for students of different ability levels in all major subject areas. Approximately 160 teachers, administrators, and students, in total, were interviewed. In addition, we collected survey data from all teachers. Case accounts based on the visits served as the primary data base. Interviews were transcribed to provide supplementary evidence during later analytic phases. Analysis proceeded using the strategies outlined by Miles and Huberman.[18]

The best way to present qualitative data is through case studies. The following two mini-cases illustrate the way in which alternative structures and some of the factors relating to quality of work life play out in two very different schools.

HILLSIDE HIGH SCHOOL

Although it lies only a few miles from an urban center, Hillside High School is set in a bucolic rural area, apparently far from problems that besiege urban schools. But its appearance is misleading. Like their inner-city colleagues, Hillside teachers work with a high proportion of "at risk" students. Over a quarter of the students are bussed in from the city's housing projects; the remainder come from predominantly blue-collar families, many of whom are unemployed. Local students self-deprecatingly refer to themselves as "rednecks."

Few Hillside graduates—30 percent—pursue their education after high school, and achievement levels of entering ninth graders are lower than the average for the metropolitan district. The dropout rate is also higher. Not surprisingly, Hillside was a discouraging place to teach for many. A veteran teacher recalls: "I was in a state of near burnout and I don't think I was inspiring many kids." Teachers in the district dreaded a transfer to Hillside. Today, however, since the restructuring effort Hillside has many applicants for each of its rare openings.

The change process at Hillside has been collaborative, but teachers point to the principal, Mary Hermann, as a catalyst for positive change since she arrived in 1986. Hermann is committed to participatory management, and stresses that her philosophy is easily expressed: "Every teacher is a leader; every leader is a teacher."

Initially, this slogan fell on largely cynical ears. As one teacher said,

I thought here's another new principal who's going to come in and tell us that this is the best starting day . . . we've ever had. About a month along, I expected we'd start getting the riot act because we hadn't done this or that. But as the year went on, I became more enamored of her style. . . . We have a principal who encourages us to go beyond the classroom in our teaching, encourages us to apply for grants and fellowships. She shows a very positive attitude toward us and also toward the students.

As one of many initiatives, the school became involved in a structured professional development program. In the spring of 1986, Hillside faculty voted to become involved with a district teacher center that provided them with resources, instructional training, and encouragement for innovative ideas. Hillside supports released time so that teams of teachers can benefit from the district's activities. After Hermann's arrival, Hillside also joined the Coalition of Essential Schools, the national school reform movement founded by Theodore Sizer, and began to introduce concepts such as personalizing instruction and extensive collaboration to redesign curricula.

The school remains traditional in many outward features, but the changes are substantial. Morale is heightened. One teacher spoke for many when she said "I'm excited when I go to school every day, and I try to get my kids to feel that excitement." Collaborative spirit, while not uniform, has increased. The same teacher says, "More teachers are working together and cooperating than I ever thought was possible. We have large numbers of teachers who meet often, work together, share ideas." Another said, "One of the things that has opened up is that if I want to do something within math, there are teachers here that I know I can go to and they will help me teach that in my classroom. . . . We all know a lot more about what is happening in other departments and in each other's classrooms."

There are dissenters. Hermann wryly divides the staff into "the four Rs—restructurers, reviewers, resisters, and reborn," the latter category being resisters who have joined with the renewal efforts. A variety of participatory mechanisms have increased the number in the restructuring camp. For example, the school's Steering Committee is comprised of elected faculty, administrators, professional staff, students, parents, and support staff. The committee sets goals, designs strategies, and implements programs using a shared decision-making process. Each member is expected to participate actively on at least one task force, such as the one that recently designed a successful Teacher-Guided Assistance (TGA) program, which is a twenty-five minute period for teachers and students to meet daily. Teachers believe the TGA period, which gives them close contact with fifteen to twenty students, has given them opportunities to provide students with extra personal and academic support that was not possible in the previous schedule.

Equally important is the annual faculty retreat that deals with professional development concerns such as cooperative learning, designing interdisciplinary units, and strategies to enhance student engagement. The retreat, which may be attended by family members, acts symbolically to unite the faculty.

Teachers candidly assess the changes they have witnessed. As one says, "I think the majority of our teachers are heavily involved. I also know that some choose not to be involved. One thing about an administrator giving faculty permission is that when you say you don't have to do this, you have to mean it. I have seen some of the people who were very negative three or four years ago come around and start working on things because they've felt like they've wanted to and needed to." Another speaks of the collaborative spirit: "All the work of the task forces, the decisions that we make, that's all been a collaborative effort. I don't know of anything that has been achieved by one person alone at Hillside in the last four years."

Teachers point to Hermann as freeing and enabling them. "If you want to try something, Mrs. Hermann believes you should go ahead and try. If you have an idea, she will say, 'How do you plan to put this into action?' After you tell her, she will say, 'Yes, we can try it.'

And after you have done it she'll pat you on the back and acknowledge even the smallest accomplishment of a teacher or student."

Teachers have initiated ideas such as special curricular and program offerings, including a team-taught, interdisciplinary academic/technical mini-magnet which offers students an option that prepares them for direct entry into the work force or further technical training, and emphasizes critical thinking skills. Another team-taught course is "U.S. is US," an interdisciplinary class for juniors that uses simulations, structured group activities, and other participatory experiences. And there is an expanded team-teaching program featuring a "bridge" to help ninth graders adjust to high school.

The restructuring has been time consuming, which has deterred some from getting involved. One "resister" says, "I am so busy planning lessons and marking papers, I don't even have time to say hello. Forget it. I think what they're doing is crazy and don't see the need for it."

CITY PARK JUNIOR-SENIOR HIGH SCHOOL

City Park is located in a run-down area of a major city, facing a cluster of small grocery stores and a pizza parlor. Behind the school is an elevated train which frequently makes classroom conversation impossible. The general appearance of the building conforms to the grim architecture of older urban schools.

The corridors and classrooms offer a warmer, more cheerful atmosphere than the exterior. Throughout the school an unusual informality prevails. Small classes of students are engaged in a lively discussion in one room; teachers can be seen engrossed in planning without an immediately discernible leader. Desks are arranged in circles and groups. Everyone is on a first-name basis; students refer to their teachers as "Herb" or "Lou." Classes are longer than usual (two-hour blocks) and students move about without bells, and do not need a pass when they go to the restroom.

City Park is an innovative, alternative public high school, administered in large part as a teachers' collective in which students, who are predominantly from low-income families in the surrounding neighborhood, are treated as responsible individuals.

The school opened in 1985 with 80 seventh graders. Previously the principal, Danna Mason, started and directed two elementary schools with progressive philosophies. City Park was conceived to provide similar education for older children. The school has grown one grade each year; in 1988-89 it had grades 7-10 with approximately

300 students. The school's fundamental philosophy, which emphasizes personalization, demands a small size.

Students choose City Park, and because of the school's belief that the family is a significant part of the educational process, parents and student are required to spend a day visiting the school before enrolling. The student body is heterogeneous in race, socioeconomic status, and academic performance.

Teachers at City Park have a variety of backgrounds. Some worked with Danna Mason, or were parents in the elementary schools that she founded. Others have made a career change from other fields or have come from private schools. However, all welcome the opportunity to work in an alternative setting.

The school's main governance unit is the school faculty that meets weekly, but instruction and student life are organized into divisions (grades 7-8, 9-10, and 11-12) and houses (two per division, with seventy to eighty students and four to five teachers), teacher teams, of which there is one in humanities and one in mathematics/science for each division, are the main units of affiliation for the faculty.

Teachers conduct two-hour blocks daily in either humanities or mathematics/science—the only main subjects. Also, each teacher and administrator conducts a one-hour Advisory, where topics such as journal writing, current events, and sex education are explored in a discussion format. Teachers who lead Advisories are considered "experts" on their students and contact parents about schoolwork and behavioral issues. There are no counselors, or other administrators with specialized responsibility for student services.

The teacher teams meet weekly for two to three hours during the school day, while students are with the other team or working at community service projects outside the school. Teams make the main decisions on curriculum, teaching, and assessment, and provide a forum for socializing new teachers, discussing strategies and problems in teaching, and brainstorming about meeting the needs of individual students.

To work at City Park, teachers must be willing to join the team. The spirit of community decisions prevails, although it permits individual discretion and flexibility in the classroom. As one teacher explains, "The team determines what I'm going to do over the next week, not necessarily how I'll do it or in what order. It is an outline."

Another teacher credits collaboration for her feelings of empowerment:

We are not disenfranchised teachers. We are empowered people. We've created meetings and structures to suit our needs. We view a student experiencing difficulty as *our* problem. Therefore, I'm not a failure as a teacher—which ultimately could translate into hating the kid for . . . giving me this difficulty.

But intense collaboration can be draining:

You do get exhausted, but I am far from burned out. I have never been so excited about a job in my life. . . . I think [teaming] makes the job of teaching a creative experience. . . . There is a human creativity working with the team now and there is a human creativity working with the kids . . . it is tapping into that creativity that makes the job exciting though it is exhausting.

Teachers collectively plan the school's interdisciplinary curriculum, which is far from traditional. For example, the science curriculum includes a unit on astronomy and properties of light, with geometry and mapping taught simultaneously. The humanities program includes Shakespeare and an interdisciplinary examination of China, South Africa, and the Mayans.

A member of the Coalition of Essential Schools, City Park focuses on mastery of a smaller body of knowledge and skills than the typical high school. Reasoning and communication skills are stressed, and the staff is working toward alternative forms of assessment.

The school's alternative structure produces results for teachers. As one says, "We really see enormous gains because we work with students for two years. That's satisfying. . . . We're not always doing the same thing. It will be my sixth year at the school and there's always something new to think about." Another teacher says that an unexpected benefit has been feelings of respect, not just from colleagues but from students: "It's clear that students are really interested in what I have to say. . . . Another sort of respect is honesty. Students will say things about themselves; they'll talk in a way that is real."

The school's annual retreat reinforces the family feeling among teachers. It plays a critical role in orienting new teachers, sharing philosophy, and team building. It also helps to initiate and reinforce the strong norms of the school, such as a social philosophy that emphasizes conflict resolution, antiracism, refusal to blame others, and the support of students and teachers.

One teacher observes, "I've grown enormously at this school. I love my job. When I tell people I teach in a public high school in [the city] and I love my job, people look at me in amazement." She compares City Park's restructured climate with her previous experience in traditional high schools. "The system creates people who try to beat the system, because it's a pecking order. The principal dumps on the teachers, the teachers dump on the kids, and the kids dump on each other. Here, what I especially like is that we expect the same things for ourselves that we expect for the students."

Key Findings

Our study of teachers' work is rich in conclusions, many of which go well beyond the framework with which we began the study. Here I briefly review some of the findings that are most critical for rethinking current and proposed practices in educational policy and in schools.

THE MOST IMPORTANT FACTORS AND WHAT THEY MEAN TO TEACHERS

The study confirms, both in the case study and survey data, that the dimensions of Teacher QWL outlined in the model do have a substantial impact on teachers' commitment to students, their school, and their work. However, not all QWL dimensions are equal in their impacts.

Above all, our data point to the conclusion that *respect* is *primus inter parus*. Where teachers are treated with respect—and, in turn, treat students with respect—the teacher's quality of work life is high *even where there is little other evidence of significant restructuring*. Conversely, teachers who do not feel respected by administrators, other teachers, and students are caught up in a work environment that cannot be fulfilling no matter how many other opportunities are available to them. Many teachers see respect and trust as synonymous: "One of the things that holds back a lot of teachers is distrust. If there is a faculty that feels they can trust one another, trust the administration without being criticized behind their backs, that faculty can go very far. They are freed up to do different things, to talk to one another without hesitation."

Another dimension of QWL that is particularly important is *having the opportunity to use existing skills and to learn new ones*. But we should not leap quickly to the conclusion that more staff development opportunities are the "restructuring answer" to this need. When teachers and administrators in our schools consider the issue of personal development, they define it more broadly than the opportunity to attend courses or seminars, as is clearly evidenced in the two cases above. First, they see two other aspects of quality of work life—shared values and goals, and mutual respect—as prerequisites to effective staff development. "A clear mission that staff can own" and "a schoolwide action plan" around which staff development takes place are viewed as critical in those schools where this dimension of QWL was particularly high. In considering an appropriate professional development culture, it was noted that "mutual support and respect should be evident among all staff" and that it was important to "listen actively and respond positively to teacher talk." Among the most potent forms of staff development in virtually every school were retreats organized by the faculty themselves, which permitted them to "get away from school for thinking time." Thus, these professional teachers saw staff development and personal skill development as inseparable from the broader culture of the school. Not surprisingly, many teachers valued development activities that were school-focused rather than initiated by the district or professional associations outside the school. Staff development that was designed, and either partially or fully carried out, by staff members was generally believed to be more valuable.

Teachers also view opportunities to work in collaboration with other teachers as important. But even in these restructured schools these opportunities were rarer than we expected—except in City Park. Collaboration was not always viewed as easy or simple, and is definitely not the same as being part of a support group. As one teacher in City Park said, "Sometimes it presents problems.... We're all friendly, but we're not necessarily friends. Occasionally it can become a problem because you can become uncomfortable criticizing somebody." Yet, real collaboration requires the tough work of codevelopment and mutual responsibility: it is the adult equivalent of "cooperative learning" in which the group must take responsibility for the quality of the outcome. Not surprisingly, this form of restructuring was not common in most of the schools, occurring most often as a consequence of *ad hoc* department or personal efforts to create a new course or unit, rather than being a regularized feature of teachers' lives. Where it developed, however, it was perceived as very enriching for both the teachers involved and for the student recipients of teacher effort.

Teachers want *feedback* on their performance, but feedback works best when it is viewed as inseparable from collaborative work environments and strong leadership within the school (to be discussed below). In the eight schools, the environment for feedback was as important as actual information received. When teachers feel that they can discuss their work honestly, and when administrators are able (and competent) to review teaching performance, feedback is extremely effective. However, the implementation of productive peer review programs is difficult, at best. As one teacher at City Park pointed out, criticizing another teacher's work in a collaborative group is difficult under the best of circumstances; under less desirable settings it may degenerate into tacit reinforcement of ineffective practices.

Resources, in the most obvious sense of amenities in the physical plant or special funds for equipment, were relatively unimportant. The schools in this study had all gone beyond the basic hurdle of creating a safe and reasonably pleasant physical environment, but the large discrepancy in resources beyond this seemed to make little difference. What mattered most to teachers was a resource—time— that was, either by policy or by practice, within the discretion of the school. Time was important because it was the backbone for staff development and collaborative work efforts.

Look at both Hillside and City Park—schools that were among those able to cope most effectively with the time constraints on teachers. In Hillside, the district generously supported time for groups of teachers to work together on curriculum in the district's professional development program. In City Park, the juggling of the schedule permits the teaching teams to have their regular weekly meetings during the school day. The only other resource that emerged as a significant issue was the availability in some schools of a discretionary "grant program" to support the development costs of individuals or groups of teachers engaged in innovation.

One surprise of the study was the lack of significance attributed to *empowering teachers* through formal participation in decision making. Those schools that had more elaborate, formal mechanisms for involving teachers in school policy did not seem, to us or to the teachers in them, to be better places for teachers than those that did not. Furthermore, when questioned about these structures, few teachers felt that they were critical. Rather, teachers and administrators defined empowerment more broadly as the need to "ensure that teachers have the resources, training, and administrative support to become involved and engaged." As one teacher said: "It is okay to have a traditionally structured high school. That is no problem [for teacher engagement]. However, I personally believe that what really satisfies a teacher is the opportunity to speak out. . . . We speak out, we're free to critique something, we're free to give advice, to pat each other on the back."

This is not to say that decision-making mechanisms are irrelevant. Teachers and administrators pointed to the need to institutionalize philosophical commitment to increasing teacher influence by creating steering committees, allocating released time for teachers to become involved in serious ways, having administrative "open-door policies," and having decentralized budgets that can support teacher suggestions and ideas. Consistent with the emphasis on collective staff development, there was consistent emphasis on the need to "provide opportunities for teachers to make important instructional decisions" through collaborative decision making. However, the type of empowerment that was most satisfying fell into the category of broad informal influence over the school, rather than the formally delegated right to participate in decisions of specific types.

THE EFFECTS OF LEADERSHIP AND SCHOOL CULTURE

Some observations that go beyond the QWL framework in significant ways are also important. The "leadership factor" was even more important than we expected. Teachers agree that no matter how talented the staff, a school with an ineffective principal is unlikely to be exciting, and schools can become exciting quite rapidly after the arrival of a supportive principal. But teachers describe the role of an effective principal largely as one that facilitates the QWL conditions described above, thus freeing the staff to reach its own potential. In particular, if we look at City Park and Hillside—and the other six schools as well—good leadership consists of:

Providing consistent policies to delegate and empower. Principals who create healthy environments for teachers "make teachers invent solutions to problems—they [the principals] aren't the only problem solvers." The effective principal, "can leave the building without things falling apart or hitting snags, and has staff empowered to respond to crises."

Spending time on the details of life in the school. Leadership in the eight schools was not efficient. Administrators were proactive, seeking out advice, and anticipating emerging problems. They "hang around," they "know what's going on in the classrooms, in the lunchroom, etc." They had an open-door policy, and encouraged drop-in visits.

Modeling risk taking. To stretch professionally, teachers must take risks in the classroom. Over and over again the teachers in these schools claimed that they were willing to do so because their principal was also willing to "bite the bullet when necessary [and] make tough decisions." One aspect of risk taking is the principal's personal willingness to confront bad teaching, coupled with supportive programs to help less effective teachers improve.

Providing leadership about values. Teachers were clear that the principal set an important tone for developing a vision and a value orientation in the school. It is important for the principal to understand and reflect the best in community ethical standards and values, and to "make clear what is valued—don't keep faculty guessing about what is important."

It is notable that each of the eight schools existed in a context where the district was exceptionally supportive of the school and teachers, or where the principal fiercely protected the school from distracting external demands and requirements.

AN EMPHASIS ON CARING FOR STUDENTS

The theme of caring as a significant aspect of teachers' work in restructured schools has been extensively developed elsewhere.[19] Caring for students and the way in which it is intertwined with teacher and student engagement is probably best summarized by a teacher from City Park:

Part of teaching is lending your ego for a kid to learn. . . . If you are only teaching a subject and not teaching kids—what you are talking about is communicating a subject. I am saying . . . that you may teach a subject well, but that you are only teaching it to the people who can pick it up exactly as you have presented it. [But] if you are teaching the kids, you see where each kid is and what [his or her] next step is. You have to perceive all of the differences. . . . You have to handle the resistance so that they may take steps for themselves. . . . *You have to do that, and that is an engaging process.*

Caring is good for students, of course, but it is also good for teachers. Caring makes schools into ethical and moral environments, not just arenas for "getting the job done." Studies of beginning teachers indicate that a significant motivation is the desire to be involved with a profession that has a moral character. This is not simply altruism, but the teacher's need to be engaged with work that has significance broader than making a better widget.

Beyond the QWL Framework: Some Conclusions for Policy and Practice

In addition to the observations addressed to the QWL framework, we have drawn broader conclusions on the issue of restructuring schools. First, we believe that the impacts of formal restructuring (such as school-site management, career ladders, or development of schools-within-schools) may be felt most profoundly in those schools where teachers' working conditions are now the least rewarding—in demoralized urban schools, and where the community does not automatically reinforce high levels of commitment to achievement in school.[20] If we look at the two cases, we see settings that would, at first glance, provide few incentives for teacher recruitment. The problems of New York City's schools, for example, have been amply and poignantly described in newspapers and journalistic accounts.[21] Yet both City Park and Hillside, in very different ways, have focused on the special needs of their disadvantaged student populations to create "high expectations," and to inspire even very experienced teachers to levels of professional engagement that are far greater than they previously experienced. Our study suggests that restructuring can make a major dent in the previously durable conclusion that teachers will always find more satisfaction in working with the children of the middle class.

It is especially encouraging that the schools we studied illustrate at least a few instances in which teachers experienced high quality of work life although they were not working with the children of the middle class. The fact that these schools seem to have achieved success in part through their experimentation with alternative structures offers evidence (and hope) that teachers can find rewarding professional lives in schools populated largely by poor students.

One conclusion is inescapable: there are many different ways to improve teachers' work—and no way is perfect. At City Park we see significant restructuring. There teachers' work is organized so differently from a typical high school that many teachers would find it difficult to adjust. Even the deeply dedicated teachers who choose to come there occasionally chafe at the demands of group process. Hillside, on the other hand, does not immediately appear to be restructured in terms of the organization of teachers, grouping of students, or administrative flow charts. Here, "restructuring" occurs mainly in the way teachers and administrators are rethinking their relationships to each other and to the students. The positive and negative features of Hillside's nonrevolutionary approach are two sides of the same coin. On the one hand, the community and most of the teachers accept the changes, but, on the other, a minority of teachers carries out the real work of reform, with continuing debate about the school's vision. It is not useful to conclude that one school has a better approach. Rather, each school has made careful compromises to choose a route that "works" in its unique environment.

Finally, we conclude that many current discussions of reform are far too limited in their emphasis on changing the structural features of schools and the formal definitions of roles as a strategy to improve schools as work places. Certainly structural changes are important. They can send critical symbolic messages about what the school should be and create environments in which teachers have the resources of time and support for innovation and improvement. However, to be effective, restructuring must nurture and reflect broader changes in values and human relationships in schools. When teachers and students believe that they are working in a caring and stimulating environment, school-specific structural changes can evolve to fit specific needs and preferences of the school.

ACKNOWLEDGMENTS. I am grateful for the assistance of Fred Newmann and for the editorial help of Anne Turnbaugh Lockwood with the case studies. Sheila Rosenblum wrote the preliminary drafts of the case studies on which the excerpts included here are based. The ideas presented in this chapter were deeply influenced by my other colleagues in the study: Stewart Purkey, BetsAnn Smith, and Richard Rossmiller. The research was supported by the Office of Educational Research and Improvement, U.S. Department of Education. Any opinions, findings, and conclusions or recommendations expressed are those of the author and do not necessarily reflect the view of the supporting agency.

NOTES

1. Mary Haywood Metz, "How Social Class Differences Shape Teachers' Work," in *The Context of Teaching in Secondary Schools: Teachers' Realities*, edited by Milbrey W. McLaughlin, Joan E. Talbert, and Nina Bascia (New York: Teachers College Press, 1990); idem, "Real School: A Universal Drama and Disparate Experience," in *Education Politics for the New Century: The Twentieth Anniversary Yearbook of the Politics of Education Association*, edited by Margaret Goertz and Douglas Mitchell (Philadelphia: Falmer Press, 1990); Annette H. Hemmings and Mary Haywood Metz, "Real Teaching: How High School Teachers Negotiate Societal, Local Community, and Student Pressures When They Define Their Work," in *Curriculum Differentiation: Interpretive Studies in United States Secondary Education*, edited by Lina Valli and Reba Page (Buffalo, NY: SUNY Press, forthcoming).

2. National Commission on Excellence in Education, *A Nation at Risk* (Washington, DC: U.S. Department of Education, 1983); Carnegie Forum on Education and the Economy, *A Nation Prepared: Teachers for the 21st Century* (New York: Carnegie Forum on Education and the Economy, 1986); Holmes Group, *Tomorrow's Teachers* (East Lansing, MI: Holmes Group, 1986).

3. Wilbur Brookover, Charles Beady, Patricia Flood, John Schweitzer, and Joe Wisenbaker, *School Social Systems and Student Achievement: Schools Can Make a Difference* (New York: Praeger, 1979); William Firestone and Sheila Rosenblum, "Building Commitment in Urban High Schools," *Educational Evaluation and Policy Analysis* 10 (1988): 285-300; Gary Wehlage, Robert A. Rutter, Gregory Smith, Nancy L. Lesko, and Ricardo R. Fernandez, *Reducing the Risk: Schools as Communities of Support* (Philadelphia: Falmer Press, 1989); Anthony Bryk, Valerie Lee, and Julia L. Smith, "High School Organization and Its Effects on Teachers and Students," in *Choice and Control in American Education*, vol. 1, *The Theory of Choice and Control in Education*, edited by William Clune and John Witte (Philadelphia: Falmer Press, 1990).

4. Robert L. Kahn, "The Work Module: A Proposal for the Humanization of Work," in *Work and the Quality of Life*, edited by James O'Toole (Cambridge, MA: MIT Press, 1974); William A. Pasmore and John J. Sherwood, *Sociotechnical Systems and the Quality of Working Life* (La Jolla, CA: University Associates, 1984); William A. Pasmore, *Designing Effective Organizations* (New York: Wiley, 1988).

5. For a fuller discussion, see Karen S. Louis and BetsAnn Smith, "Teachers' Work: Current Issues and Prospects for Reform," in *Productivity and Performance in Educational Organizations*, edited by P. Reyes (Newbury Park: Sage, 1990), pp. 23-47.

6. Firestone and Rosenblum, "Building Commitment in Urban High Schools." Interestingly, teachers in many other countries with quite different educational systems, such as Sweden and the Netherlands, have begun to express similar concerns. See Karen S. Louis, Lennert Bodstrom, and Ulrich Teichler, *Review of Educational Policy in the Netherlands* (Paris: Organization for Economic Cooperation and Development, 1990).

7. Firestone and Rosenblum, "Building Commitment in Urban High Schools"; Susan Moore Johnson, "Teachers, Power, and School Change," in *Choice and Control in American Education*, vol. 2, *The Practice of Choice, Decentralization, and School Restructuring*, edited by William Clune and John Witte (Philadelphia: Falmer Press, 1991).

8. John L. Cotton, David A. Vollrath, Kirk L. Froggatt, Mark Lengnick-Hall, and Kenneth R. Jennings, "Employee Participation: Diverse Forms and Different Outcomes," *Academy of Management Review* 13 (1988): 8-22.

9. Judith Warren Little, "Norms of Collegiality and Experimentation: Workplace Conditions of School Success," *American Educational Research Journal* 19 (1982): 325-340.

10. Bryk, Lee, and Smith, "High School Organization and Its Effects on Teachers and Students."

11. David K. Cohen, "Teaching Practice: Plus Que Ça Change...," in *Contributing to Educational Change: Perspectives on Research and Practice*, edited by Philip W. Jackson (Berkeley, CA: McCutchan Publishing Corp., 1988).

12. Susan Rosenholtz, "Effective Schools: Interpreting the Evidence," *American Journal of Education* 93, no. 3 (1985): 352-388; idem, *Teachers' Workplace: The Social Organization of Schools* (New York: Longman, 1988).

13. Susan Loucks-Horsley, Catherine Harding, Margaret Arbuckle, Lynn Murray, Cynthia Dubea, and Martha Williams, *Continuing to Learn: A Guidebook for Teacher Development* (Andover, MA: Regional Laboratory for Educational Improvement of the Northeast and the Islands, 1987).

14. Charles H. Sederberg and Shirley M. Clark, "Motivation and Organizational Incentives for High Vitality Teachers: A Qualitative Perspective," *Journal of Research and Development in Education* 24 (1990): 6-13.

15. Marilyn M. Cohn, Robert B. Kottkamp, Gary N. McCloskey, and Eugene F. Provenzo, "Teachers' Perspective on the Problems of Their Profession: Implications for Policy Makers and Practitioners" (Unpublished paper, Washington University, St. Louis, MO, 1987).

16. Mary Haywood Metz, Annette Hemmings, and Alex Tyre, *Phase I of the Teacher Working Conditions Study: Final Report* (Madison, WI: Center for the Study of Effective Secondary Schools, University of Wisconsin, 1988), Karen S. Louis and Matthew B. Miles, *Improving the Urban High School: What Works and Why* (New York: Teachers College Press, 1990).

17. The schools are described briefly in Karen S. Louis, Stewart Purkey, BetsAnn Smith, Mary Anne Raywid, Sheila Rosenblum, and Richard Rossmiller, *Alternative School Structures and the Quality of Teachers' Work Lives, Final Report* (Madison, WI: Center for the Study of Effective Secondary Schools, University of Wisconsin, forthcoming).

18. Matthew Miles and Michael Huberman, *Qualitative Data Analysis* (Beverly Hills, CA: Sage, 1984).

19. BetsAnn Smith, Mary Anne Raywid, and Stewart Purkey, "Making Caring Concrete: The Cultures of Effective High Schools" (Paper presented at the Annual Meeting of the American Educational Research Association, Chicago, 1991).

20. Karen S. Louis and BetsAnn Smith, "Breaking the Iron Law of Social Class: The Renewal of Teachers' Professional Status and Engagement," in *Student Engagement and Achievement in American High Schools*, edited by Fred Newmann (New York: Teachers College Press, forthcoming).

21. Samuel G. Freedman, *Small Victories: The Real World of a Teacher, Her Students, and Their School* (New York: Harper & Row, 1990).

CHAPTER IX

Opening the Black Box of Professional Community

JUDITH WARREN LITTLE

The stories we tell one another about special teachers we have had—or have missed out on—underscore the profoundly personal and individualistic nature of teaching. At the same time, teachers are pressed to become less individualistic and more "collaborative," in part as a remedy for the supposed ills of isolation. Are these pictures at odds or in harmony? Unexplored aspects of teachers' individual identity and professional relations provide the point of departure for this essay. In the discussion that follows, I join insights derived from teachers with an emerging literature on individualism and community in American society to examine the dynamics of teachers' professional affiliation in secondary schools. My aim is to contribute to the evolving discussion and debate on the nature and consequences of teachers' individual and collective involvements in teaching—their pervasive privacy and their colleagueship.

Three conditions give urgency to these explorations. First, we have witnessed repeated attempts to calibrate workplace obligations, opportunities, and rewards in ways that attract and retain capable and committed teachers. Getting the incentives right may be a matter of offering teachers sufficient scope for independent action without abrogating legitimate institutional interests in the priorities, performance, and commitment of the teacher workforce. Second, teachers now confront external circumstances and pressures that fundamentally complicate the task of teaching. Dramatic shifts in the composition of the student population, for example, make it more and more difficult for teachers to succeed by relying on their individual resources. The task of teaching is rendered more and more complex; it is arguably the case that even the most knowledgeable and enthusiastic teachers cannot credibly do the job alone. Such externalities place pressure on teachers

---

Judith Warren Little is Associate Professor in the Graduate School of Education, University of California at Berkeley.

to embrace a common set of priorities and to organize a collective response to the complexities of teaching.

Finally, questions surrounding individualism and community assume a special urgency by virtue of the very nature of teachers' work. Schoolteaching entails entrustment with the education of the young; it engages the teacher as a moral agent of the broader public. Ideally, teachers display a command of and enthusiasm for subject-matter knowledge, but also satisfy an "ethic of care" in relation to children and adolescents. Thus, the individualistic or collective stance of teachers toward their work matters because teaching presents, in its content and in its conduct, an intellectual, social, emotional, and moral model for children. One might argue that a special standard of collective and civic responsibility is at stake.

My thinking on these topics owes much to the accounts that teachers have offered in field studies of secondary school teaching spanning three years. In interviews and in their interactions with one another, teachers trace the phenomenological contours of identity and community. They illuminate conceptions of "being a teacher" that distinguish teachers from members of other occupations and, within teaching itself, distinguish groups of teachers from one another. In these ways, teachers show the personal career niches that high school teaching makes possible, together with the ties among colleagues that are forged by will or by circumstance. They sketch the interplay of individual and institution, of professional identity and professional relations.

Perspectives on Independence and Community

Any discussion of professional community among teachers sits against a backdrop of teaching's pervasive and persistent privacy.[1] Many of the proposed virtues of teacher collaboration schemes or school restructuring plans center on overcoming the individual limitations and organizational failings that result from privatized teaching and isolated teachers. The rationales that support such plans generally include a litany of problems associated with a norm of classroom privacy. Laments about privacy center on teachers' isolation from adult companionship and the support of knowledgeable peers; put this way, the problems center on the deprivations teachers experience by virtue of their solitary classroom existence. Other criticisms center on the potential losses to children and to the public at large when personal autonomy translates into freedom from scrutiny directed at classroom practice, apparent relief from defending professional judgment, and the virtual absence of collective responsibility for performance. In response, reform proposals evince a certain unquestioning optimism regarding the benefits that might be expected to follow from penetrating "the walls of privatism"[2] and fostering more vigorous exchange among teachers.

Much of the pessimism surrounding privacy seems a reasonable response to more than two decades of case study research in schools; much of the optimism directed at close colleagueship also seems warranted. Yet these tendencies toward wholesale pessimism or optimism have helped to reinforce a narrowly constructed and compartmentalized view of teachers' work lives, obscuring the situated meanings and unanticipated consequences of privacy and colleagueship.

Recent challenges call into question the almost wholly negative or skeptical view of teachers' privacy and the relentlessly optimistic view of teachers' collaborations. These commentaries offer a more affirmative view of teachers' classroom independence, while field studies of teachers' careers suggest a more comprehensive view of the individual prerogatives that teachers exercise both in and out of the classroom. The consequence of such analyses has been to render "privacy" and "community" not as either/or conditions but as fluid, dynamic, and situationally specific norms of interaction and interpretation that give meaning to "being a teacher."

Such a perspective is implicit in the metaphor of the teacher as an independent artisan whose success comes from consistent and highly localized "tinkering" with the craft at hand.[3] Huberman argues that the metaphor of the independent artisan is true both to the prevailing organization of teaching and to the way that teachers, over the longer term of a career, come to find satisfaction and success in their work. This model squares well with most descriptions of schools as workplaces: that is, it accords with a view that schools are organized to exert little influence on teaching practice or its improvement.[4] The organization of time and space, combined with professional norms of autonomy and equal status, reinforce teachers' fundamental independence on matters of professional practice. In effect, Huberman leaves policymakers with the challenge of making the best use of the inevitable independence of classroom teaching.

Nonetheless, Huberman's model leaves largely unaddressed the question of civic purpose to which schools ultimately must respond. Can a pool of independent entrepreneurs, no matter how skilled, meet the aspirations for intellectual, moral, vocational, and civic education held out by the public? A partial answer to this issue may be found in a distinction between individualism and individuality. Hargreaves distinguishes between destructive forms of individualism that compromise the social good and constructive forms of individuality that give life to the relation between teachers and students.[5] Based on his study of teachers' use of allocated preparation time in Canadian elementary schools, for example, Hargreaves elaborates two forms of individualism that might be considered deliberate strategies for preserving and extending individual control over one's work.[6] Each is a principled, rational response to the work of teaching as teachers experience it. Each, in specific circumstances, might be examined for its effect on classroom practice. The term "strategic individualism" applies to the ways in which teachers buffer the complex demands of the work by limiting intrusions.[7] "Elective individualism" encompasses those individual prerogatives that teachers preserve in an effort to fulfill an ethic of care and responsibility toward children.

These critics join in rejecting the notion of isolation as professional pathology, though they do not dismiss its problematic aspects. Without placing naive faith in teachers' unconstrained independence in matters of professional practice, they prompt us to specify more closely both its drawbacks and its prospects. This represents a shift from a language that emphasizes privacy and isolation to a language that encompasses both the possibilities and the problems that reside in teachers' autonomous action. It proposes an expanded conception of "being a teacher" in the multiple arenas in which teachers pursue independent initiative and seek independent control of their work—in the classroom, among colleagues, and in pursuit of a career.

Defenses of teachers' independence are reinforced by those who find individualism deeply embedded in the broader American society. In *Habits of the Heart*, Robert Bellah and his colleagues examine the fundamental strains of individualism in American culture and pose related problems regarding the possibility for community and commitment.[8] "Individualism lies at the very core of American culture," according to their analysis (p. 142). At the center of this culture is "the autonomous individual, presumed to be able to choose the role he will play and the commitments he will make" (p. 47). To advocate for the open classroom door, for a more collective and less private enterprise of teaching, is not only to remain inattentive to the fundamental and persistent conditions of schoolteaching, but also to confront closely held values of western society.

Challenges to the nearly unrelievedly negative stance toward teachers' privacy thus serve to open up a wider range of conceptual and practical possibilities, and expand the arenas in which teachers are seen to exercise independent initiative and seek individual control (productively or not, for good or ill). In parallel fashion, recent commentaries dispute the overwhelmingly positive view of teachers' collaboration, and begin to specify some of the dimensions along which teachers' experience of professional community might be charted. Until very recently, analyses of teachers' collegial relations have had a characteristically optimistic cast, even when they have portrayed truly collegial work as a phenomenon achieved rarely and with difficulty. But notions of professional community are now also in flux. On one hand, opportunities for collaboration have proliferated both within the school and among wider networks of teachers who share common interests or circumstances. At the same time, the broad optimism attached to "collaborative cultures" has been tempered by critiques that center not merely on pragmatic obstacles but also on fundamental conceptual inadequacies and ideological dilemmas.

To the arguments regarding organizational impediments to collaboration among teachers have been added certain reservations based in the apparent purposes and consequences of teachers' shared work. Coining the term "contrived collegiality," Hargreaves observes that teachers are increasingly being invited to collaborate with one another and are being offered greater material resources to do so; at the same time, however, they are expected to come together in the service of agendas defined by others.[9] The most recent reform initiatives in Canada, the United States, England, and elsewhere have all spurred initiatives in which teachers are brought together to implement curriculum policies framed at some distance from local schools and classrooms. Hargreaves and others concentrate on the nature and consequences of institutional controls over teachers' work. They take special heed of the steady escalation in formally orchestrated "collaborative" work, most commonly under the auspices of the employing district or school. Here we confront the tensions between institutional imperatives and teachers' own professional inclinations. We are made alert to the possible conflict between bureaucratic and professional (educational) concerns and to the phenomena of institutional coercion, control, and surveillance for purposes that may be quite at odds with the central purposes of teaching.[10] Placing ourselves in teachers' shoes, we are inclined to ask, Who promotes or suppresses which forms of professional community among teachers, and for what apparent purposes? At the same time, teachers do have a record of successful overt and covert resistance to institutional initiatives (on the grounds that they violate principles of autonomy, for example). Taking the institutional perspective, and recalling that education is a crucial civic undertaking, we might ask, What do we make of a formal institution that can so little compel its members' loyalty and action by appeal to institutional obligations?

In a world and an occupation in which individualism prevails and in which individuality is treasured, what are the obligations, opportunities, and rewards of community among teachers? What bonds are formed among them, and on what basis? What kinds of claims do teachers actually make on one another? Elsewhere, in an effort to remedy "conceptually amorphous and ideologically sanguine" notions of collaboration and collegiality, I have suggested ways in which structured occasions of joint work might be examined for the degree to which they required or produced genuine interdependence among teachers and yielded demonstrable benefit for students.[11] (We have avoided assuming, throughout our field studies, that frequent and intensive exchange among teachers necessarily reflects norms that are favorable to academic achievement and standards of equity. In Hammersley's account of "staffroom news," for example, or Woods's description of "staffroom humour," exchanges among teachers served to bolster teachers' claims to adequacy in the face of troublesome relations with students.)[12] I still maintain that it will be fruitful to examine these overt and relatively structured professional relations in terms of their prospects for influencing individual classroom choices and consequences. Such an enterprise distinguishes both certain structural dimensions of professional relationship—interdependence, intensity, and inclusivity—and the substance of belief and expertise displayed in exchanges among teachers. But I also argue here that an emphasis on structured occasions of "helping" or "sharing" or other "joint work" may blind us to the more fluid, moment-by-moment interplay of self and society in schools. In looking for community only where teachers gather in some organized forum, we are likely to miss some of the most potent features of teaching as an occupational community, and of schools as organizational cultures—the way persons act or do not act in one another's presence (or outside it), form their views in relation to one another, and construct interpretations of one another's actions. Quite apart from the dangers that come from an ideological naiveté are those that derive from an overly narrow construction of what counts as collegueship among teachers in the first place.

By most accounts, collective orientations and involvements in secondary schools are far overshadowed by individualistic pursuits. Schools would seem to supply only the most tenuous influence on teachers' individual dispositions and practices. Yet certain between-school and within-school patterns deserve attention, showing the situationally variable ways in which teachers take one another into account in the ordinary fabric of school life. Teachers' own words and actions begin to open up the "black box" of individualism and community.

Occupational Community and "Consciousness of Kind"

An occupational community, as defined by Van Maanen and Barley, is "a group of people who consider themselves to be engaged in the same sort of work; whose identity is drawn from the work; who share with one another a set of values, norms, and perspectives that apply to but extend beyond work-related matters; and whose work relationships meld work and leisure."[13] At the heart of such a community is a certain "consciousness of kind"[14] expressed in "the social dimensions used by members themselves for recognizing one another, the social limits of such bonds, and situational factors which amplify or diminish the perceived common identity."[15] Elsewhere I have observed the relative inattention to meaningful groups within schools:

Few studies take account of all of the ways in which groups are constituted, or the manner in which the "groupness" provides a set of lenses through which to portray a school's culture or cultures. Subgroup analyses reveal not only differences of perspective and practices, but also differences in institutional leverage. . . . Individual teachers may hold multiple membership in the internal groups of the school. . . . Secondary teachers, for example, may be members of a department and members of a coaching staff; they may teach part time in two or more departments; their orientation toward their subject (and department) may be colored by the number of low-achieving or high-achieving students they teach (track assignment) or by the apparent fit between the school curriculum and "cutting edge" developments in the field.[16]

The boundaries and meaning of group membership may be anticipated but not fully captured in the nominal labels we routinely apply. We cannot simply assume what it means to be a "teacher" or a "high school teacher" or a "math teacher," for example. Beyond the distinctions made by nominal labels are the connotative dimensions that "lead some members to separate themselves from others who do denotatively similar work."[17] In a critical treatise on the nature of community, Gusfield asks: "When do people define themselves as having important characteristics in common, and when do these become the basis for communal identity and action?"[18]

We began our search for the meaningful boundaries of "professional community" by acknowledging the probable import of organizational subunits such as departments[19] and by giving closer scrutiny to naturally occurring reference groups within the school (which may not coincide entirely with formal structures). Such group boundaries, and the norms of interaction and interpretation that mark them from one another, are revealed in part by the selective use of "we" (and "they") in teachers' accounts and observed interactions.

Applied to teaching, "consciousness of kind" is at root a sense of having adopted the identity of "teacher" in the first place. Nias detailed the multiple ways in which British primary teachers' sense of self was infused by "being a teacher." Yet she also found that "it is possible to teach for years, successfully and with the affirmation of one's head teacher and colleagues, without incorporating 'teacher' into one's self-image."[20] One in six of the fifty mid-career teachers interviewed by Nias did not "feel like a teacher." Judging by Cusick's inventory of the nonteaching work, family involvements, recreational interests, church or community activity, and other commitments that competed with teaching for high school teachers' time and loyalty, we might anticipate a parallel phenomenon among American secondary teachers.[21]

Our analyses point to four aspects of high school teaching that plausibly enhance or erode teachers' sense of being a teacher and contribute to their "consciousness of kind." The *students* one teaches—their present circumstances, their dispositions or talents, and their probable futures—shape the meanings attached to being a good teacher or a good colleague. *Instructional assignments* confer certain status, opportunities, and rewards that may wax and wane over time and across circumstances. Membership in particular *departments* represents direct participation in an occupational community close at hand, with varying measures of congeniality, cohesiveness, intellectual rigor, and the like. Finally, the *subject* in which one specializes supplies its own resources (or restrictions) for identity and community, both inside and outside the school. It is in their affiliations with a disciplinary tradition that teachers may find a powerful avenue to a more cosmopolitan web of relationships beyond the boundaries of school or district.

(Involvement in teachers' unions, of course, is another potentially "cosmopolitan" relationship that spans the organization of schools and membership in the wider occupation.[22])

Although these features differentiate conditions of independence and community among teachers, groups, and schools, they do not exhaust the possibilities. They exclude, for example, the affinities that arise out of teachers' common personal circumstances or interests (say, children of the same age or common recreational interests). They do, however, permit us to trace "consciousness of kind" to commonalities in the circumstances and interactions of teaching. Each of these features may be examined for its independence-preserving and community-building aspects. Each presents resources on which teachers may rely (or obstacles with which they must contend) to forge their own sense of self and community. And each constitutes an arena of professional life that is plausibly subject to policymaking and to the exercise of leadership.

STUDENTS AS A RESOURCE FOR IDENTITY AND COMMUNITY

The meaning of "being a teacher" is expressed as a disposition toward students. Teachers' orientations toward students vary both between and within schools. Teachers differ, for example, in the goals they express for the students they teach.[23] They seek and achieve quite variable levels of personal attachment. In a powerful sense, teachers live a life in the classroom, whether rich or impoverished; their dealings with students may draw them further into "being a teacher" or may yield cynicism and indifference.

But the teacher-student relation, whatever form it takes and whatever level of success and satisfaction it yields, is salient for teachers in all schools. When asked "What's important for us to understand about you as a teacher here, in this school?" teachers talk often and at length about students. They speak of the school's students generally, and of the students who populate their own classes. In doing so, teachers locate themselves at the center or at the margins of the school's symbolic and material resources or rewards. At Oak Valley High School, the largest of our field sites with nearly 3000 students and more than 100 teachers, an English teacher describes a level of parental expectation, public support, and professional recognition that link a teacher's "pride" to the school's successful students:

I think [Oak Valley] is a place that's pretty pride-filled, if that's appropriate. . . . The kids coming in the classroom are being pushed to do well. . . . You have teachers who are in general enjoying their jobs and getting a reward from it. And from the outside, going to conferences and all, it's pretty thrilling to have people know I teach at Oak Valley. They'll say, "Oh, Oak Valley!" and they've heard of us. So there's a sense of pride here that, I think, affects all the different levels (Transcript 0V04301, lines 45-97).

This English teacher's sentiments are echoed consistently by other teachers in the traditional academic departments. But the "pride," to the extent that it is felt, is in fact constructed differently at "all the different levels." In this and other academically oriented comprehensive high schools, we find a pronounced difference between teachers in traditional academic departments and teachers of conventionally defined "vocational" subjects. The value placed on "college-bound" students creates the standard of worth both for students and for teachers. Teachers of industrial arts, business, consumer/family studies ("home ec"), or vocational agriculture must seek alternative grounds on which to establish their contribution or to make claims on school resources. The symbolism surrounding the phrase "college-bound" marginalizes a certain segment of students, teachers, curricula, and goals by denying them any affirmative identity (they are, emphatically, "non-college-bound"). Teachers of "non-college-bound" students at Oak Valley dispute the numbers of college acceptances touted by the school's administrators, and criticize what they consider to be an inappropriate concentration of resources. Nonetheless, they find it difficult to escape the lower status attached to their clientele and their curriculum. An industrial arts teacher complains: "The pride in voc ed is in the people teaching it. There's limited pride, limited acknowledgement out there. . . . They [the administrators] almost make you feel second class."

Whom teachers teach, and how those students are seen by others, is thus a major element in the identity of "teacher." Teachers are situated by their student clientele. But one's self-image as a teacher—or a "good teacher"—is also bolstered or eroded by the daily ebb and flow of the classroom. Regardless of the categorical labels attached to students, a teacher's competence and confidence are tested in the moment-by-moment exchanges among individuals and in the

---

Note: Schools mentioned in this chapter are designated by pseudonyms. Quotations from Oak Valley teachers are taken from transcripts coded to indicate the school, the teacher, and the year of data collection.

dynamics of specific classes. In a five-period teaching day, teachers readily distinguish between the "good" classes and the "tough" ones; it is not uncommon for teachers to experience widely fluctuating levels of "efficacy" from one class to another. Indeed, the variance in measured levels of performance efficacy is nearly as great within teacher (across classes) as between teachers.[24] The definition of "good" and "difficult" classes is not straightforward; certainly it is not summed up by students' prior academic achievement alone. In any event, one might argue that the burdens or blessings of privacy assume quite different significance in the course of the school day. So, too, do the support, indifference, or animosity of one's colleagues.

From these observations emerge two curiosities. First, we have begun to wonder how teachers' engagements with one another reinforce, alter, compensate for, or in other ways mediate the salience of "student" in shaping the success and satisfactions of teaching. What teachers require or value from a community of peers is plausibly tied to teachers' encounters with students both in and out of the classroom. Second, we have begun to trace the ways in which teachers influence (or fail to influence) the student clientele available to them. Teachers in these schools are pleased when they are assured of "good" students, though the definitions of "good" do not accord neatly or simply with records of academic achievement. But "good" students do not always appear to be within reach. Teachers at urban Valley High School, for example, decry the "creaming off" of their best students when a new school opened nearby and express a certain hopelessness over the remaining student population. Vocational teachers at Oak Valley lament a perceived increase in "dumping ground" placements; they believe themselves to be enjoying fewer and fewer of the "student" resources the school has to offer.

INSTRUCTIONAL ASSIGNMENT

The policies and practices governing the nature of the teaching assignments that teachers acquire supply the local meaning that "math teacher" or "English teacher" or "art teacher" comes to have in daily work.[25] The instructional assignment assumes special importance in light of a conception of career that highlights persons' relation to work and the social identity it offers. (This is precisely the conception held out by Van Maanen and Barley's definition of the "occupational community.") Teachers attribute the success and satisfaction they find in their work to the specific assignments they acquire. In their stories of entering and staying in teaching, teachers highlight turning points that center on teaching assignments—points at which they succeeded (or were thwarted) in securing a desirable school placement and a favorable configuration of courses and students.

Teachers' accounts present three levels at which "instructional assignment" is differentially subject to individual influence, the source of individual pride or embarrassment, and the basis of community. First, teachers express their consciousness of where high school teaching fits in an academic hierarchy. By the tales of "getting to high school" or "moving up to high school," many position high school teaching at the pinnacle of a status hierarchy in K-12 teaching; a few position high school teaching between work in middle schools (typically less favored) and opportunities to teach in community colleges (a source of pride for those who hold or seek them).

Second, teachers achieve (or attempt) influence over their assignments to individual schools. Their reports suggest strategies for controlling individual career pathways that could not be anticipated by reference to districts' teacher selection practices or local contract language regarding transfer rights. Teachers describe "shopping" among districts, or assessing the trade-offs between public and private school positions.

Finally, patterns of actual teaching assignment on a yearly or semester basis achieve a good or poor fit with teachers' subject preparation and preferences. Students are the first of many professional resources that may be differentially distributed within and between secondary schools. Teachers are differentially successful in negotiating preferred schedules, topics, and students.[26] We expect that the specific patterns of distribution, and the meaning attached to them by teachers, will bear a relationship to teachers' daily performance and career commitment. It remains uncertain whether or how the configuration of assignments creates a certain de facto community through circumstance.[27]

THE DEPARTMENT

Subject area organization modeled on higher education creates both possibilities and limitations for teachers' professional identity and community. Despite criticisms of subject departmentalization,[28] it remains one of the fundamental facts of life in the work of most secondary teachers.[29] The department is perhaps the most prominent domain of potential interdependence among teachers, and one that has shown itself to be remarkably resilient in the face of repeated efforts to forge other forms of school organization.[30] At suburban Oak Valley High School, with its 3000 students and more than 100 staff, departments are the primary frame of reference for most teachers. Yet the departments provide very different kinds of homes for the teachers who inhabit them. Here, a third-year teacher describes the "fit" he found with the English department:

I came here [to interview] and I was really impressed right away with the teachers that were here in the English Department. They weren't the kind that were sitting back during the breaks, smoking cigarettes and complaining about kids and how bad they are and all that. . . . They were really energetic and involved in what they were doing and . . . sharing ideas about what they were doing in class, what was working, showing students' work, you know . . . (Transcript 0V07701, lines 43-61).

In this instance, a teacher's sense of confident autonomy in the classroom rests in part on the place he finds within a like-minded community within the department. Yet there are limits to the like-mindedness. This teacher, like most others in the department, lists members of other departments among his closest associates.[31] He also points to systematic differences within the department with regard to classroom practice. By his description, echoed closely by others, this is a department that takes pride in being an intellectual center without expecting or achieving consensus with regard to the subject or the methods by which it is best taught. Its members display and discuss their course outlines, lesson plans, and student assignments, and show one another samples of student work, but they also accord one another a wide degree of latitude with regard to classroom pedagogy. Individuals gain the respect of their colleagues by satisfying criteria that combine classroom prowess with other kinds of professional activity. Some, though not all, publish fiction and poetry, are active in professional associations, and lead writing workshops for teachers from other districts. A picture of the group is prominently displayed in the department office, and the office swirls with activity throughout the day. Teachers dignify one another's individuality, but also expect one another to be both productive and sociable members of the group.

Other departments provide very different grounds for individual teachers' work. A science department generates competition among its members by its practices of teacher assignment and the allocation of classrooms, laboratory space, and equipment. The psychic rewards that secure the commitment and enthusiasm of new teachers in this department are jeopardized when senior members of the department hold hostage the most favored teaching assignments. Members of a social studies department hold competing views of what Ball and

Lacey have labeled "subject paradigm" and "subject pedagogy."[32] Unlike the members of the Oak Valley English department, these teachers are polarized by their differences.

Although their salience may vary within and across schools, departments represent a naturally occurring ground for teachers' interactions. In future analyses, three aspects of departmental life will command special attention: the department as a meaningful reference group for teachers with regard to curricular and instructional priorities; the department as a source of professional expertise and a model of professional commitment; and the department as a resource for influence within the school, specifically with regard to control over human and material resources.

SUBJECT SPECIALIZATION

Persistent stereotypes paint high school teachers as resolutely "subject-centered." Until very recently, however, there have been few efforts to penetrate that stereotype to discover the meaning of subject specialization for teachers' conceptions of task, their actual work in schools, and their commitment to teaching. The few exceptions suggest some of the possibilities that await a more extensive probe. A comparative study of secondary art and science teachers in England reveals differences across subjects in teachers' orientation toward the discipline and toward the reward system and career possibilities of teaching.[33] Meaningful differences within subject disciplines are expressed in part as differences in individuals' "subject paradigm" and "subject pedagogy."[34] Such differences serve both to bond departments and to divide them. One of the four English departments studied by Ball and Lacey formed a cohesive subculture with shared views of the subject and the way it should be taught. A second department found itself in agreement on pedagogy despite differences over subject paradigm. Both these departments, in which all members were English specialists with full-time assignments to the department, were positioned to operate as relatively powerful instruments of curriculum policy. The remaining two departments, by contrast, were divided by substantive issues (disagreements over paradigm and pedagogy).

To what extent and in what manner does the subject constitute a form of affiliation among teachers? One plausible answer is that secondary teaching closely approximates a world of entrepreneurial individualism in which teachers and students alike pursue self-interested activity in a "shopping mall high school."[35] By this view, individual teachers draw upon the resources of subject specialization to construct a personal niche to which they bring idiosyncratic preferences for content priorities, pedagogical style, and favored instructional assignments. Community at the level of the school, in so far as there is one, resides in a set of tacit agreements that preserve the widest possible latitude for independent action. At the level of the occupation, "consciousness of kind" might amount to no more than diffuse participation in an abstract community of scholars within a disciplinary tradition. Surveys of nearly 700 teachers suggest that attendance at subject-related conferences is a common (nearly universal) form of participation in a professional community. But conference attendance alone communicates little about the nature and extent of one's links to a subject discipline or one's affiliations with others who teach it. Further, this form of participation in "community" is affected by fluctuations in local resources, board policies governing released time, and the like.

It is perhaps less important to know the frequency or scale of teachers' participation than to grasp the meaning of such involvements for the teachers who pursue them, and to understand the way in which district policies and practices promote or inhibit those involvements. We know little of these out-of-school involvements and the extent to which they supply teachers with intellectual stimulation, emotional satisfaction, personal recognition, or status in the broader occupation. The permeability of the school walls is of special interest for secondary teachers, given the demands placed on "staying current in one's field."

We might productively distinguish between the school or district (the employing organization) and the wider occupation of teaching as meaningful domains of action and affiliation. Membership in subject-matter associations, networks, and other informal collaborative enterprises is an unexplored and potentially consequential element in teachers' professional identity and career satisfaction. A small supplemental study of participants in two Urban Mathematics Collaborative projects has enabled us to trace the way in which subject affiliations and departmental ties are maintained or attenuated by relationships in the larger occupation or community.[36]

In sum, a school's prevailing stance toward its students, its formal (typically departmental) design, and the demands and opportunities of daily work (instructional assignment) appear to constitute the principal organizational ground on which secondary teachers construct identity and community. In addition, subject specialization provides a source of identity and collegial relationship that reaches to the teaching occupation more widely and to connections in higher education, industry, the arts, and other arenas. Although these are not the only contributors to one's "sense of self" or "consciousness of kind," they are prominent in teachers' talk. They provide windows into the intersection of teachers' independent action and their participation in a professional community both inside and outside the school.

The Claims Teachers Make on One Another: Mutual Obligation and Mutual Support

More often than not, secondary teachers have been portrayed as going their own way within an institution in which school-level goal consensus is (for many reasons) difficult to achieve and in which the linkage between institutional goals and individual practice is insubstantial. Efforts to detect "community" among high school teachers have not been fruitful. Cusick concluded that there were no meaningful "professional networks" among the staffs of two midwestern high schools he observed; rather, teachers engaged in a form of competitive entrepreneurialism to control course offerings and content, student enrollment, discretionary time, and the like.[37] Their work lives were a mosaic of personal and professional commitments that included second jobs and other out-of-school involvements, chosen and sustained quite independent of institutional interests. Departments were administrative conveniences rather than intellectual homes or instruments of curriculum policy.

Whole-school studies (especially those of elementary schools) tend to emphasize community as "goal consensus."[38] In some secondary schools, most commonly independent schools, small size coincides with singularity of purpose in much the same way. More often, however, secondary schools appear to be generally absent any powerful mechanisms by which institutional and occupational obligations come to hold sway over personal prerogative. Rather, teachers' affiliations approximate "community as a voluntary gathering of autonomous individuals."[39] Professional community defined in this way would seem to have only the most insubstantial hold on teachers. Comprehensive high schools stand in dramatic contrast, for example, to religious or utopian communities in which there are both symbolic and structural mechanisms that subordinate personal to communal interests.[40] The broadly permissive character of such professional relations is underscored by those unusual cases in education in which teachers' individualism is substantially constrained by public and powerful expressions of mutual obligation, and in which personal prerogative is expressed fully by institutional goals. In the "total world" of Bethany Baptist Academy, teachers describe institutional obligations and collective responsibilities that stand in startling contrast to those present in Cusick's comprehensive high schools.[41] Bethany's teachers (all themselves born-again Christians) submit not only their work but also their lives to the scrutiny and the pragmatic control of the larger institution. They attend Wednesday and Sunday services, participate in evening meetings, make home visitations, and in other ways blur the boundaries between professional and personal time, space, and activity. Teachers both witness and participate in rituals that secure and sustain commitment and that define the patterns of obligation that keep commitment alive.

Taken together, Cusick's observations of the self-interest reigning in "typical" comprehensive high schools and Peshkin's observations of the rituals and rhetoric required to sustain Bethany Baptist's level of collective commitment underscore the utilitarian individualism of the wider society and the generally permissive collegiality of schools. Bellah et al. (1985) frame the dilemma this way:

[I]f the entire social world is made up of individuals, each endowed with the right to be free of others' demands, it becomes hard to forge bonds of attachment to, or cooperation with, other people, since such bonds would imply obligations that necessarily impinge on one's freedom.[42]

A major question, then, is the extent to which a "consciousness of kind" is manifest in a pattern of mutual obligation and mutual support. Again, descriptions of the broader American culture have their echoes in teachers' views. Personal freedom, in the society at large ". . . turns out to mean being left alone by others, not having other people's values, ideas, or styles of life forced upon one, being free of arbitrary authority in work, family, and political life."[43] This is strikingly reminiscent of (in accord with) teachers' views of autonomy: freedom from scrutiny, the right to make professional judgments that fit personal preference, and the implicit obligation to solve one's own problems. Autonomy may be expressed as the limits of departmental constraint on course content, pedagogy, and treatment of students.

Where do we find autonomy tempered by obligation to the group? For example, is "sharing the load" part of a definition of collegueship, and for whom? Here, teachers' independent interests and preferences may be in conflict with principles of service to students. The past chair of Oak Valley's English department describes the group's stance toward teaching assignments in a way that expresses collective obligations to teach remedial classes:

So I think the school is pretty much philosophically doing what it says it should do and that's provide the college-bound track to most of the students. I know that we in the English Department feel very strongly that our objective is to get the kid out of that remedial track and get him into the regular track and I know that that's, it's, we talk about it all the time. . . . Our "remedial, non-college-bound," we rotate. . . . And everybody in the department will be involved in those courses and that's the way it goes (Transcript 0V04301, lines 451-462, 534-535).

The same department expects its members to "add to the wealth" and to subordinate personal curriculum preferences to a principle of departmental curriculum coherence:

We started something a couple of years ago where every teacher is, not forced, but encouraged to pick up a new prep every other year. And the idea behind that one is so that courses didn't become so specialized to teachers that if a teacher were to leave the department and all of a sudden the course, you know somebody's stuck teaching it and doesn't really know how it's supposed to go and all that, and tried to remove the idea of special interest classes and say, "Look, if it's in our department then it's worth being taught and so let's have people who can teach it." (Transcript 0V04301, lines 569-587).

Where independence is in tension with collective obligations, membership in a professional community appears to take on the form of elective and sporadic "involvements." Americans' penchant for "getting involved," according to Bellah et al., signals a distinctive and peculiar relationship between self and society.[44] Getting involved is a way of both pursuing and protecting one's personal interests; it is therefore both possible and legitimate to remain uninvolved. This argument has its direct echoes in teachers' insistence that voluntary staff development is preferable to mandated participation. Examples proliferate in our chronicles of secondary teachers' work. Teachers active in the urban mathematics networks report quite varied success in securing the "involvement" of their departments in activities of the network. In most instances, involvement was secured by displays of personal enthusiasm and by appeals to self-interest or anticipated personal benefit. Although the teachers who participate display a consistent and intense concern for "reaching the kids," there are few instances in which their initial involvement could be explained by appeals to the collective obligation that is part of being a "math teacher." "Given such assumptions about the [self-interested] purposes of involvement," say Bellah and his colleagues, "what kind of vision can one have of the public good?"[45]

These examples suggest that the nature and extent of community might be traced through situationally specific rights and obligations on matters of professional practice both within the school and in the larger occupational domain. In doing so, we discover empirically the kinds of claims that teachers can and do place on one another. Community emerges in the form of multiple ties with differential significance to individuals and to the institution, and with differential capacity to engage a teacher's loyalty and action.

Conclusion

In this essay, I have examined the ties between teachers' individual interests or inclinations and their membership in a broader professional community. The consequence of "opening up" our conceptions of independence and collegiality is to render them at once more conceptually robust and more empirically sensitive. It becomes apparent that "privacy" of teachers can be grasped only in the context of the organization and occupation of teaching, and that the character of professional independence is closely linked to the nature of professional community. "Being a teacher" is not a single identity grounded only in classroom life, nor is professional community a seamless fabric, a single unity to which one is committed or not.

Recent debates and discussions—both in regard to schools and in commentary on modern society—provide us with the set of lenses and conceptual dimensions by which we might move beyond the "conceptually amorphous and ideologically sanguine" stance toward independence and collegiality in teachers' professional work. This analysis introduces dimensions of colleagueship that have gone largely unattended in a research literature that to date has achieved only a modest level of conceptual discrimination. In reexamining the distinctions between a norm of privacy and a norm of collegiality, it begins to distinguish strong from weak ties among teachers, and the way in which the norm of privacy is itself a form of collegial relation. To an emphasis on the forms and processes of collegial exchange, it adds a focus on the knowledge and beliefs that teachers express to one another either directly or indirectly. It extends colleagueship beyond the school walls and thereby renders problematic the critically unexamined link to value consensus. It acknowledges the multiplicity of locally meaningful reference groups. From a policy standpoint, this pursuit enables us to grasp the forces that contribute to teachers' performance and commitment and the specific ways in which those forces are linked to the contexts of the school and the occupation of teaching.

ACKNOWLEDGMENTS. The research that informs this paper was supported by the Center for Research on the Context of Secondary School Teaching (Stanford University) with funds from the Office of Educational Research and Improvement, U.S. Department of Education; by the National Center for Research on Vocational Education (University of California, Berkeley) with funds from the Office of Vocational and Adult Education, U.S. Department of Education; and by the Educational Development Center, Inc., with funds from the Ford Foundation.

NOTES

1. Judith Warren Little, "The Persistence of Privacy: Autonomy and Initiative in Teachers' Professional Relations," *Teachers College Record* 91, no. 4 (1990): 509-536.

2. Michael Fullan, *The Meaning of Educational Change* (New York: Teachers College Press, 1982).

3. Michael Huberman, "The Social Context of Instruction in Schools," in *Cultures, Careers, and Contexts*, edited by Judith Warren Little and Milbrey W. McLaughlin (New York: Teachers College Press, forthcoming).

4. Tom Bird and Judith Warren Little, "How Schools Organize the Teaching Occupation," *Elementary School Journal* 86, no. 4 (1986): 493-511.

5. Andy Hargreaves, "Individualism and Individuality," *International Journal of Educational Research* (in press); idem, *Elementary Teachers' Use of Preparation Time, Project Report* (Toronto: Ontario Institute for Studies in Education, 1989).

6. Hargreaves, "Individualism and Individuality." A third form, which Hargreaves labels "constrained" individualism, results from obstacles placed in the way of teachers' collective action—obstacles that range from administrative style to the organization of time, space, and responsibilities during the salaried work day. This form of individualism is better seen as a set of conditions akin to the familiar portrait of teachers' enforced isolation than as a deliberate and principled response that teachers make to their work.

7. See also, David J. Flinders, "Teacher Isolation and the New Reform," *Journal of Curriculum and Supervision* 4, no. 1 (1988): 17-29.

8. Robert Bellah, Richard Madsen, William M. Sullivan, Ann Swidler, and Steve Tipton, *Habits of the Heart: Individualism and Commitment in American Life* (Berkeley, CA: University of California Press, 1985).

9. Andy Hargreaves, *Contrived Collegiality: The Micropolitics of Teacher Collaboration* (Toronto: Ontario Institute for Studies in Education, 1990). See also, Andy Hargreaves and Ruth Dawe, "Paths of Professional Development: Contrived Collegiality, Collaborative Culture, and the Case of Peer Coaching," *Teaching and Teacher Education* 6, no. 3 (1990): 227-241; Gunnar Handal, "The Effect of Changing Frames on Teachers' Collective Practical Theories of Work" (Paper presented at the Annual Meeting of the American Educational Research Association, San Francisco, 1989).

10. Linda M. McNeil, *Contradictions of Control* (New York: Routledge and Kegan Paul, 1986).

11. Little, "The Persistence of Privacy."

12. Martyn Hammersley, "Staffroom News" and Peter Woods, "The Meaning of Staffroom Humour," in *Classrooms and Staffrooms: The Sociology of Teachers and Teaching*, edited by Andy Hargreaves and Peter Woods (Milton Keynes: Open University Press, 1984), pp. 203-214; 190-202.

13. John Van Maanen and Stephen R. Barley, "Occupational Communities: Culture and Control in Organizations," *Research in Organizational Behavior* 6 (1984): 287.

14. The term "consciousness of kind" was coined by Franklin Giddings in an early work on theories of human society, and is cited and further developed in Joseph Gusfield, *Community: A Critical Response* (Oxford: Basil Blackwell, 1975). Van Maanen and Barley also make use of the Gusfield treatment in discussing the phenomenological dimensions of work group boundaries. See their "Occupational Communities: Culture and Control in Organizations."

15. Van Maanen and Barley, "Occupational Communities: Culture and Control in Organizations," p. 295.

16. Little, "The Persistence of Privacy."

17. Van Maanen and Barley, "Occupational Communities," p. 295.

18. Gusfield, *Community: A Critical Response*, p. 30.

19. W. R. Scott, *Work Units in Organizations: Ransacking the Literature* (Stanford, CA: Center for Research on the Context of Secondary School Teaching, Stanford University, 1989); Leslie S. Siskin, "School Restructuring and Subject Subcultures" (Paper presented at the Annual Meeting of the American Educational Research Association, Chicago, 1991).

20. Jennifer Nias, *Primary Teachers Talking: A Study of Teaching as Work* (London: Routledge, 1989), p. 181.

21. Philip A. Cusick, *A Study of Networks among Professional Staffs in Secondary Schools* (East Lansing, MI: Institute for Research on Teaching, Michigan State University, 1982).

22. Nina Bascia, "Teachers' Unions and Notions of Professional Community" (Paper presented at the Annual Meeting of the American Educational Research Association, Chicago, 1991.)

23. Milbrey W. McLaughlin, *Strategic Dimensions of Teachers' Workplace Context* (Stanford, CA: Center for Research on the Context of Secondary School Teaching, Stanford University, 1990); Center for Research on the Context of Secondary School Teaching, *CRC Report to Field Sites* (Stanford, CA: Center for Research on the Context of Secondary School Teaching, Stanford University, 1989). See also Sara Lawrence Lightfoot, *The Good High School* (New York: Basic Books, 1983) and Mary H. Metz, "How Social Class Differences Shape Teachers' Work," in *The Contexts of Teaching in Secondary Schools: Teachers' Realities*, edited by Milbrey W. McLaughlin, Joan E. Talbert, and Nina Bascia (New York: Teachers College Press, 1990), pp. 40-107.

24. Stephen W. Raudenbush, Brian Rowan, and Y. F. Cheong, *Contextual Effects on the Self-efficacy of High School Teachers* (Stanford, CA: Center for Research on the Context of Secondary School Teaching, Stanford University, 1990).

25. See, for example, C. Bennet, "Paints, Pots, or Promotion? Art Teachers' Attitudes toward Their Careers," in *Teachers' Lives and Careers*, edited by Stephen J. Ball and Ivor Goodson (London: Falmer Press, 1985); Stephen J. Ball and C. Lacey, "Subject Disciplines as the Opportunity for Group Action: A Measured Critique of Subject Subcultures," in *Classrooms and Staffrooms: The Sociology of Teachers and*

Teaching, edited by Andy Hargreaves and Peter Woods (Milton Keynes: Open University Press, 1984), pp. 232-244; and Patricia Sikes, Lynda Measor, and Peter Woods, *Teacher Careers: Crises and Continuities* (London: Falmer Press, 1985), chap. 7.

26. Philip Cusick, *The Egalitarian Ideal and the American High School* (New York: Longman, 1983); M. K. V. Finley, "Teachers and Tracking in a Comprehensive High School," *Sociology of Education* 57 (October 1984): 233-243; Barbara Neufeld, "Inside Organization: High School Teachers' Efforts to Influence Their Work" (Doctoral dissertation, Graduate School of Education, Harvard University, 1984).

27. Joan E. Talbert, *Teacher Tracking: Exacerbating Inequalities in the High School* (Stanford, CA: Center for Research on the Context of Secondary Teaching, Stanford University, 1990).

28. See, for example, Theodore Sizer, *Horace's Compromise: The Dilemma of the American High School* (Boston: Houghton Mifflin, 1984).

29. Leslie S. Siskin, *Different Worlds: The Department as Context for High School Teachers* (Stanford, CA: Center for Research on the Context of Secondary School Teaching, Stanford University, 1990); Milbrey W. McLaughlin, Joan E. Talbert, and Patricia Phelan, *1990 CRC Report to Field Sites* (Stanford, CA: Center for Research on the Context of Secondary School Teaching, Stanford University, 1990).

30. Siskin, "School Restructuring and Subject Subcultures."

31. Marian Eaton, "Communication Networks in Four High Schools" (Paper presented at the Annual Meeting of the American Educational Research Association, Chicago, 1991).

32. Ball and Lacey, "Subject Disciplines as the Opportunity for Group Action."

33. Sikes, Measor and Woods, *Teacher Careers: Crises and Continuities*; Bennet, "Paints, Pots, or Promotions?"

34. Ball and Lacey, "Subject Disciplines as the Opportunity for Group Action." See also, F. T. Elbaz, *Teacher Thinking: A Study of Practical Knowledge* (London: Croom Helm, 1983).

35. Arthur Powell, Eleanor Farrar, and David K. Cohen, *The Shopping Mall High School: Winners and Losers in the Educational Marketplace* (Boston: Houghton Mifflin, 1985).

36. Gary Lichtenstein, "The Urban Math Collaborative in Los Angeles: Why Does It Work?" (Paper presented at the Annual Meeting of the American Educational Research Association, Chicago, 1991).

37. Cusick, *A Study of Networks among Professional Staffs in Secondary Schools*.

38. Susan Rosenholtz, *Teachers' Workplace* (New York: Longman, 1989).

39. Bellah et al., *Habits of the Heart*, p. 206.

40. Rosabeth M. Kanter, *Commitment and Community* (Cambridge: Harvard University Press, 1972).

41. Alan Peshkin, *God's Choice: The Total World of a Fundamentalist Christian School* (New York: Teachers College Press, 1986).

42. Bellah et al., *Habits of the Heart*, p. 23.

43. Ibid.

44. Ibid.

45. Ibid., p. 167.

Section Three
CHANGING ROLES AND RELATIONSHIPS OF TEACHERS AS LEARNERS AND AS LEADERS

CHAPTER X

Teaching to Learn

PAMELA L. GROSSMAN

A friend recently noticed that I was reading a copy of *Learning to Teach* by Richard Arends and commented that I was too close to retirement to learn how to do it correctly now. At the time I laughed, but in reflection I know that it is never too late to learn to teach. That is the basis for the excitement, strength, and motivation of the Puget Sound Professional Development Center renewal program. We at the middle level can learn better methods and strategies whether we are student teachers or veterans of twenty-five years.

Nanna S. Brantigan, 1991

The middle school teacher quoted above fulfills multiple roles in her daily life. She teaches language arts to seventh graders, serves as the school librarian, presents at conferences nationwide on team-teaching and cooperative learning, engages in action research, and participates actively in the restructuring of her own school. In addition, she has served as both the on-site supervisor for student teachers and as the Teaching Associate for the core seminar in a pilot middle school teacher education program offered through the Puget Sound Professional Development Center. Her story illustrates the core contention of this chapter that engagement in the preparation of the next generation of teachers provides rich opportunities for teacher learning.

Pamela L. Grossman is Assistant Professor of Education in the College of Education, University of Washington, Seattle.

Conceptions of Teacher Learning

When we speak of teacher learning, we are speaking of many things. Buchmann, for example, defines teacher learning as both "developing specific skills, dispositions, and understandings for enabling youngsters to learn worthwhile things in school" and "bringing one's education, experiences, and knowledge of people to bear on one's work over time."[1] Within the first definition, teacher learning can consist of improvement of pedagogical skills, changes in attitudes or beliefs regarding teaching, or the acquisition of particular knowledge. Each of these goals for teacher learning suggests differing approaches to learning, as we do not acquire a skill in the same manner in which we change a belief. The second definition highlights the relationship between new learning and changes in classroom practice, a particular variety of learning from experience. In this conception of teacher learning, the everyday work of teachers becomes the crucible for teacher learning, as they transform their practice to reflect what they have come to know and believe over time. The most "authentic assessment" of teacher learning within this definition resides in teachers' actual classroom practices, for one can come to know something within the first definition without being able to bring it to bear upon one's practice.

Research on teacher learning comes from many sources. Some research has looked at teachers' acquisition of generic pedagogical skills,[2] while other research has looked at the development of beliefs and perspectives about teaching.[3] Recent work on teachers' subject-matter knowledge has explored the ways in which teachers acquire knowledge and construct new understandings about the subject matter they teach, and the relationship between subject-matter knowledge and teaching.[4] Research on staff development provides yet another resource for research on teacher learning.[5] Each body of research illuminates a different facet of teacher learning. The nature of teacher learning in each of these research traditions, however, has been implicit rather than explicit. While several of these lines of research take a developmental perspective on what teachers know and are able to do,[6] the processes of teacher learning have not been the central focus of these investigations.

For too long a curious dichotomy existed between conceptions of student learning and conceptions of teacher learning. While research in cognitive psychology and anthropology demonstrated the complexity of student learning and the persistence of students' prior conceptions, staff developers and teacher educators continued to act as if teacher learning were relatively unproblematic—one could simply tell teachers that telling students is insufficient. Recent research suggests that assumptions regarding student learning hold for teachers as well.[7] Teachers must also be able to situate their new knowledge and understanding within the context of their actual classrooms. When teachers acquire new knowledge outside the contexts of teaching, they may find it difficult to bring this knowledge to bear upon actual classroom practices.[8] As Lampert argues, teachers' attempts to bring their new research-derived understandings about the nature of children's thinking into their teaching lead to unforeseen practical dilemmas. In order for learning within Buchmann's second definition to occur, teachers must both see the connections between their learning and their everyday work as teachers and resolve the tensions between abstract principles and the complexity of classroom practice.

Contexts Which Support Teacher Learning

In discussing the processes involved in learning to teach, Feiman-Nemser argues that "formal arrangements for teaching teachers and helping them to improve do not fit with what we know about how teachers learn to teach and get better at teaching over time."[9] She identifies two perspectives on the professional development of teachers, one which focuses on the individual teacher as the agent for change, and a second which focuses upon the school itself as the context in which teacher learning does, or does not, occur.[10] Shulman argues that schools as they currently exist are not structured to support the capability of teachers to learn from experience; in order for learning to occur, teachers must have the opportunity to get feedback on what they are actually doing as they teach and to understand fully the consequences of their actions.[11] Because the limits of individual rationality post obstacles to accomplishing these tasks, Shulman argues for the importance of collegiality in learning from experience, a contention supported by the work of Little.[12] Through observing one another's teaching, colleagues can help each other see more accurately and completely what each teacher is doing and the consequences of those actions. Collegiality, then, is an important feature of contexts which support teacher learning.

What contributes to the development of norms of collegiality and collaboration? Little argues that "nonroutine tasks tend to drive the formation of collaborative relations."[13] According to this analysis, opportunities for teachers to engage in new tasks, including developing curricula at the school or district levels, mentoring beginning teachers, participating in school-based management, or engaging in the work of a professional development school, support the development of collegiality, which in turn contributes to a context which supports teacher learning.

Schools that provide a supportive context for teacher learning must also define teachers' engagement in these novel tasks as contributing to their own professional growth, either as classroom teachers or as members of a larger professional community.[14] By expanding their conception of teachers' work beyond the classroom walls, administrators, as well as teachers, can value learning that does not provide specific ideas for classroom teaching, but may provide new ways of thinking about teaching more generally or new skills for fulfilling their expanded roles on site councils, interdisciplinary teams, or in teacher education programs.

Finally, contexts that support teacher learning create specific structures to promote reflection and experimentation with teaching. The nature of these structures may vary widely, but their presence reminds us that opportunities for learning can be structured into organizations; without explicit structures, learning from teaching is left largely to chance.

The second wave of reform has provided a number of novel tasks for teachers, including participation in school-based management, work as mentor teachers, and involvement in teacher education through professional development schools. In this chapter I examine the specific example of a professional development center as a changing context for teaching which offers both opportunities and constraints for teacher learning.

Opportunities for Teacher Learning through Engagement in Teacher Education

The professional preparation of beginning teachers and the education of students form the entwined raison d'être of a professional development school.[15] Professional development schools assume that these responsibilities will be shared by educators at the school site and university faculty. Explicit in the concept of a professional development school is the assumption that all teachers are learners who are engaged in ongoing inquiry into their practice.[16] Less explicit in discussions of professional development schools are the processes through which participants will come to see themselves as a community of inquirers into teaching and into the nature of the learning that can result from inquiry.

In the Puget Sound Professional Development Center, a team composed of a university faculty member, a middle school principal, a middle school teacher, and a student teacher proposed the skeleton for a pilot middle school teacher preparation program to be run through our professional development center. Our program, now in its second year of implementation, brings together university faculty, teachers, principals, and counselors to share in the responsibility for both the field experience and a core seminar for preservice teachers. Middle school teachers can participate directly in the preparation of preservice teachers through three distinct roles: cooperating teacher (often defined as a team of teachers responsible for one or two student teachers); site supervisors, responsible for supervision and evaluation of student teachers at their school site; and teaching associate, responsible for team-teaching the core seminar along with university faculty members. Each of these roles provides distinct opportunities for professional development; each role also contains its own constraints to the realization of these opportunities for teacher learning.

THE CORE SEMINAR

At the center of this preservice program lies a core seminar for all students. The course is team-taught by a middle school teacher and three or four university professors with different areas of expertise. This core seminar collapses four required courses in the general teacher education program—general methods of teaching, educational measurement and evaluation, multicultural perspectives, and crucial issues in education—and incorporates content related to middle school philosophy and curriculum and to early adolescence. Throughout the seminar, issues and strategies related to special education are woven into the fabric of the course. Curriculum deliberations involve not only the seminar instructors, but site supervisors and cooperating teachers as well. Instruction of the seminar is shared by all team members, and middle school teachers from our professional development schools come to class occasionally to teach specific topics.

The core seminar has several purposes. One of its central purposes is to connect the two major components of the teacher education curriculum—the curriculum of the university and the curriculum of the field experience. Assignments for the seminar are often carried out at the school site, as students are engaged in writing case studies based upon data collected at the school site. For example, students write a case study of an exceptional student in one of the classes they are observing. For this assignment, they shadow the student throughout the day, collect other information regarding the student's individual educational plan, analyze the data, and write a case study which synthesizes their observations with their readings and discussions from the seminar.

The concept of reflective practice provides one leitmotif for the course. Students are expected to provide reasons for their pedagogical decisions and to scrutinize their decisions from the perspective of the readings and class discussion, as well as from the perspective of their observations in schools. The team of instructors attempts to model reflective practice by making our own teaching transparent to students. We provide a running commentary on our teaching dilemmas, our own reasons for various pedagogical decisions, and the class critiques the decisions on the basis of their own experience. The seminar becomes a common case of teaching in which we all participate and which is therefore available for analysis and reflection.

The seminar also strives to create a perspective on the joint construction of knowledge and the problematic nature of teaching. Because we have created a course that crosses the boundaries of academic disciplines, as well as the worlds of school and university, we have created a curriculum in which none of us is expert; we all have much to learn from each other. The multiple perspectives regarding teaching are represented in the very construction of the teaching team. As our class discussions represent, vividly at times, reasonable people disagree about many aspects of teaching. This planned disagreement helps represent to students the fundamental complexity of teaching and the lack of unambiguous answers in education.

The intent of this core seminar, then, is to create the hub of the wheel around which other experiences in teacher education are organized. Students learn to question what they see and hear from us as well as from their experiences in schools. They learn that knowledge can be constructed rather than transmitted and that colleagues can disagree and still respect each other. These expectations for students help shape the nature of their field experiences, as students carry these perspectives with them to their school sites.

THE COOPERATING TEACHER

The role of cooperating teacher is most familiar to the teachers in our program. A number of the middle school teachers have served as cooperating teachers in the past, sometimes for more than one university program. While theoretically the role of cooperating teacher offers a rich context for teacher reflection and renewal, the very familiarity of the role and the meanings traditionally associated with it may also work against teachers' use of this role as a route to personal professional development.

Serving as a cooperating teacher can provide opportunities for reflection both about one's own practice and about teaching more generally. Trying to explain what they do, and the reasons for those actions, to a novice may help experienced teachers make more explicit their tacit knowledge regarding students, classrooms, curriculum, and instruction. As Karen McElliott, a cooperating teacher in our program, commented, "This has made me more explicit about what I do. You can't keep your mouth shut and hope they'll figure out what's going on. You need to explain, elaborate, ask." Observing student teachers may also contribute to reflection by experienced teachers, as the beginner's mistakes can reacquaint teachers with skills that have become routinized over time. In helping student teachers analyze their practice, cooperating teachers may clarify their own craft knowledge and their understandings of the relationships between, for instance, classroom management and curriculum.[17]

Both explanations and observations can also serve to stimulate cooperating teachers' reflections on classroom practice, which in turn may stimulate new learning. Cooperating teachers often commented that having a student teacher in their classroom "forced" them to verbalize the reasons for their actions; the very process of verbalization may require cooperating teachers to reexamine both their actions and their reasoning. Teachers may rethink their actions subsequent to a discussion with a novice teacher or may come to understand more clearly the connections, or lack of connections, between their goals and their actions. Having a beginner in one's classroom provides at least the opportunity to stop and reflect. Many of the cooperating teachers in our program used the words "forced to reflect" as they considered the benefits of being a cooperating teacher. As Karen McElliott commented, "The experience forces you to be reflective. You have to ask yourself *why* am I doing this and *should* I be doing this?"

Serving as a cooperating teacher also holds the possibility for acquiring new knowledge about teaching, including new methods of instruction, alternative approaches to curriculum, or different perspectives on classroom management. Fresh from their university classes, student teachers bring word of these new ideas and are eager to try them out in actual classrooms. In theory, this partnership with student teachers can serve as a source of new knowledge. As McElliott remarked, "Student teachers share ideas from their methods courses . . . mention books. I test what I know against what they're learning." Other cooperating teachers in our project talked about the feeling of being on "the cutting edge" of new knowledge through their association with the project and gave examples of new ideas and perspectives they had encountered through their student teachers.

Finally, the role of cooperating teacher within our professional development center holds the potential to open the classroom door to new relationships with colleagues at both the school and university and to forge a broader professional identity as a teacher educator. To take the role of cooperating teacher seriously is to expand one's definition of one's task from educating children to educating the next generation of teachers. This new role offers the opportunity to learn more about adult learning, about teacher education, about the world of educational policy and research in teacher education. In talking about what she had learned as a cooperating teacher, McElliott mentioned her realization that "teachers really do have a responsibility to the profession. That's part of what we need to do. Find the best student teachers we can to replace us and . . . fight for better working conditions for these future teachers."

To suggest that serving as a cooperating teacher in our professional development center holds the potential for teacher learning in these areas is not to claim that such learning inevitably occurs. A number of factors, both historical and structural, work against the realization of the learning the role theoretically could promote.

The very familiarity of the role of the traditional cooperating teacher poses formidable obstacles to recasting the role as an opportunity for teacher learning. As a number of our teachers have told us, in the past being a cooperating teacher has been seen as a reward for past performance. Rather than an incentive for further professional growth, taking on a student teacher has been seen as an "on-site sabbatical," a chance to retreat from the demands of the classroom, as the student teacher assumed increasing responsibility for teaching. No specialized knowledge was seen as necessary to fulfill the role, nor did the role require a new relationship to the university. Becoming a cooperating teacher in the past has not meant rethinking one's own practice or expanding one's professional identity. While many cooperating teachers have assumed these responsibilities on their own initiative, no explicit structures existed to support teachers' growth in this role.

Being cast as the "expert" in relationship to the student teacher may also provide obstacles to teacher learning. When student teachers bring in new ideas regarding curriculum, instruction, or classroom management, areas in which experienced teachers may have regarded themselves as expert, cooperating teachers may become defensive about their practices, rather than open to rethinking what they do. One cooperating teacher commented on the desire to "play it safe" when other adults are in the room. Defining cooperating teachers as "experts" may work against the very experimentation with teaching techniques that student teachers need to see modeled, as the connotations of expertise may preclude the possibility of necessary failures. In their determination to model exemplary practice, cooperating teachers may come to see less than perfect practice as a failure, rather than as an opportunity to think out loud with the student teacher about the dilemmas of classroom practice and the difficulties inherent in experimenting with new approaches to teaching and to teach student teachers how to learn from mistakes.

The division between experts and novices may also work against cooperating teachers taking advantage of the new knowledge and ideas brought by student teachers. While our cooperating teachers have mentioned instances of becoming aware of new methods or approaches from student teachers, relatively few talked about working to integrate these new ideas into their own classroom practice. New approaches may threaten the delicately balanced routines that manifest the teachers' expertise in the first place.[18] Student teachers, then, do not have the opportunity to see experienced teachers struggle to implement a different approach to teaching, nor do cooperating teachers take advantage of the opportunity to try out new methods or approaches in their classroom.

The reasons underlying the constraints to teacher learning do not necessarily lie with the individual cooperating teacher, but with the lack of explicit structures to promote learning in the sense of bringing new knowledge to bear upon classroom practice. Changing one's teaching is difficult in the best of circumstances, and changing any one aspect of teaching may cause new, unanticipated dilemmas to arise.[19] Change is all the more difficult in the presence of an audience. If we expect that cooperating teachers' new knowledge or understanding will affect classroom practice, together we will need to create more explicit structures that build experimentation with teaching into the very role of the cooperating teacher. We also need to create structures in which cooperating teachers can meet together to reflect on their teaching and on the dilemmas involved in balancing their responsibilities to student teachers with responsibilities to students. Our first attempt to create such a structure through an ongoing workshop for cooperating teachers was met with great enthusiasm. Cooperating teachers appreciated the time set aside to reflect on the nature of their roles and broader issues related to teaching and learning to teach. This structure, however, still stops short of supporting actual changes in classroom practice.

THE SITE SUPERVISOR

A less familiar role in the preparation of new teachers in our model is that of the site supervisor. Rather than using university-based personnel to supervise and evaluate student teachers' field experiences, we have delegated these responsibilities to experienced teachers at our professional development center sites. The supervisors meet weekly with the student teachers throughout the year, orient them to the school site and key personnel, and observe and evaluate the student teachers using the university's evaluation system. In addition, the supervisors meet monthly with members of the teaching team from the core seminar. The preservice teachers consistently identify the site supervisors as one of the strongest features of our model. They appreciate the ready access to a supervisor who is knowledgeable about the particular contexts of both the school and district and who is committed to their development as beginning teachers. While the benefits to the preservice teachers seem clear, there are also potential benefits for the experienced teachers who fulfill this role.

One opportunity for learning is similar to that available to cooperating teachers. Through both observing novices and engaging in discussions with them about teaching, supervisors are challenged to make their own understanding of teaching more explicit. The need to provide feedback to student teachers has challenged supervisors to find a more precise vocabulary with which to communicate about teaching. While in disagreement with some aspects of the university evaluation system, the supervisors appreciate the access it provides to a common technical vocabulary for observing and discussing aspects of classroom instruction.[20] In addition to making explicit their more intuitive knowledge, supervisors have commented on the stimulus provided by the observation for reflection on their own teaching. As two of our supervisors discovered, evaluating the lack of closure in a student teacher's lesson prompted them to reexamine their own problems in closing lessons. As one of the site supervisors, Karen Gosney, commented, "Whatever I see in them, I try to analyze in my own teaching." She talked about her discussions with one student teacher who planned marvelous activities but found it difficult to connect the activities with what he wanted students to learn. This discussion stimulated her to "go back and ask, 'Why am I doing this? What do *I* want students to learn?'" This supervisor saw her role in teacher education as a "wonderful chance for me to grow in my own teaching."

Site supervisors also see their new roles as a redefinition of their relationship to teaching. They see themselves as active contributors to the preparation of the next generation of teachers, extending their influence beyond the sphere of their own classrooms. As Gosney commented, "Perhaps being part of the 'big picture' of teaching is what I really like the most. I don't feel isolated in the classroom. I have experience that makes me feel valued, respected, a contributor." One important feature of the role of site supervisor is that teachers do not need to leave teaching to expand their role. As Gosney remarked, "being valued in a mentoring capacity makes me happy to be in the classroom." Little argues that "as they mature personally and professionally, teachers also seek involvement and influence beyond the classroom."[21] Through participation in preservice education, teachers can expand their influence without abdicating their primary responsibility to classroom teaching.

By virtue of their responsibilities, site supervisors are thrown into novel relationships with their peers. When relationships between student teachers and cooperating teachers create conflict, the site supervisor is the first person to know and often the first person to act. Supervisors have served as mediators in these situations, a role that can cause both discomfort and professional growth. While talking with peers about aspects of their teaching that trouble student teachers does not come easily to site supervisors, in the process they may acquire new skills in communicating with colleagues about difficult topics related to practice. When one cooperating teacher argued that the classroom techniques advocated by the student teacher would simply not work in his school, the site supervisor mentioned that other colleagues at the school were using these same approaches. These conversations challenge the norms of nonintrusiveness and isolation among teachers, as the practices of cooperating teachers become the concern of the site supervisor. The role itself creates new negotiated relationships at the school site, since the university supervisor must mediate between collegial responsibilities to the cooperating teacher and responsibilities for the supervision of student teachers.

We have created a few explicit structures that provide some of the conditions necessary for learning. In monthly meetings with all the supervisors and several of the instructors from the core seminar, supervisors have the chance to share their emerging knowledge of supervision and the difficulties associated with their job. While they learn that they are not alone in their dilemmas, they also acquire new approaches to supervising and mediating between teachers and student teachers.

These monthly meetings also provide information about the university's intentions and goals and a chance for supervisors to contribute to curriculum deliberations. Supervisors bring student teachers' concerns to the attention of the seminar instructors and together we discuss dilemmas and tensions in educating new teachers. These meetings provide supervisors with a "behind the scenes" look at the role of university coursework in preparing new teachers and the challenges of articulating coursework and field experiences. For example, supervisors and seminar instructors discussed what beginning teachers needed to learn about lesson planning and the disjunction between what they heard in class and what they saw at the school site. With a fuller understanding of the university's reasons for requiring lesson plans for beginners, supervisors were better equipped to help student teachers work on planning. Supervisors also gained an awareness of the ways in which they inadvertently contributed to "mislearning" on the part of students with regard to lesson planning. When bemoaning one student's failure to write a lesson plan for a lesson she had evaluated, one supervisor wondered how the student could have thought that she did not need a lesson plan. During the course of the discussion, the supervisor remembered that when the student teacher had asked her about lesson planning, she had commented that she no longer wrote elaborate lesson plans; in the context of our discussion, she suddenly realized that the student may have "learned" that good teachers do not write lesson plans, a lesson the supervisor had not intended to teach. These discussions help surface the ways in which the university and school site can work at cross-purposes in the preparation of teachers.[22]

A second structure consists of a cross-site supervisor who works with supervisors and student teachers at all four sites of our professional development center. The site supervisor and cross-site supervisor do at least one common observation of a student teacher and share their perceptions with each other. This structure provides opportunities for supervisors to get feedback on their observations. Areas of disagreement between the two supervisors can also provoke reflection.

These newly acquired skills serve on-site supervisors in good stead as teacher leaders, while their role challenges prevailing norms of teaching. The divided loyalties inherent in the role of on-site supervisor—between school site and university, between student teachers and school colleagues—can be a potential deterrent to, as well as a stimulus for, professional growth and learning.

The first obstacle to learning, not surprisingly, is the lack of time available to supervisors not only to fulfill teaching and supervisory responsibilities but to reflect on what they are learning in the process of supervision. The role of the supervisors provides access to a number of other classrooms and opportunities to see a variety of teaching approaches. While supervisors have many opportunities to acquire new ideas for teaching, they may find it difficult to spend the time changing their own practices in light of the other demands on their time. A second obstacle involves the lack of feedback on one's own teaching. Unlike cooperating teachers, supervisors do not have another adult in their own classrooms to provide feedback as they question their own practices or experiment with new approaches.

THE TEACHING ASSOCIATE

The final role in which classroom teachers participate in the preparation of preservice teachers is the role of teaching associate. The teaching associate is part of the team that plans and teaches the core seminar for the student teachers in our program. The teaching associate is expected to contribute to curriculum development for this innovative course as well as share responsibilities for instruction.

The role of teaching associate requires the teacher to reconsider what beginning teachers need to know and how they can best acquire that knowledge. Again, the role requires teachers to make their craft knowledge explicit in curriculum deliberations with the teaching team. As Nanna Brantigan, the current teaching associate, commented:

One of my contributions to the seminar should be that of a practitioner's craft level of knowledge about middle school education, and I do feel that I have substantial knowledge in this area. However, this knowledge now needs to be documented and validated as part of a body of knowledge that is important for student teachers to have. I have read and reread much of my middle school literature in addition to the assigned course materials in order to more thoroughly integrate the seminar goals with the reality of life in a middle level school.[23]

During curriculum planning sessions, practitioners' and researchers' assumptions about middle school education may be challenged by other team members. As Brantigan implied, claiming the importance of a particular aspect of the curriculum also requires providing support for those claims, a requirement that may be more familiar to professors, used to citing sources at the drop of a hat, than to teachers. In these curriculum deliberations, teaching associates may begin to look more critically at the existing literature and deepen their own understanding of how middle school philosophy and curriculum fit into a broader theoretical framework about teaching and learning.

By virtue of literally being in two places at once, in both a field site and in university coursework, teaching associates have the potential of developing a broad understanding of teacher education with its inherent tensions and dilemmas. They are in the best position to see the fit, or lack of fit, between the instructional, curricular, or assessment approaches advocated by the university seminar and the practices students are likely to encounter at the school site. These potential disjunctions again provide opportunities for reflection, as well as for the acquisition of new knowledge and approaches to teaching. The teaching associates have described encountering for the first time the language of instructional scaffolding or of concept attainment and concept formation and the theories of learning that underlie these approaches. Already familiar with methods that draw upon these assumptions, teaching associates are able to build upon their existing craft knowledge and acquire a language that enables them to talk to both university and school-site colleagues as well as a better understanding of the theoretical assumptions underlying particular methods. As representatives from the field, teaching associates are often called upon by students to explain the disjunction between images of practice offered in university courses and practices encountered at school sites, which again provides an opportunity for reflection and the potential impetus for action.

These opportunities for learning are constrained, however, by the ways in which the role is currently structured. In commuting between the two worlds of school site and university classroom, the teaching associate may feel lost by the roadside. With not enough time at either site, they may feel disconnected from changes occurring at their own schools. Brantigan writes of her frustration with her inability to attend meetings at her own school because of the seminar: "Rather than being a bridge between the building and the university this year, I sometimes feel estranged from my school program."[23] Responsibilities to the university may conflict with responsibilities to the school site. This estrangement may also make it difficult to bring new knowledge and insights gained through participation in the seminar to bear upon either school or classroom practices.

While each of these roles in teacher education contains its own unique opportunities and obstacles for teacher learning and renewal, common to all roles is the need to balance the demands of teaching students, teaching prospective teachers, learning for oneself, and bringing one's new knowledge and understanding to bear upon teaching. The very complexity of these demands suggests the need for a community response, rather than leaving it to the individual to manage the dilemmas inherent in these sometimes conflicting roles.

Communities for Learning to Teach and Teaching to Learn

The promise of professional development schools lies in the potential to create communities of learning about teaching. All of us must balance the roles of practitioner and learner, with the inherent assumptions of expertise and uncertainty. We all have much to learn from each other; we must all abdicate the authority for knowing the answer to every question raised by student teachers. But in creating such centers for teacher learning, we must also grapple with questions concerning the necessary conditions for a school in which all participants are indeed learners. How can we exploit and support opportunities for learning inherent in new roles for teachers and faculty?

Changing contexts for teaching can create rich opportunities for teacher learning. Emerging evidence from professional development schools and from restructured schools suggests that by fulfilling new roles within these sites, teachers can acquire new knowledge and understanding about teaching and broaden their sense of professional responsibility to include school governance and decision making or the preparation of tomorrow's teachers. Less evident is whether or not teachers draw upon their new knowledge to change existing school or classroom practices. Numerous obstacles—structural, historical, practical, individual—exist to forestall changes within classrooms. As we engage in the rethinking of schools, we need a clearer understanding of both the nature of these obstacles to teacher learning and how we can overcome them.

Just as research on children's learning has led to understanding the social context of cognition, research on teacher learning must look toward interactive theoretical models that look at both the individual and the social organization of schooling to understand teachers' learning. Creating opportunities for teacher learning by creating new roles will not suffice, in the absence of a better conceptual understanding of the nature of teacher learning and of explicit structures within schools that support teacher learning over time.

This chapter provides initial speculations about the ways in which teachers can learn about teaching through engagement in new roles and tasks associated with the changing contexts of schooling. As we engage in the effort to change the contexts in which teachers work, we also need research that will help us understand more clearly the various forms of teacher learning and the features of contexts that support them. We too have much to learn, if we are to realize the potential of professional development schools as learning communities, in which learning to teach and teaching to learn become part of the everyday landscape of teaching.

ACKNOWLEDGMENTS. I wish to thank Nanna Brantigan, Karen Gosney, Ann Lieberman, Karen McElliott, Anna Richert, and Sam Wineburg for their helpful comments and contributions to this chapter.

NOTES

1. Margret Buchmann, a review of *Teachers' Professional Learning* (James Calderhead, editor), *Journal of Teacher Education* 41, no. 5 (1990): 54-62.

2. See, for example, Jere E. Brophy and Thomas L. Good, "Teacher Behavior and Student Achievement," in *Handbook of Research on Teaching*, 3d ed., edited by Merlin C. Wittrock (New York: Macmillan, 1986), pp. 328-375; N. L. Gage, *The Scientific Basis of the Art of Teaching* (New York: Teachers College Press, 1978).

3. See, for example, Sharon Feiman-Nemser and Robert Floden, "The Cultures of Teaching," in *Handbook of Research on Teaching*, 3d ed., edited by Merlin C. Wittrock (New York: Macmillan, 1986), pp. 505-526; Kenneth Zeichner and B. Robert Tabachnik, "The Development of Teacher Perspectives: Social Strategies and Institutional Control in the Socialization of Beginning Teachers," *Journal of Education for Teaching* 11 (1985): 1-25.

4. See, for example, Deborah L. Ball and G. Williamson McDiarmid, "The Subject-Matter Preparation of Teachers," in *Handbook of Research on Teacher Education*, edited by W. Robert Houston (New York: Macmillan, 1990), pp. 437-449; Lee S. Shulman, "Those Who Understand: Knowledge Growth in Teaching," *Educational Researcher* 15, no. 2 (1986): 4-14.

5. See, for example, Ann Lieberman and Lynne Miller, *Staff Development: New Demands, New Realities, New Perspectives* (New York: Teachers College Press, 1978).

6. David C. Berliner, "In Pursuit of the Expert Pedagogue," *Educational Researcher* 15, no. 7 (1986): 5-13; Shulman, "Those Who Understand."

7. David K. Cohen, "A Revolution in One Classroom: The Case of Mrs. Oublier," *Educational Evaluation and Policy Analysis* 12 (1990): 327-346; Lee S. Shulman, "Teaching Alone, Learning Together: Needed Agendas for the New Reforms" (Paper presented at a conference on Restructured Schooling for Quality Education, Trinity University, San Antonio, TX, 1987); Kenneth Tobin, "Constructivist Perspectives on Teacher Change" (Paper presented at the Annual Meeting of the American Educational Research Association, Boston, 1990).

8. Cohen, "A Revolution in One Classroom": Magdalene Lampert, "Teaching about Thinking and Thinking about Teaching," *Journal of Curriculum Studies* 16, no. 1 (1984): 1-18.

9. Sharon Feiman-Nemser, "Learning to Teach," in *Handbook of Teaching and Policy*, edited by Lee S. Shulman and Gary Sykes (New York: Longman, 1983), p. 150.

10. For discussions of this perspective, see also Judith Warren Little, "Norms of Collegiality and Experimentation: Workplace Conditions of School Success," *American Educational Research Journal* 19 (1982): 325-340; idem, "Conditions of Professional Development in Secondary Schools," in *The Contexts of Teaching in Secondary Schools*, edited by Milbrey W. McLaughlin, Joan E. Talbert, and Nina Bascia (New York: Teachers College Press, 1990); Shulman, "Teaching Alone, Teaching Together"; Kenneth A. Sirotnik, "The School as the Center of Change," in *Schooling for Tomorrow: Directing Reforms to Issues that Count*, edited by Thomas J. Sergiovanni and John H. Moore (Boston: Allyn & Bacon, 1989); Ann Lieberman, ed., *Building a Professional Culture in Schools* (New York: Teachers College Press, 1988).

11. Shulman, "Teaching Alone, Teaching Together."

12. Little, "Norms of Collegiality and Experimentation."

13. Little, "Conditions of Professional Development in Secondary Schools," p. 195.

14. Ibid.

15. Holmes Group, *Tomorrow's Schools: Principles for the Design of Professional Development Schools* (East Lansing, MI: Holmes Group, 1990).

16. Ibid.

17. As the use of the conditional implies, we know very little about whether this reflection or learning actually takes place. My analysis should be regarded as speculation only; the investigation of these speculative statements provides an avenue for further research in teacher education.

18. Gaea Leinhardt and Donald Smith, "Expertise in Mathematics Instruction: Subject Matter Knowledge," *Journal of Educational Psychology* 77 (1985): 247-271.

19. Cohen, "A Revolution in One Classroom"; Lampert, "Teaching about Thinking and Thinking about Teaching."

20. Dan C. Lortie, *Schoolteacher: A Sociological Study* (Chicago: University of Chicago Press, 1975).

21. Little, "Conditions of Professional Development in Secondary Schools," p. 214.

22. Sharon Feiman-Nemser and Margret Buchmann, "Pitfalls of Experience in Teacher Preparation," *Teachers College Record* 87 (1985): 53-65.

23. Nanna Brantigan, "Still Learning to Teach: The Voice of a Teaching Associate" (Seattle, WA: Puget Sound Professional Development Center, University of Washington, 1991).

CHAPTER XI

Learning to Lead: Portraits of Practice

LYNNE MILLER AND CYNTHIA O'SHEA

In this chapter we focus on teacher leadership as it is practiced at one elementary school in Gorham, Maine. The Narragansett School, a K-3 elementary school, has been engaged in an ongoing process of reflection and reconstruction for almost five years. Much of its work has been documented previously.[1] Narragansett's restructuring effort is distinguished by its focus on "what children know and how they know it"[2] and by its expectation that teachers who conduct systematic and collaborative inquiry in their classrooms will invent new ways to organize instruction and to assess performance. The school makes an explicit connection between the intellectual engagement of teachers and the engagement of the students they teach. It assumes that when teachers take leadership in matters of instruction and school organization, authentic change happens. Serving over 400 children, Narragansett defines itself as:

a center of inquiry . . . serious in purpose, joyous in accomplishment . . . where teachers are more than technicians. They are those who instruct, engage in thoughtful reflection, seek out research and conduct their own, and regularly meet with colleagues.[3]

The emergence of teacher leadership at Narragansett School has been both gradual and dramatic.[4] Beginning with formalized roles for team leaders, teacher leadership has come to assume a variety of forms. Some teachers took leadership in developing new instructional arrangements, such as multigraded, team-taught classes. Others designed new assessment tools, concentrated on expanding their teaching strategies, or led staff development seminars for their colleagues in the school. A teacher/scholar position was created—a rotating

---

Lynne Miller is Professor of Education, University of Southern Maine at Gorham. Cynthia O'Shea is the Principal of Narragansett School in Gorham.

position in which a teacher on leave from the classroom for a year conducts systematic investigations into learning and teaching on behalf of the whole school faculty.

In the pages that follow, the development of teacher leadership at Narragansett School is explored through portraits of four teacher leaders. The purpose of this chapter is to show how teacher leadership emerges, what teacher leaders do, and how teacher leaders think about themselves as they take on new roles. Data for the study were collected through written responses to questions, interviews, observation, and analysis of documents.

Portraits of Practice

MARY JO O'CONNOR: LEADERSHIP FROM EXPERIENCE

Mary Jo O'Connor is a respected member of the Narragansett School community. She has established herself as an accomplished classroom teacher, a conscientious colleague, and a committed parent. There is nothing flashy about Mary Jo. She goes about her business in a way that neither calls attention to herself nor seeks recognition and approval for her achievements. She is a "teacher's teacher," grounded in classroom practice and comfortable with the daily routine of schools and teaching. A graduate of a small New England college, Mary Jo majored in elementary education before entering teaching; she had accompanied her husband to Japan and took time out to raise her family before she committed herself to a full-time teaching career. She has been at Narragansett School for seven years.

In the fall of 1990, Mary Jo assumed the newly created position of teacher/scholar at Narragansett. She viewed the position as "multidimensional in design . . . allowing me to be released from the classroom for a year to work intensely on areas identified by myself and other staff." The move from classroom teacher to teacher/scholar was neither abrupt nor dramatic for Mary Jo. She saw her new role as a logical extension of her development over the past few years:

As a teacher working in a school which not only encouraged—but celebrated—reflective practice, I had been making changes in my teaching in small incremental steps over the last four years. Each time I would make changes, I found myself self-correcting along the way, making adjustments based on my own tacit understandings, as well as on current research.

Two years previously, Mary Jo had decided to stay with her first-grade class for another year. Curious about the next step for the children she taught and intrigued by the implications for student learning if expectations and routines were not interrupted, she approached her principal with her plan. The next year, she moved to second grade along with her class. What followed set the stage for Mary Jo's transition to teacher/scholar.

The next year was a tremendous learning experience not only for me, but for my students as well. During that year I was sure enough with my students' ability levels that I implemented a new approach to reading instruction. Using qualitative research methods I was learning in a graduate course at the university, I was able to get some answers about the ways children liked to be taught reading. The research left many avenues open for further exploration.

As a classroom teacher, Mary Jo had come to incorporate research and inquiry into her practice. When the teacher/scholar position was announced, Mary Jo applied without hesitation. She saw herself as ready for the challenge of the job. She viewed the year away from classroom teaching as an opportunity to explore the issues of early literacy acquisition that had begun to interest her. After being a leader in her classroom, Mary Jo was ready to become a leader in a larger arena:

I had seen myself as a leader in my own classroom, charting curriculum, making a difference; I now felt ready to assume a new leadership role, out of the classroom, but still viably connected to teachers in a very unique but important way.

In her role as teacher/scholar, Mary Jo is involved in a variety of activities—some intended and others improvised along the way. She has focused her scholarly inquiry on issues of literacy acquisition in the primary grades. Melding nicely with this work has been an opportunity to design a curriculum notebook for language arts. The notebook reflects the school faculty's current understandings about how children learn to read and write. Also connected to this line of investigation is ongoing work with two other teachers in the area of alternative assessment. As part of this collaborative effort, Mary Jo is helping to articulate an expanded notion of assessment, one that showcases student skills and achievements beyond paper and pencil tests. A model for portfolio-based assessment is being developed and tested.

As Mary Jo's role has developed, she has stimulated teacher dialogues and collaboration. She has had the time and the opportunity to share ideas about teaching and learning with her teaching colleagues. She has become a "sounding board" for teachers, who often drop in to chat with her in the course of the school day. "I don't have all the answers for sure, but I do share a common understanding of children and the dailiness of teaching." As a result of these informal interactions, teachers have invited Mary Jo into their classrooms to do demonstration lessons, to observe, and to work with small groups of students. "I have become an available and willing partner, working with them and for them."

Mary Jo also works closely with a group of teacher assistants. The teacher assistants at Narragansett play an important role in the school's restructuring effort. They perform duties that free teachers from clerical responsibilities and assist them in classroom instruction. Teacher assistants not only collect milk money and run off dittos; they also teach small groups of students, provide tutorial assistance, and collect data about student learning for teachers. As teacher/scholar, Mary Jo serves as the liaison between the assistants and the whole school program. She helps make the connection between what the assistants do and the school's commitment to ongoing inquiry. Mary Jo and the assistants meet once a month in a formal setting where they discuss diverse educational topics, ranging from whole language practices to classroom management. She also meets with the assistants on an informal basis—individually and in small groups.

This simple accounting of Mary Jo's worklife provides some insight into the depth and breadth of her role as teacher/scholar. She notes, "This job has afforded me the opportunity to transcend much of the educational rhetoric and to more closely understand that good education is basic and grounded in common sense." The job has taught her other things as well. As a teacher/scholar, Mary Jo has had the chance to view teaching from a new perspective, as someone looking in. She has discovered, or rather rediscovered, that teaching is complex, intellectual, and challenging work.

In my early years of survival teaching, I had almost internalized that teaching was a static entity—very few changes in curriculum were made from year to year; my approach remained the same. As I began to have meaty conversations with other teachers, I began to examine my own practices more closely. In this role, I've seen close-up the variety and intricacy of teaching. I know now and appreciate that teaching is complex and certainly not static.

She has incorporated the importance of teaching as learning into her view of teaching. She locates teacher development at the center of school life: "For teachers to be truly effective, they must first see themselves as learners. Teachers don't have all the answers but need to commit themselves to the spirit of reflective practice and ongoing inquiry." Mary Jo not only views teachers as learners; she sees them as leaders as well and makes explicit the connection between learning and leading. "I see teachers as leaders in their classrooms making change in curriculum to meet the needs of their students, inventing assessment pieces, and investigating current theories."

Mary Jo has also come to see teachers as the source and sustenance of meaningful change. Change cannot, to her mind, be mandated from above. It must percolate from below.

Teachers are at certain stages in their own development. When ready, teachers will accept that change is needed, begin to understand it, then eventually become the agents of change themselves. Change cannot be hurried or forced on people—if so it will be short-lived.

Finally, Mary Jo has recognized her own abilities and promise. Her sense of efficacy, already strong in her classroom, has expanded to include the whole school—and beyond.

Perhaps what I have learned most is to trust and believe in myself. I am making the most of an exciting opportunity in the position of teacher/scholar. I know that I can organize my time so that I am productive and effective. I'm learning to trust my instincts more, continue to think about things differently, and in this position, build a model for schools which underscores my belief that teachers are the keys to fundamental, lasting school improvement.

SALLY LOUGHLIN: LEADERSHIP FROM KNOWLEDGE

Sally Loughlin is a relative newcomer to Narragansett and to teaching. Graduated five years ago from a select liberal arts college where she was an honors major in economics and government, she entered the teaching profession through the back door.

By the time that I realized that working directly with people and examining how they think was the most energizing type of work for me, I was already a graduate with no teaching classes. When I did obtain enough credits to become certified, I still had no clue as to what teaching was about.

When she was first interviewed for a job at Narragansett School, Sally impressed the principal as someone "who would be outstanding or a complete disaster—nothing in between." The principal took a risk and hired Sally, who quickly emerged as a different kind of teacher leader. Her leadership role at Narragansett is neither prescribed nor formalized. She has earned leadership by dint of her intelligence, her driving curiosity, her search for new knowledge, and her power as a classroom teacher.

I focus on children as thinkers. My teaching revolves around the idea that everyone can become smarter if they reflect on their own thinking. I want my students to be advocates for their own learning, to know how they learn best and to examine critically the work they are asked to do.

Sally's growth as a teacher mirrors her growth as a leader. As she moved away from textbooks as the basis for instruction and from traditional tests as the basis for assessment, Sally staked out new territory both for the children she taught and for the colleagues with whom she worked.

When I began to teach, I had a vague notion that teachers took a few years to develop their files and then just kept playing that same old song. In my ignorance, I was quite sure I had an easy job. Good fortune brought me to an environment where people were expected to do their best. I began to realize that each day was mine—it's my movie. I'm the writer, director, and star, if I want to be. I am not, as I originally thought, a bit part in someone else's production.

What Sally decided to do with her newly discovered power was to systematically redefine teaching, learning, and assessment as they occurred in her classroom.

She began, characteristically, by seeking new knowledge. She read voraciously and became intrigued by the notions of intelligence proposed by Howard Gardner and the organization of thinking developed by Robert Sternberg. The recent research in cognitive sciences was particularly engaging for her; she acquired an appreciation for work in the area of metacognition.

I have always been fascinated with the mind and its infinite possibilities. I often imagined my students' minds to be full of thoughts that I never get to witness or appreciate. Right now, I'm having a great time experimenting with some very basic variables and I'll bet that years from now I will continue to wonder how the brain works and how to get people to become advocates for their own learning.

Only after spending considerable time expanding her knowledge base did Sally begin to put her new ideas into practice. Her classroom began to take a different turn. She developed heterogeneous reading practices, initiated independent projects with her children, established learning stations in the content areas. She struggled to connect content to process, always raising questions with her students about what they knew and how they knew it. She focused on strategies for learning and on making explicit the purpose of every task and assignment. Her first visible project outside her own classroom was a team-teaching arrangement with a special education teacher. Every afternoon Sally and her special education colleague combined their classes to teach science to a multigraded and diverse group of youngsters. They developed a "science laboratory" where students worked collaboratively on real-life tasks, such as setting up a bird museum. The students and their teachers also formed a tee-shirt design and manufacturing business, where students received fees for their designs.

Sally's emergence as a teacher leader originated with her willingness to think out loud and in public about the knowledge she was acquiring about learning and thinking. She became codirector of the school's staff development program and helped redirect the program from one driven by workshop presentations by experts to one based on systematic, collegial inquiry. She became an informal, and then formal, spokesperson for the school in the area of alternative assessment of student learning. She was one of four teachers who developed a slide presentation on assessment for a national conference. She took leadership in developing new assessment tools for her classes, in sharing them with her colleagues, and in developing a K-8 portfolio system for the entire district.

Sally's leadership in the school in areas of teaching, learning, and assessment is clearly acknowledged and valued by her colleagues. Having no title other than classroom teacher, she has exercised considerable influence on the school and the district. Sally's appraisal of her own leadership is characteristically precise and could as easily be applied to her stance as a teacher.

Leadership is informal, unofficial, offers unobtrusive support, and helps identify opportunities. True leadership enables others to be more powerful; a successful leader assists others to identify their own leadership potential.

For Sally, knowledge is power. And power is to be shared.

I believe that everyone is doing the best they can and that everyone can become an able thinker. My role is not to decide for others what they should do; my role is to guide them so they can be as happy with their decisions as I am with mine.

WALLY ZIKO: LEADING FROM VISION

Wally Ziko has been reinventing himself as a teacher for over fifteen years. He has been teaching in Gorham at the Shaw Junior High School since 1977. He began as an industrial arts teacher, but left that program to develop a technology laboratory for junior high students. Wally has been a dreamer and an entrepreneur all his life. To casual acquaintances he may appear to be preoccupied and he usually is. His personality type has not always been understood or valued in schools.

I was always a misfit in school. I knew that I was different and that I didn't fit into the system. As I look back on it, I realize that the system at that time was not tolerant of a wide range of abilities and differences. I really didn't do well until I got to college when people started leaving me alone. The other reason that contributed to my eventual success was that following high school, I spent two years in the seminary; eventually when I did go to college, I was more mature. Also, I went to a Jesuit university that was intolerant of intellectual laziness but did tolerate my being an eccentric.

In the six years that he has been operating the technology laboratory in Gorham, Wally has received four grants from the state department of education and three grants from Apple Computer. In addition, he has taught university courses, is a published author, and has been highlighted in trade publications for his innovative use of technology in education. Wally is not a formal member of the Narragansett staff, yet is considered a major player in the school's restructuring efforts. His association with Narragansett began three years ago when the former superintendent saw the connection between restructuring and technology.

Connie Goldman (former superintendent) saw that schools had very little new power or tools to get things done in a system. It was important to use the core of what existed and build on that. She saw that the paraprofessional strand for teachers could be used to free teachers to use their energy to identify needs and make changes. She also appreciated that the computerized portfolio project could drive meaningful change in curriculum and assessment. So, as superintendent with an understanding of the whole system, she literally introduced the right hand to the left hand.

When the Narragansett staff began collaborating with Wally, they were relieved to find him respectful of their own accomplishments and easily accessible as a colleague. An informal working relationship was initiated, leading ultimately to Wally's role as a teacher leader at the school.

The Narragansett staff appreciated Wally's ability to stretch their imagination about what technology could make possible in a school; Wally appreciated the groundwork that the Narragansett staff had done in curriculum and assessment. A major key in sustaining this unique relationship was the availability of time for both Wally and the school staff. The district provided a full-time assistant to Wally, so he could leave the junior high school and work regularly at Narragansett. The teacher assistant program, already in place at Narragansett, was used to provide released time for teachers during the regular school day. What emerged from this frequent interaction between practicing experts in technology and instruction was a project to develop a computerized portfolio for each Gorham elementary student.

The computerized portfolio project was the result of Wally's vision and his ability and willingness to involve others in translating his vision into practice. The vision is quite compelling. It requires that we imagine a new scenario for parent-teacher conferences. The teacher sits in front of a computer and turns it on rather than opening a rank card. With the computer on, the parents see actual artifacts that their child has produced and that were saved via a computer scanner. At the same time, the parents can hear their child read passages of his or her own work or the work of others. This is made possible by a voice recorder that has been connected to the computer. Finally, parents see a project that their child has done and they listen to the child's report of his or her findings. This part of the data has been saved on the computer by a special hook-up and a video camera. Parents, children, and teachers alike are able to see and hear authentic tasks and assess progress over a period of time. In Wally's vision, this collection of data would be available on a yearly basis and could be compiled over a child's entire public school experience. When students graduate from high school, each would have a diploma in one hand and a compact disc portfolio of who he or she is as a learner in the other hand. They could then offer this to trade schools, colleges, or businesses as an accurate representation of what they are capable of doing.

Wally and the teachers at Narragansett are in the process of developing the form and content of the portfolio project. They have developed a sample video-disc and are seeking funding to support the project. Wally's role as a teacher leader is still emerging. He continues to reinvent what he is doing and how he does it.

What do I do? At any one given minute I might be an educational technology curriculum developer and coordinator, an in-service provider, a computer technician, a computer network manager, a computer software trainer, an alternative assessment project coordinator and promoter, a graphic artist and publisher, an educational philosopher and advisor, a writer or a grant writer and administrator. But in the end, I teach. I have a regular classroom position with all its responsibilities, possibilities, and problems.

It is important to note that although Wally is a full-time teacher at the junior high school he has managed to become a teacher leader in another school within the district.

In his role as a teacher leader, Wally has developed powerful insights about schools, the process of change, and the possibilities of leadership.

I work in a profession that cannot escape its nature. Traditional schools remain frantically preoccupied with authority. Schools attempting reform alternate frantically between a preoccupation with authority and a preoccupation with leadership.

He puts his faith in teachers as the legitimate agents of change and as leaders in instruction.

It is clear to me that in times of change in institutions like schools it is better that teachers change faster than schools: the reverse is painful for both the schools and teachers, but much more for the teachers.

And he puts faith in himself as a teacher and as a leader of teachers. "After working in schools for fifteen years, the most wonderful feeling follows on the realization you are middle-aged and were born to teach."

CAROLYN MCGOLDRICK: LEADERSHIP FROM RESPECT FOR CHILDREN

Carolyn McGoldrick has been in and out of public school teaching for over twenty years. She began as a fifth-grade teacher in Massachusetts in 1970. After teaching there for three years, she married and relocated in Maine where she taught a second grade in Gorham for five years before leaving to stay home with her children. While out of the classroom, Carolyn kept in touch with former colleagues and what was going on in schools. Through her involvement as a parent, reading to her own children, she developed an affection for children's literature and its power in reaching the whole child. She developed her knowledge and expertise and became a source for recommending book titles to her teacher friends who wanted to address specific issues in their classrooms.

Her return to public schools was mediated by these experiences. At a time when the Narragansett library was without a librarian or an adequate collection of books, Carolyn was hired as a consultant. She developed thematic monthly storytime packets and trained and supported parent volunteers charged with carrying out the program. The packets were designed to address a specific affective need. The program was a success with children, teachers, and parents alike. It had the added benefit of bringing Carolyn back into the system that she had left six years before. This was the first time the school had hired a part-time teacher as a consultant to satisfy a building need. Free of classroom responsibilities, Carolyn explored and implemented aspects of education that, while important, were often overlooked as part of the official curriculum.

When a librarian was finally hired, Carolyn was no longer needed in the role she had created, but she had become a valuable resource to the school. Opportunities surfaced which kept Carolyn involved in the school in new ways. The Gorham school system had committed itself to a new elementary social studies approach that focused on self-understanding and on relationships with others; no one had been designated to design the curriculum. At the same time that the social studies curriculum was being developed, Narragansett School was awarded a state grant for restructuring. The grant application emphasized children's self-awareness and the connections between self-esteem and children's ability to learn about learning. Carolyn immediately saw the link between the new social studies curriculum and Narragansett's restructuring proposal. With the support of the school's principal and teachers, she assumed a new position. Carolyn was hired to write lessons about self-awareness and self-esteem and to help teachers implement them in their classrooms. Since this was a three-year project, Carolyn began her work in the seven classrooms of first graders. Her plan was to move with the children as they progressed to second and third grades. Carolyn spends most of her time in classrooms teaching children. The regular teachers use this time to observe the lessons being taught and to watch their students as learners.

Because of Carolyn's knowledge, her belief in the importance of self-esteem, and her skill in working with children, she quickly won the respect of her colleagues.

As they watched Carolyn McGoldrick work with children, teachers often commented on the instant rapport she established with them and her ability to engage them intellectually and affectively. From Carolyn's point of view, this ability stems from her willingness to listen carefully to what children have to say. She sees her classes as being alive with mutual respect and productivity.

I have always respected children. I have never adjusted my vocabulary or my faith in their ability because they are young. I treat children the way I want to be treated. As a teacher, I am motivated to reach the whole child. To me education goes deeper than teaching subject matter—it's working with human beings. I never feel as though I am doing my job unless I pay attention to the whole child.

While Carolyn has always held the belief that to be effective one must pay attention to the whole child, she feels that the structure of schools was not set up to encourage that.

When I first started teaching, I could have been on Mars for all the sense it made. I used to think of myself as a person who was responsible for filling empty holes. It was only intuitive that I attended to the whole child. I wasn't taught that that was an important aspect of teaching. The focus was on the program and trying to get each child to fit the program. That process was fraught with frustration on everyone's part.

In her new role, Carolyn is in a position to help teachers change fundamentally the ways that the school structures learning. After three years, she has been instrumental in influencing how children view themselves and how teachers view the learning process. Through her visible and direct work with children, Carolyn has modeled attitudes and behavior that other teachers at Narragansett not only value but also apply to their own teaching. She has taught in every classroom in the school and is welcomed as a colleague, friend, and teacher of teachers.

Carolyn's insights about teacher leadership have developed along with her role. She views reflective practice as a key element.

I have come to understand the importance of reflective practice. Today whenever I am in doubt, I stop and ask myself if what I'm doing makes sense. If not, I make changes until it does make sense. Oftentimes this calls for bravery. We need to develop the courage to speak out against practices that don't make sense for people. We need to question ourselves and we need to encourage our students to do the same.

Carolyn recognizes the strong impact of demonstration and modeling. She has said that when thinking of leadership, a quotation from Emerson comes closest to her feelings: "They're so busy watching you, they can't hear what you say." She honors the sheer power of a good example and she leads by being one.

Learning to Lead: Lessons from the Field

The four accounts of teacher leadership presented here offer insights into the diversity, complexity, and power of new roles as they are developing at Narragansett School. The experiences and reflection of Mary Jo, Sally, Wally, and Carolyn have deeper meaning and value to the extent that they provide a framework for describing and promoting teacher leadership beyond the parameters of one school in Maine. A critical reading of the four portraits leads to some important understandings about teacher leaders.

There are multiple and diverse paths to teacher leadership. Each teacher leader studied followed a unique trajectory toward the role. Each led from a particular strength; each strength has developed over time and was rooted in classroom teaching, the daily life of the school, and the particular dispositions and concerns of the individual. Mary Jo's strength was her experience and reputation as a veteran teacher; Sally led from the power of her knowledge and intelligence; Wally from the force of his vision and invention; and Carolyn from the firmness of her commitment to children.

Teacher-leader roles are improvised, informal, and serendipitous. None of the teacher leaders held a formal leadership role at the school. Narragansett had previously developed a Lead Teacher position at each grade level; yet none of the four leaders held these positions. Rather, their leadership was forged through a coming together of building-level needs and their own particular talents, interests, and readiness levels. Mary Jo's graduate course work promoted her interest in research; Sally's interest in cognitive studies emerged just as the school's interest in learning how children learn was becoming clarified; Wally's knowledge of technology answered the school staff's need for adequate tools for assessment; and Carolyn's status as volunteer parent and substitute librarian filled a void at the school and ultimately led to the creation of a new position. This is not to say that all teacher leadership is informal and emergent, but rather to emphasize the worthiness of improvisation and invention in the development of teacher-leader roles.

A general ethos in the school, as well as supportive conditions in the district, nurture and sustain teacher leaders. Each of the teacher leaders made reference to both the ethos that had been established at Narragansett School and to the opportunities for leadership that the principal provided. For Mary Jo, the school "celebrated" reflective practice. Sally saw Narragansett as a place where people "were expected to do their best." Wally found in the school a haven for his ideas which had not been embraced by his own school's staff. And Carolyn discovered a match between her deeply held convictions about children and the espoused beliefs and ongoing practices of the school. The role of the principal is key here, both as the clear voice of the mission of the school and as the guardian of the vision the staff had developed. As Sally said: "What I said about my own leadership, I learned from watching the principal. That's where it starts."

The teacher leaders also garnered support from the school district, especially from the superintendent. As Wally indicated, the superintendent had "an understanding of the whole system." She linked people to each other and provided the time and the opportunity for meaningful interactions to occur. She supported the creation of the teacher/scholar position, hired paraprofessionals to free teachers from clerical tasks, and promoted dialogue and reflection whenever and wherever possible. When she left the superintendency, she was followed by a man who shared her commitment to teacher leadership and the spirit of inquiry. He continued the policies and practices that she had initiated.

Teaching and leadership are complementary functions; they are woven of the same cloth. All four of the teacher leaders defined themselves primarily as teachers. Becoming teachers of adults as well as of children seemed to them a logical extension of their roles. In fact, they all spoke of themselves as having gone through common stages of development. They spoke of themselves as first being novice teachers, ill at ease in the profession and uncertain about their own abilities to adapt. They commented on the growing awareness of the limits and routinization that public schools placed on their colleagues and on themselves, and they identified a moment in time when they began to see teaching in a different light, as having the potential for intellectual work and for professional and personal growth. These transitions from teaching as routine to teaching as active engagement to teaching as leading were both gradual and ongoing.

As teacher leaders, the four carved niches for themselves in a school that was itself in the process of reflection and self-renewal. They became more firm in their commitments as teachers as they became more comfortable in their roles as leaders. They recognized that teachers are key to school improvement and the restructuring of education. They strengthened their faith in themselves and in their colleagues. And they discovered, in their new leadership roles, that, as Wally said, they were "born to teach."

Notes

1. Connie Goldman, "What Is This Thing Called Restructuring?" unpublished paper, 1988; "Narragansett School Field Notes" (Gorham, Maine: University of Southern Maine, 1988); Lynne Miller, "Teacher Leadership in a Renewing School," in *Teacher Leadership*, edited by Robert McClure (Washington, DC: National Education Association, forthcoming); Connie Goldman and Cynthia O'Shea, "A Culture for Change," *Educational Leadership* 47, no. 8 (1989): 41-43.

2. Cynthia O'Shea, "Field Notes" (Gorham, Maine: University of Southern Maine, 1990).

3. "Narragansett School Field Notes," p. 5.

4. Lynne Miller, "Teacher Leadership in a Renewing School."

CHAPTER XII

Teacher Leadership in a Teacher-Run School

PATRICIA A. WASLEY

Across the country there is despair over the flagging quality of public education. Everywhere people are looking for classrooms from which students emerge able to participate in and contribute to contemporary society. Everyone is searching for teachers who can lead our schools to new practices which can be responsive to changing student needs. That search is manifested in a variety of ways: weekly newspaper articles on exceptional teachers; a spate of books about the odds teachers face (*Among School Children, Small Victories, Walking Trees*);[1] state by state legislation which promotes teacher leadership and school change; and television specials ("Schools That Work" and "Solving the Education Crisis"). Underlying all these examples is a kind of unspoken hope that teachers can lead our students to more productive lives and salvage our hopes for public education.

Several years ago, in order to better understand teacher leadership and its potential to improve schooling, I studied a small group of experimenting teachers who were in positions of leadership.[2] I knew that teachers had been taking leadership roles in districts for years and I believed that those teachers might contribute greater depth to the growing conversation about the potential of such leadership positions for improving educational experiences for students.

I learned that current roles tell a great deal both about the possibilities that teacher-leader positions bring to the improvement of educational practices and about the problems that arise as a result of these roles. In theory, all the positions I studied were created to bring about changes in faculty practices on behalf of better student learning. Whether or not teacher leaders could actually match these theoretical intentions seemed to depend on a number of conditions. Teacher leaders were successful if (a) they worked with willing colleagues and

---

Patricia A. Wasley is Senior Researcher for School Change, Coalition of Essential Schools, Brown University.

had time to collaborate; (b) there was shared agreement on the need for change; (c) they were not diverted to administrative work, such as scheduling assemblies and organizing volunteer teas; (d) the instructional focus of their work supported changing practices rather than reinforcing current common practices; (e) their role had been created and implemented by those who were supposed to change as a result of the teacher leader's work; (f) that role was flexible enough to provide different kinds of collaborative relationships for a faculty with diverse needs.

When most or at least some of these conditions were in place the possibilities for improved practice were compelling. I visited classrooms where teacher leaders were working with students who were engaged in rigorous work, functioning as historians, journalists, film makers, archivists, environmentalists, social activists. Youngsters worked at problem solving, simulating think tanks in which experts struggle with confounding problems that face our nation and others. Students shared the fruits of their intellectual labors and were articulate about the gains they had made. They pointed out the connections among disciplines and the advantages of the technology they were using. Perhaps most important, their classrooms were places that the students, their teachers, and I found interesting. They were at once casual, intense, varied in pace depending on the activity, sometimes noisy, sometimes quiet, sometimes conflicted, but always places where students were doing the learning, were engaged, and had left passivity in the hall or in front of their television sets at home.

In addition to illustrating the problems and the possibilities for teacher leadership, that study proffered two confounding paradoxes. By their very nature teacher leadership roles suggest that shared leadership is possible in the midst of hierarchical systems. Principals and department heads must share their authority and responsibility if teachers in leadership positions are to have a legitimate opportunity to bring about change. District offices must be willing to expand the leadership team in a school if the roles are to be authentic. Given the years of hierarchical practices in schools, traditional norms are challenged when teachers have leadership responsibilities.

At the same time, if teacher leadership positions are to be effective, teachers must be willing to learn from their colleagues. Teachers have spent years going outside their schools for new ideas and for growth opportunities. In addition, because of salary structures, most teachers have equal status, differentiated only by the number of years in the district. Frequently there is an inherent mistrust of anyone who rises above the rest, an immediate relegation of teacher leaders to the ranks of administrators, even if the teacher leader spends part time in the classroom. Another common attitude is often reflected in such statements as "Any teacher who has taught next door to me for years can't know more than I do! We've been in the same faculty meetings for years, struggled with the same students. We've even taken a couple of the same courses in the summer. I like him (or her) a lot, but we teach different subjects."

Despite these two unresolved paradoxes, interest in teacher leadership continues to grow and expand. Shortly after I finished this study, I was invited to Aguilar Elementary School.[3] It is a K-6 elementary school serving 700 students in a small urban center in the high southwestern desert. Eighty percent of the students are Hispanic, 15 percent are Anglo, and the rest are Native American, Afro-American, and Asian. In its seventh year, Aguilar had 50+ staff members. Aguilar recently joined "Re:Learning" but had been working for a number of years to find better ways to support their students. (Re:Learning is a partnership between the Education Commission of the States, a number of states, the Coalition of Essential Schools at Brown University,[4] and some 100 member schools across the country. The objective of the partnership is to create educational systems which support schools as they redesign their practices to help students learn to use their minds well.) Aguilar was also experimenting with multi-aged grouping in a program called Winter Exploration (WE). They had begun an early intervention program that had a number of components. A year before, the principal had taken a new position, and the teachers undertook the management of the school in order to protect the changes they had begun to make. They believed they were pioneering in the field of teacher leadership, and invited me to help them think about their work. In this chapter I report on Aguilar's rather remarkable story, using numerous quotations taken from taped records of my group sessions with the faculty. Then I reexamine teacher leadership through the lens of Aguilar; its case offers fresh insights on the problems and possibilities for educational change.

Aguilar Elementary School

As the yellow school buses roll into the school yard, the morning sun illuminates a big school. Students swarm around, playing, while teachers usher them this way and that. The atmosphere is lively.

Several languages zing through the air; the intonations are cheerful and energetic.

Students and teachers move into the building and into the classrooms, ready for the day to begin. While it is a warm, caring place, Aguilar reflects a number of the pressing challenges a majority of our schools face. A minority of its students come from two-parent homes. A majority of the parents work and as a result have little time to tend to their children's academic progress. Few students are gaining the essential skills they need in order to participate in our complex society. The surrounding community is very poor. Many students come to school hungry; many are disconnected from the purposes of schooling.

Like many schools across the country, the staff at Aguilar has rallied to address these challenges. Rather than railing over changing conditions while clinging to traditional practices, these teachers have determined that they must find better ways to serve their students. The changes they wish to make are difficult because they require that everyone involved—teachers, parents, administrators—question familiar, comfortable practices which no longer seem to be effective. They have mustered the courage and the flexibility to suggest alternatives. Then, toughest of all, they have begun to experiment. All this takes extra time and new reserves of energy. Everyone knows that both these resources must come from a professional commitment to students, for there is no money to compensate teachers for extra time and effort.

CHANGING LEADERSHIP IN A CHANGING SCHOOL

Aguilar Elementary School is a young school in a growing district. For seven years, Al Stevensen was the principal. A twenty-six year veteran in the district came with him to open the school. She described Mr. Stevensen as follows:

> He was an easy, laid back kind of guy, and I think he purposely hired very strong people who had a very deep philosophy about what they were doing, people who were not afraid to stand up and express opinions. He was very child oriented, always reinforcing the idea that everything we did should be based on what is good for children. He let the teachers and the staff know that we were the professionals: "You know what you're doing. I trust you. Go to it." He involved us a great deal in the decisions as we developed and built this school. It is no accident that this school has turned out the way it has.

In the summer of the school's seventh year Mr. Stevensen sent a letter to the staff to announce his retirement. Although it was not common practice at the time, two of the teachers were invited by the central office to sit on the committee for selecting a new principal. Tim Senoza, a teacher who had been at the school for two years, was selected. The veteran teacher described him:

He shared Al's philosophy, but was more of a pusher, a mover, and a shaker. He said to us, "Come on. We can do all kinds of wonderful things. There is lots that can be done for these kids that we're not doing now." He brought us together socially. We did a lot of eating together, and we celebrated everything. We got involved with a foundation which supported us in thinking about restructuring. They brought lots of speakers in who told us about different possibilities. Tim kept telling us, "This is our chance. What do we want to do?"

Another teacher commented:

For two years, the staff worked together to develop a mission statement and goals. We started our early intervention program which has a lot of pieces to it—peer tutoring, adult tutoring, summer school. We stopped pulling some kids out for remedial help.

And the veteran teacher again:

We just started doing all of this stuff. No one told us to. We talked a lot about who we were, what our kids were, what our philosophy is, and then more ideas came up to the top. We all felt that we wanted multi-aged grouping and we wanted a more experience-oriented curriculum. And we wanted our kids to feel comfortable in a large school. We wanted them to know more adults than just their teacher and more kids so they wouldn't feel lost. And so we started our Winter Exploration (WE) program, which is still evolving.

Then, in the summer of 1989, the staff received a letter from the principal saying that he had taken another job. Members of the staff described their reactions to the principal's leaving:

We were happy for him, but it sent us into a panic. We thought "What's going on here? We've got all these programs going. We're the biggest elementary school in the district. How are we going to . . .?" I mean this is not an easy task. So several of us got together and came up with a plan for a team of teachers to run the school.

Another teacher put it this way:

It wasn't a statement against principals. In fact, our principals had really helped us to get to the point where we were ready to take more responsibility. It's just that we knew that if someone came who didn't like what we had started . . . .

Other teachers added their concerns about what happens to innovative programs in schools when leaders leave: "Who'd want to deal with a staff like us?" "I've worked in several schools. Each new principal has different ideas about what should be done." "Or how things should be run." "Remember that library program we started at Watervale Elementary? That died after our principal left."

The dilemma is a common one. Educational leaders change jobs frequently. The reasons for this are quite simple: it is necessary in order to move up the very limited career ladder. Department heads become assistant principals. Principals in small elementary schools move to larger elementary schools before moving to secondary schools or to the central office. Teacher leaders become staff development or curriculum specialists working out of the central office, or they move to assistant principalships. Everyone on the staff at Aguilar had experience with changes in leadership. At this particular time the staff was fearful, based on previous experiences, that they might lose momentum during the transition to a new principal, or worse, that the work they had begun might be dismissed as unimportant while the new administrator set to work on a more personally compelling agenda.

PLANNING FOR A TEACHER-MANAGED SCHOOL

After learning that Mr. Senoza was leaving, a self-selected committee of eight teachers quickly gathered to discuss their options. The committee was aware that a number of the elementary principals would likely be interested in transferring to Aguilar. They also knew that there was no one on the staff who expressed any interest in moving into administration. In addition, the staff was in the midst of several experimental programs that were important to them. They were about to begin the third year of the WE program—an experiment in interdisciplinary instruction with multi-age grouping of students. Their continuing hope was that as they became more comfortable with the very different teaching practices involved in WE, they would redesign the regular school program to include multi-age grouping and team teaching. They had just completed their third year of the early intervention program with its multiple foci. Several staff members had submitted a proposal for additional funding to the U.S. Department of Education. They received a grant of $101,000—no small feat for a group of teachers. That award would strengthen and sustain their early intervention program for a year, and they were in the midst of determining best uses for the money.

Energy was high on the staff. Everyone felt that they were building a more powerful, more caring and progressive place for students. They had been innovating and experimenting for a couple of years and their efforts had taught them that they need not be bound by traditional structures or practices. Moreover, they had watched two principals run themselves ragged in their large elementary school. A senior teacher observed:

Currently, no matter how large the elementary school is, there is only one principal. Period. It doesn't make any difference if the school is bigger than a junior high or a middle school, both of which have assistant principals. The elementary schools are perceived to need only one administrator. We've watched firsthand. It's too big a job for any one person. So we thought about how we might improve that situation.

The planning group generated a plan to establish a management-team approach to running the school and went to the superintendent with their plan. His response was:

I think it's great. Why don't you try for it, but you have to do a couple of things. You'll need to get waivers from the State Department of Education. You'll need to prepare job descriptions for each of the team members and describe how the team will work. You'll need to make a presentation to the board, and you'll need to get the agreement of the entire staff.

The planning group conceived of a management team of four people—a "facilitator" and three coordinators. Each would have special responsibilities but all would work together to coordinate their efforts in running the school. All members of the team would receive a stipend in addition to their regular salaries. The total amount available for stipends would be determined by subtracting a veteran teacher's salary from the principal's salary. The difference would be divided among the team members according to their responsibilities. The facilitator, to be selected by the planning group and approved by the staff, would be released entirely from teaching and would receive a stipend of $3,000. The three coordinators would be selected by the staff. Each coordinator would teach full time and would receive a stipend of $1,500.

The special responsibilities envisioned for each member of the team were as follows:

The facilitator. The facilitator would have responsibility for the day-to-day running of the school, would attend all district-level administrative meetings, and would be the liaison between the central office and the school staff. Other responsibilities would include: doing all the paperwork required by the district and the state, evaluating teachers who were up for comprehensive evaluation (required every third year); making employment recommendations to the superintendent; carrying out board policies; maintaining student records and personnel records; coordinating community relations; overseeing building and grounds; overseeing instructional matters.

The coordinator for staff evaluations. The staff evaluations coordinator would supervise the peer evaluation program, including assuming responsibility for appropriate documentation; contact the assistant superintendent on all evaluations that required growth plans; chair the peer evaluation committee and communicate its work to the rest of the faculty.

The coordinator for building and grounds. The coordinator for building and grounds would be responsible for maintaining a safe environment; for coordinating the work of the custodial staff; for ordering supplies and materials, including textbooks; for dealing with all maintenance issues; for coordinating bus schedules; and for maintaining the inventory of the school's equipment.

The coordinator for academics. The academics coordinator would be responsible for the instructional program in the school. This responsibility would include working with staff assignments, keeping track of students' cumulative folders, organizing plans for professional development and curriculum development, participating in committees dealing with curriculum and instruction.

The planning group wrote up this plan and approached the State Department of Education. An official of the department described its position as very supportive—"sort of like the Wizard of OZ giving the Tin Man a heart when he had a heart all along. We conferred upon them the right to do what they already had the right to do." There were no policies in place that prevented a team from running a school.

The planning group then brought the staff together during the summer. They explained what they were proposing and why, and held a staff vote—everyone from custodial staff to teachers. A woman who had some administrative training and had been in the district a long time was suggested by the planning team for the facilitator's position. A member of the planning team, she had already agreed to take the facilitator's role if the staff were supportive. The rest of the management team would be selected by the staff once the board approved the plan. The vote was 35 to 2 in support of the plan for a management team. Comments like the following describe how the staff felt about the plan:

One of the things about this staff is that we don't think of all the worst possible scenarios to figure out why something won't work. We just think, "Hey, that sounds really neat. Let's try it."

We like the ownership of our own work. We thought if we vote to do this we will really be in charge of our own program. We wanted it to work. Then we took the proposal to our parent group. It was summer and so we had a small percentage [of parents present], but the really interested, active parents came and we presented it and they voted to support it, too.

The planning group and the facilitator then approached the board with the plan. After a grueling and very difficult session the board approved the plan by a 4 to 1 vote. The board viewed the proposition as both interesting and problematic. As one teacher noted, "they were reticent to pay elementary teachers a stipend even though high school teachers receive stipends all the time." The board also perceived that the management team approach would create tension with the existing principals' group. At the same time, the board enjoyed a reputation for innovation and were convinced by the superintendent that new ideas should gain a hearing. Like the teachers, board members had attended a number of sessions sponsored by a foundation on the need for change. They approved the experimental team on a year-to-year basis.

The assistant superintendent in charge of principals stated that she would supervise the facilitator in the same way principals are supervised. The rest of the management team would be supervised by the facilitator. The staff then proceeded to recruit people to fill the other three positions on the management team.

When the 1989-90 school year began, the management team was in place.

We knew it was going to be chaotic that first year. We were pioneers and none of us really knew what to expect. So we just dug in and worked hard to define roles and figure out who was going to do what. The first year was hard but we made it, and we had lots of ideas about how to improve things for the second year.

Over the summer months, the board unanimously approved the management team for another year.

A Teacher-Run School in Action

At the time of my visit in October, 1990, the staff had made a few revisions in their original plans for the management team. One of the management team members stepped down because the additional responsibility took too much time away from her students. A replacement team member was just learning the ropes. The staff had conducted a session to clarify who makes what decisions, and was operating under those new understandings. Parents talked about the school as an exceptional place, and indicated that they were happy to support the teachers. Parents' Night attendance was way up. Two of the seven board members believed that they represented the board's opinion that, at least for this second year, the school was well managed.

PROTECTING CHANGES BEING MADE

The major purpose for establishing the management team was to protect the changes the staff was in the midst of making when the principal left. A brief look at their most ambitious projects will illustrate how their work was proceeding.

The early intervention program was established to give children who are likely to fail a series of boosts to make their academic success more possible. The program had several components ranging from the conduct of workshops for parents to a six-week summer school for a multi-aged group of thirty children who ended the school year the farthest behind. Each of the early intervention programs was managed by a committee, and each committee was in the process of putting in place the previous year's recommendations gathered from parents, students, and staff members.

The WE program, in its third year, consisted of interdisciplinary courses offered to multi-aged groups of students by self-selected teams of teachers. As the WE committee was planning for the 1991 program, they were rethinking a number of their previous practices. Teachers were in the process of building new teams with a stronger interdisciplinary focus, and they hoped to experiment more with the nine Common Principles of the Coalition of Essential Schools—student as worker, teacher as coach, among others—because these were new to the staff.

Other changes in their school program had occurred since they began to manage the school. The special education teacher mainstreamed her students and began working with them in the regular classroom. The school improvement committee—a committee begun under Mr. Senoza—continued to work on issues related to site-based management and professional development. A committee was in its second year of dealing with Aguilar's participation in Re:Learning. All told, there were some fifteen working committees, each designed to address changes the staff wished to make in the school.

In addition to continuing the programs begun earlier, the management team approach gave those programs a new thrust. During the 1989-90 school year, a peer evaluation committee established a process for annual review. Their belief was that in a teacher-run building they should share responsibility for the quality of instruction. A second objective of the peer review program was to break down the isolation in which teachers traditionally work so that they might begin to learn from one another. The staff talked animatedly about the peer evaluation program. Some of the comments were:

Last year, we all wanted this to work well so we were very—well, kind. I feel a transition in this now. I feel like we're going to get a little tougher with each other; we want to really talk about things we see.

This was pretty exciting. I've taught here all these years and have never seen the people teach who are next door to me. Now I am able to see how they deliver curriculum, how they handle discipline problems, how they manage the flow of things in the classroom.

And to have another person from your level, an experienced person, come in and observe you and then dialogue with you is just a tremendous learning experience.

But it was tough. A lot of us felt nervous about it. Some said, "Wait a minute. That's not what I signed up to teach for. I'm not an administrator. I don't want to go in there finding fault with people."

We were all nervous. And we learned a lot about our differences.

I asked about the differences in instruction they were seeing. They agreed that some people used more cooperative learning techniques but that the majority of the staff used pretty traditional methods and resources. I asked whether they believed they would eventually take a stand in favor of one type of instruction over another. A lively debate ensued. Several noted that all teachers need a variety of instructional methods, and that the old should not be discarded altogether. Others claimed that they need more staff development in order to know more about different methods. Others noted that they were going to have to face it—some teachers would never change, and that they were going to have to say something. A teacher in his second year at the school said, "What is remarkable here is the overall climate. Forcing methods of instruction could undermine what the staff has begun. They need to evolve." As the complexities of this conversation opened up, the volume went up and emotions rose. One of the veterans said, "Whoa! Hold it. We're starting only our second year of peer observations. Each year we'll move forward. We have to keep track of the benefits we're gaining as well as think of how to make these observations more powerful. Lighten up!" The rest of the group laughed and then admitted that they were not a particularly light group.

Teacher Management: Comments by Teachers

In their discussions with me the staff expressed the view that managing the school had provided important benefits, had brought some unanticipated challenges, and had taught them a few good lessons as well.

BENEFITS

The benefits were important to sustain their drive to keep going. For instance, outsiders were interested in what they were doing, which had a double benefit. The staff at Aguilar clarified their purposes for visitors, but also learned from hearing what other schools were doing.

A veteran teacher said, "We are helping each other more. I have gotten to know my colleagues better, so we talk things out together, which reduces the stress teachers feel. I help Tanya, who takes everything very seriously, to be less—well, serious." Nodding emphatically, Tanya responded, "We've become better friends. It makes the pressure of change easier to manage."

A newcomer in the school said:

One thing I've noticed being here is that children and their needs are being discussed everywhere, everywhere. In the lounge. In the bathroom. I think the reason why people feel good and successful here is that the focus is on the children. It is very intense here, much more caring of students. And, the management team approach encourages everyone to be a leader where they feel they can effect positive change. That is one of the best aspects of this school.

There was a good deal of discussion about stress, which was also perceived to have beneficial effects, as the following comments suggest.

The thing is, that it's a different kind of stress than fighting with the principal, fighting with the system, always being told you have to do something when you know philosophically it is wrong.

There's a big difference between the stress you create for yourself and stress that's created outside of you. I have control over the stress I create. I can say to myself, "I'm overdoing it, and I'm going to put this committee or responsibility aside right now." When outside forces create stress, I have no control.

All this has been important to me. Mr. Senoza was a good principal, and I liked working with him. Still, I have had run-ins with other principals. Those experiences tended to make me want to work alone in my own room. I wanted to do this in order to have some say in the running of the school. I am normally an introvert, but my colleagues asked me to get involved and so I have. It has been very positive for me personally.

The other thing is that we've been able to hire people to come into the school who want to work in a school like this. Let's face it. We all work more hours in order to get our lessons done, to plan WE with our team members, to conduct observations and dialogues, and we're all on a million committees. Our new teacher is an example. When we interviewed him, we really grilled him. In fact, I think we did more talking than he did because we really wanted him to know what he was getting into.

The newcomer responded to this last comment:

Truth of the matter is that I thought it was probably more psycho-babble rhetoric! They said they were running the school by a team of teachers. . . . It was intriguing enough for me to be willing to drive 150 miles per day. And you know, they—we—are running the school and it has been a great experience for me. One thing that surprises me is, really, considering all the things they've done here and the new appropriation of responsibility, I don't see any more problems or difficulties doing this than arise in the other places I've worked. I've encountered few difficulties here, and plenty of help.

CHALLENGES

The staff talked openly about the challenges they faced. At the beginning of their second year of managing the school, they identified a number of unresolved issues.

Stress. The stress level among staff was very high. Everyone talked about it. "I eat, sleep, and dream this place!" "In a school like this, we expect more of ourselves. We place more demands on ourselves and we all give a lot more time." They knew that they must find ways to preserve energy if they wanted to maintain staff and their efforts. No answers seemed readily available although people were trying a variety of strategies.

Communication. Communication among staff, the fifteen committees, and the management team posed a major challenge. Several teachers spoke to the problem.

We opened the door for people to participate, and they started believing in it when they saw that their opinions counted; now they want to do it all the time and on every issue. Everyone wants to be heard.

The more programs we run, the less time we have to communicate. I spend a lot of time trying to contact teachers I need to communicate with, and I am frequently unable to get to them when I need to.

The facilitator also spoke of her concerns about communication:

I often have to share decisions made by various committees. The most frequent response I hear is, "Why wasn't I told about this?" The problem is that we have so many committees going, and we try to put the minutes of the meetings in people's mailboxes, but people don't have time to read it all. So they feel left out of the communications loop.

In addition, the management team was having difficulty communicating among themselves. Early in their second year they had not had a single meeting to coordinate their efforts. Several members of the team noted that they seldom met in the first year, that it was difficult for them to get together as they had not been given any released time to work together, and that their individual responsibilities and other committee meetings took place after school.

Decision making. Decision making constituted another major challenge. In the faculty meeting where the staff were told by the evaluation committee when and how the evaluation observations would be done for the 1990-1991 school year there was a great deal of tension in the room. The evaluations coordinator believed that the committee had taken the feedback the whole staff had given and had incorporated their suggestions and that the staff had vested the committee with the right to make decisions. She made it perfectly clear that the committee would not be flexible as they had been the previous year with scheduling evaluations and that people needed to follow the schedule. The plan was presented with little time for discussion. It appeared that the committee did not believe that discussion was necessary. Some of the staff were disgruntled. Time ran out at the meeting and a number of staff left feeling that several issues were unresolved. The committee felt some frustration as well.

The facilitator talked about the difficulties they faced with decision making:

We have so many committees that no one can attend all the meetings they'd like to, so everyone ends up being left out of some decisions, which makes people unhappy. I am stumped as to what to do. We make all the meetings open so that anyone who wants to can participate. And sometimes people complain about decisions made even when they could have attended but chose not to. That's when I really want to tear my hair out! I don't know what to do with those people.

Staff who felt left out of decisions agreed that meetings were open, and also agreed that it was impossible to attend all the meetings they were interested in. They noted, however, that there were times when they had to forego participation in order to help students. Recognizing the dilemmas, they were not willing to concede that all avenues for legitimate participation had been explored.

A number of staff members talked about the obscurity which clouded decision making in general. The staff recognized a need to clarify who has the authority to make what decisions. After a lengthy meeting, a list of agreements was distributed—which decisions would be made by management team members, by committee members, or by the whole staff—but it was clear that many staff still felt that the issue of decision making was murky. In addition, most decisions were made by majority vote, and they all felt the tension which resulted when there was significant division.

Role clarification. Another challenge was role clarification. The facilitator's role was the most confounding. The teachers in the school and personnel in the state department clearly believed that the school was run by a team of teachers, while board members and central office administrators described the school as run by a kind of principal. The facilitator was caught between the role as perceived by those higher up on the hierarchical ladder, and by her own colleagues with whom she worked daily—many of whom were fiercely committed to establishing the legitimacy of a teacher-run school. There was a kind of unspoken tension caused by the disjunction between these perceptions.

The teachers were proud of the extra responsibility they had all undertaken, and wanted recognition for their shared responsibility. They were also supportive of the risk that the facilitator had agreed to take on their behalf and believed that she, like everyone else, was trying hard to make things work. Several staff felt that the role was not open for discussion. There was some distrust over the fact that this position had not been selected by the whole staff, but appointed by the planning team. The staff recognized that the management team and the planning group did not feel that the district in general would support the management team approach if they felt that the staff disagreed about how it should be done. As a result, the staff which generally did not hesitate to open controversial discussions, remained quiet about the facilitator's role in order to secure the legitimacy of the management team first. There was no indication that anyone wanted to do away with the facilitator's role or replace the person serving as facilitator; they simply wanted to have the opportunity to talk about how it was working and to suggest possible revisions in much the same way they were critiquing other innovations. Given the tenuousness of the management team, the topic seemed particularly sensitive.

Paradoxically, the staff also found it difficult to make the shift from a principal to a management team. Individual management team members noted that everyone tended to go first to the facilitator for everything. The janitors went to the facilitator instead of to the building and grounds coordinator. Individual staff members ran their ideas for professional development by the facilitator instead of by the academic coordinator. Everyone had to be reminded to go to the appropriate person.

In addition, there were unanticipated problems which again raised questions about role clarification. Earlier in the year the staff noticed that several staff members were coming late. They asked, whose responsibility is a problem like that? The facilitator did not believe that she could facilitate for the staff and function as the disciplinarian as well, nor did she want to watch people's comings and goings. She felt that the disciplinary role was traditionally the principal's role, but she was not a principal, and that there should be alternatives. Many of the teachers wanted her to take that responsibility, believing that was why she had been released full time from teaching and given the largest stipend. One staff member suggested that it might be the responsibility of the peer observers. It was an issue on which they were still working.

Other role clarification issues surfaced as the management team members noted that their duties were much larger and more complicated than had been anticipated. The academic coordinator, the building and grounds coordinator, and the evaluations coordinator all taught full time and, like everyone else, worked on several committees. Each of them was struggling to find ways of involving the staff in decisions rather than establishing policies in an authoritarian manner. They felt the separation from the rest of the staff that their new roles created, and they noted that they would like more time to meet together to form a stronger support group and a better team.

Time. Everyone on the staff talked about the lack of time. They needed time to work together in order to build stronger programs for students. A person who had been on the management team the first year quit because she believed that her outside responsibilities took time away from her students and that this directly contradicted her purposes in assuming management responsibility for the school. Full-time teachers on the management team noted that it was difficult for them to take full responsibility for their assigned duties because they were in class. There was no released time available for them to work together, and no support for occasional release when needed. All staff noted that because of so many meetings they could do little else during the regular school day than teach and attend meetings. Individual planning and preparation had to be done at home. Heightened involvement between specialists and regular teachers meant more meetings, as did increased parental involvement. Teachers were eager for more time to work together to plan their curriculum and to share instructional techniques, but they described the days as absolutely jampacked and meteoric in tempo.

New staff. Introduction of new staff proved another challenge. The staff seemed clear that this school was not for everyone and noted that several people had already left for more traditional settings. They believed that this was a positive thing. Furthermore, they were aware that this innovation—a teacher-run building—had been undertaken because the staff was uniquely willing to "give it a shot." The challenge lay in how to bring new people into a staff that shared common goals and a spirit of innovation so that the newcomers felt equal partnership. During their first year of managing the building, the staff noted that some newcomers felt left out of the decision making. When included, they often lacked the valuable historical background which helped to shape certain decisions. Newcomers to the WE program and to the summer school program did not know about the philosophy upon which these programs had been built. The school had never had an explicit means of inducting new staff members into the school. Not until the beginning of the second year, when several second-year returnees voiced their concerns, did it occur to the veteran staff that they needed a system for inducting newcomers. They were just beginning to discuss the kinds of possibilities—a buddy system, a mentoring partnership, or some sort of seminar for newcomers—with which they might experiment.

Coherence. The staff agreed that it was difficult to keep track of everything they were doing and to make sure that it all fit together. There were some fifteen committees in operation. The staff was not at all sure that there wasn't some overlap between committees or whether all fifteen were completely necessary. "Whenever we think of something that needs to be done, we form a committee. I'm not sure that we ask what existing committee might undertake a new task. I'm also not sure that we ever examine old committees to see whether we still need them."

Legitimate participation. The last challenge dealt with legitimate participation in the new management system. A number of staff worried that there were teachers who were silent partners, who didn't say much about what they thought should happen. Staff worried that these people felt left out or that they disagreed with the directions the school was taking, but were too intimidated by the more vocal staff members to speak up. Others mentioned that there was a small group of dissenters, who complained no matter what and dragged the potential of the entire staff down with them. Everyone wondered how best to provide them with a voice without allowing them to undermine what the majority wanted to do. In another vein, four people suggested that the management team and the original planning group did not allow open conflict, that they kept the time for discussion too short in meetings, and used meetings to announce decisions made rather than to offer possible decisions and allow the staff the opportunity to have input. These staff members were worried that, while these actions revealed sincere hopes to protect the team concept, the management team was not allowing others to voice their legitimate concerns and as a result was undermining the potential of the very thing they were trying to create.

LESSONS

The staff agreed that in their first year of managing the school while attempting to carry on the changes they had begun they had learned several important lessons—some old, some new.

We learned about the importance of documenting decisions that are made in meetings, to have a historical record.

Yes, all of us have experienced selective memory. Things get so confusing sometimes that it is hard to keep track of exactly what we said we were going to do. Time and again we've had arguments because different people heard different things. So we've learned to review decisions made at the end of each meeting for clarification and to commit those to the minutes. It helps to avoid more conflict later on.

We've learned that we have to work on alternative structures for meetings so that we can involve everyone. The funny part is that some of us were taking cooperative learning classes, but didn't think to apply it to the work the adults do until we wanted to review everything we'd been working on last year.

We put everyone in small groups and had them summarize what they thought should be changed in all the areas where we had been working. It was a great meeting and everyone participated. I don't know why we don't do that more often.

We learned this summer that we really have to plan ahead. We were so busy during the school year with all the aspects of the early intervention program that we left the planning for the summer school until the summer. There we were with six weeks of programs to run and not enough time to plan it as thoroughly as we would like.

The big problem was that we believed that we had planned it adequately because we had run it the summer before. What we didn't plan for were the changes in staff and the need to coordinate the curriculum. While the parents and kids loved what was offered, we knew that we could have done a better job.

I think we've learned to get things out in the open. I personally hate conflict, but I know that we can't work together unless we know who's thinking what. We're still not very skilled at it.

I don't think we know the best ways to air conflict yet. Doing it in an open forum, asking people to say what they think, necessarily becomes very personal at times. We need to get the issues out in a way that is less personal, less painful.

We have learned that there is more to be done. We'd like to find more ways to involve parents—those who work and can't get here during the day.

We want to look at alternative assessment. We haven't even begun to think about that.

We'd like to figure out how to measure the effects of the early intervention program by tracking some of the kids through high school.

Some of us want to team like we do for WE permanently, but WE has been a whole staff project and so we need to discuss that with everybody else.

We need a professional library. We go to workshops and discover that people are reading things that would really help us—but the materials are hard for us to get. We should have them right here for all of us to share. We might be able to use part of our grant for that.

We need to do more work on our curriculum to make sure that the kids are getting everything they need.

The changes we've made at Aguilar are changes that we felt were important here for these children—the children we have here. It's not like a recipe. It's not like saying, "Okay, everything we've done here is terrific and you ought to try it in your school." So many of the reports we've read suggest that we adopt the ideas of another place. Or a new principal comes in and says, "We did this at my other school. I think we should do it here, too." We looked at our population. We tried to identify needs as we saw them as the children presented them to us and tried to devise something that will fit our students' needs. It's not a blueprint. I think, instead, we have learned to look within and ask, "What does our population of kids need?"

We've learned another thing. You can start a new program and you can change, but the change never stops. One change makes you change something else which makes you change something else. Like the WE program—we had to build an all-day kindergarten program if we wanted kindergarten kids to participate. Now some teachers want to do WE all the time. See what I mean? Once you start, it's hard to stop."

As the staff developed this list of lessons they felt they had learned, each individual seemed to draw energy from the ideas of others. They generated enough projects and directions to last well into the next century. The room was full of energy, full of a feeling of challenge and potential—like the energy one feels among team members at the beginning of a race or a game. There was no flagging, no sense of exhaustion here.

A New Web of Questions

Teacher leadership at Aguilar is impressive—the staff developed a climate of experimentation, an innovative new management structure, and vested confidence in one another. However, as is to be expected with any new role, the Aguilar approach to teacher leadership spins its own web, and raises new questions. Each of the questions forces a more thorough examination and understanding of the most important issues related to teacher leadership.

Does Aguilar have a teacher-run school? Or are the perceptions of the board and the central office correct? For example, is the facilitator really a principal with a different title and some collegial support? If the facilitator is really a pseudo-principal, what gains have been made? If this is not the case and the role is legitimate, what is the difference and what are the costs and the benefits to students and adults? What are the advantages of a teacher-run school? Is the fact that the staff feels empowered to run their own school enough of a rationale? Should other school faculties be encouraged to run their own school? What does this say about the role of the principal? Does it suggest that the principal's role is in need of changing just as classroom practices are in need of revision?

Do the projects which the staff has designed affect the quality of experience that students have in the classroom? The underlying purpose for the creation of the management team was to protect the changes the faculty had begun to make in projects such as WE, early intervention, and peer evaluation, each of which was designed to respond to the needs of students. To date, the Aguilar teachers have only their collective observations about WE to help them determine whether it is making a difference for their students. Because it was an extra program, they were not formally assessing student performance, but agreed that students seemed more motivated during WE than they did during the regular school day. Their assessment of the summer program was really focused on whether students and parents were satisfied with the program, or what changes they would recommend, rather than on an investigation of whether the program led to a difference in achievement. Furthermore, while all these projects were aimed at helping students, none of them specifically addressed changing practices. Teachers described much of the pedagogy in the building as traditional—many teachers used texts, had reading groups, seated children in rows, expected students to recite information gained. Even in their exploration of multi-age grouping and interdisciplinary work, teachers indicated that they were using fairly traditional methods. Each teacher was preparing his or her specialty while colleagues provided management support. My observation here is not designed to judge these methods but to consider a critical component of the purposes of their projects and of teacher leadership in general. If the projects are designed to improve the quality of students' learning, will doing more of the same really make a difference?

Will the management of the school influence the kind of instructional techniques and methods used? Perhaps the most essential question is whether undertaking the management of the school makes it more likely that teachers will provide students with better educational experiences. Will teachers eventually provide students more opportunities to think critically and to solve problems when they themselves have those opportunities or will students continue to find themselves filling in blanks and looking for teacher-approved answers? Turning the question a bit, is the net gain of participation in management of the school worth the time that teachers must take away from curriculum, instruction, and student assessment? This dilemma extends beyond those involved in the management team to the whole staff. The members of the management team indicated that they worked to include others in the decision making that falls under their respective responsibilities. Does staff participation in decision making and in peer evaluation, among other things, make them better able to provide students with powerful learning experiences? Or does the time they spend on management issues decrease the energy available to examine instructional practices?

Where does the coherence of the school's efforts come from? Aguilar is a large school. With a staff of more than fifty teachers and some fifteen committees, some confusion and overlap of effort is inevitable. One of the teachers pointed out that the greatest advantage of the school was that all teachers had the opportunity to contribute leadership where they felt most comfortable or most interested. This suggests a kind of leadership density model[5] designed to foster greater investment and creativity in a larger number of the people on the staff. While this is clearly desirable, it is equally desirable to consider the coherence of the entire effort. Surely someone or some group should be assessing the quality of each project and committee in light of the overall goals of the school. It is entirely possible that one committee might be engaged in work which contradicts or undermines the efforts of another. I was not sure whether this problem already exists in the case of two separate committees on school improvement. If the management team never meets, who is taking responsibility to make sure that the school, its committees, and its projects are headed in a direction which will improve schooling rather than rearranging responsibilities for traditional school experiences? Who works to ensure that each new effort fits into the overall goals of the school so that the school can move forward in significant ways rather than simply diffusing its efforts?

What effect does a transition in leadership have on the work of change and on teacher leadership in general? At Aguilar, teachers were fulfilling leadership roles long before Mr. Senoza left. They established the management team in order to protect the work they had begun. Teachers, principals, and superintendents change jobs frequently in order to move up the relatively limited career ladder and it is not uncommon for new leaders to arrive with their own agenda and to overlook or devalue the work already underway. Several of the Aguilar teachers shared previous experiences they had had where their efforts had been dismantled because of a change in leadership. This common occurrence contributes to the cynicism teachers feel when confronted with a new initiative to improve schools. The action taken by Aguilar's staff indicates that this is an issue worth investigating more thoroughly. If the teachers established the management team in order to further their efforts to change, and if running the school detracts from efforts to change, an earlier question bears repeating: What gains are made?

In broader terms, if we hope that teacher leadership positions will enable the larger faculty to improve the quality of education, do these positions not require some constancy? If teachers in leadership positions move too frequently, the potential for serious change is diminished. Unfortunately, Aguilar provided an example here. Each year the management team had to go to the board to get approval to run the school for the next school year. As I write, the superintendent who supported them has left, and three board members are up for reelection. The teachers face a great deal of uncertainty, and everyone is fearful of what will happen if the team approach is not approved again. Several staff members who have invested heavily in the experiment claim they will leave teaching should it not be approved.

Teacher Leadership Reexamined

Teacher leadership became the focus of national attention as traditional practices in schools worked for fewer and fewer students each year. As the urgency for better schools grows, more and more people are convinced that in order to engage students, to help them learn to use their minds well, to keep them in school, we must change the kinds of interactions that take place in classrooms. The hope is that teacher leadership positions will facilitate, promote, and direct that kind of change. Earlier findings reinforced the idea that the primary focus of any teacher leadership position should be to change the nature of the interactions between students and their teachers.

Given the dedication, the willingness, and the professional commitment I see in the teachers at Aguilar, and in other teacher leaders around the country, I am hopeful about teacher leadership and its potential to improve schooling in the country. The staff at Aguilar and their colleagues in the school district indicate that traditional hierarchical structures are more flexible than many might imagine. They also demonstrate that given the opportunity to create their own forms of teacher leadership, teachers can and do learn from their colleagues. Teachers at Aguilar point out several additional considerations important to any discussion of teacher leadership. If teacher leadership positions are created to support and facilitate change, their efforts should fit into a coherent whole. Transitions in leadership both at the teacher leader level and at other levels should be anticipated in order to guarantee as much constancy to a particular change effort as possible. Furthermore, teachers do not work in a vacuum, but in a system. They work in partnership with school board members, central office administrators, principals, parents, and community leaders on behalf of the children they serve. Teachers cannot assume important leadership roles without the support of these partners, nor can they make necessary changes if they do not have the support of these partners over time. Most important, everyone in this partnership must be resolute that the central purpose of any of the changes they wish to make, of any work they hope to do, is to more powerfully engage the minds of the young people they serve.

Notes

1. Tracy Kidder, *Among School Children* (Boston: Houghton Mifflin, 1990); Samuel G. Freedman, *Small Victories* (New York: Harper and Row, 1990); Ralph Fletcher, *Walking Trees* (Portsmouth, NH: Heinemann Educational Books, 1991).

2. Patricia A. Wasley, *Teachers Who Lead: The Rhetoric of Reform and the Realities of Practice* (New York: Teachers College Press, 1991).

3. Aguilar Elementary school is a pseudonym, as are names of staff members mentioned in this chapter.

4. The Coalition of Essential Schools was founded by Theodore Sizer in 1984 to implement the ideas suggested for creating more engaging secondary schools. See Theodore Sizer, *Horace's Compromise: The Dilemma of the American High School* (Boston: Houghton Mifflin, 1984).

5. See M. S. Meyer, *Every Employee a Manager* (New York: McGraw-Hill, 1971) and Wasley, *Teachers Who Lead*.

Name Index

Adelman, Nancy E., 77
Arbuckle, Margaret, 155
Arends, Richard, 179
Astuto, Terry, 90, 109

Bacharach, Samuel B., 58
Ball, Deborah L., 195
Ball, Stephen J., 169, 170, 177, 178
Banks, Steven R., 78
Barley, Stephen R., 163, 167, 177
Barrett, Peter A., 89
Bascia, Nina, 57, 154, 177, 195
Beady, Charles, 155
Bellah, Robert, 160, 173, 174, 175, 176, 178
Bennet, C., 177
Bentzen, Maxine M., 89
Berliner, David C., 195
Berry, Barnett, 77
Bird, Tom, 176
Blue, Harold G., 88
Bodstrom, Lennert, 155
Boyer, Ernest, 35
Brantigan, Nanna S., 179, 191, 192, 193, 194, 196
Brookover, Wilbur, 155
Brophy, Jere E., 194
Bryk, Anthony, 155
Buchmann, Margret, 180, 181, 194, 196
Bush, George, 99
Bussis, Anne M., 18, 35

Carey, Neil B., 77
Carini, Patricia, 36
Castle, Shari, 89
Chanin, Robert, 83, 85, 89
Cheong, Y. F., 177
Cherlin, A. J., 136
Clark, David L., 90, 109
Clark, Shirley M., 156
Clune, William A., 58, 155
Coady, Joan, 77
Cohen, David K., 155, 178, 195
Cohn, Marilyn M., 110, 135, 136, 137, 156
Colbeck, Carol, 57
Coleman, James S., 109
Comer, James Bryant, 10, 89
Conant, James, 81

Conley, Sharon C., 58
Cooperman, Saul, 77
Cotton, John L., 155
Crowson, Robert, 58
Cusick, Philip A., 164, 172, 173, 177, 178

Daley, Suzanne, 10
Darling-Hammond, Linda, 11, 34, 35, 36, 77, 78
David, Jane L., 58
Dawe, Ruth, 176
De Bevoise, Wynn, 36
Deming, W. Edward, 104, 109
Dewey, John, 6, 8, 34
Drucker, Peter F., 34
Dubea, Cynthia, 155

Eaton, Marian, 178
Eisenhower, Dwight D., 81
Elbaz, F. T., 178
Elmore, Richard F., 58
Emerson, Ralph Waldo, 209
Etzioni, Amitai, 136
Evenden, Edward S., 88

Farrar, Eleanor, 178
Feiman-Nemser, Sharon, 181, 194, 195, 196
Feistritzer, C. Emily, 77
Fernandez, Ricardo R., 155
Finch, Mary E., 137
Finley, M. K. V., 178
Firestone, William, 155
Fletcher, Ralph, 10, 235
Flinders, David J., 176
Floden, Robert, 194
Flood, Patricia, 155
Freedman, Samuel G., 156, 235
Froggart, Kirk L., 155
Fullan, Michael, 36, 176
Futrell, Mary Hatwood, 83, 84, 85

Gage, N. L., 194
Gallagher, Robin, 108
Gamble, Guy C., 88
Gardner, Howard, 202
Garner, Wendell R., 35
Gendler, Tamar, 24, 36

237

NAME INDEX

Giddings, Franklin, 177
Giroux, Henry A., 94, 108
Glickman, Carl D., 35
Goertz, Margaret, 154
Goldman, Connie, 204
Good, Thomas L., 194
Goodlad, John I., 35, 36, 77
Goodson, Ivor, 177
Gosney, Karen, 189, 194
Grossman, Pamela, 179
Gusfield, Joseph, 164, 177

Haberman, Martin, 36
Hall, Richard H., 58
Hammersley, Martyn, 162, 177
Handal, Gunnar, 176
Hannaway, Jane, 58
Harding, Catherine, 155
Hargreaves, Andy, 160, 161, 176, 177, 178
Hemmings, Annette H., 154, 156
Hermann, Mary, 143, 144
Hirsch, Christopher R., 58
Hlebowitch, Peter, 77
Houston, W. Robert, 195
Hoy, Wayne, 136
Huberman, Michael, 142, 156, 159, 176
Hutton, Jerry B., 77

Irvine, Jacqueline J., 77

Jackson, Philip W., 10, 58, 155
Jennings, Kenneth R., 155
Jervis, Kathe, 10
Johnson, Lyndon B., 81
Johnson, Susan Moore, 155

Kahn, Robert L., 155
Kanter, Rosabeth Moss, 58, 178
Kerr, Donna H., 35, 77
Kidder, Tracy, 235
Kirp, David L., 36
Klagholz, Leo F., 77
Knapp, Michael S., 10
Knudsen, Jennifer, 37
Koerner, James D., 78
Koretz, Daniel, 35
Kottkamp, Robert B., 135, 136, 137, 156

Lacy, C., 170, 177, 178
Lampert, Magdalene, 181, 195
Lareau, Annette, 136
Lawton, Theresa A., 35
Lee, Valerie, 155

Leinhardt, Gaea, 195
Lengnick-Hall, Mark, 155
Lenz, Victor, 137
Lesko, Nancy L., 155
Lichtenstein, Gary, 37, 178
Lieberman, Ann, 1, 10, 36, 89, 137, 194, 195
Lightfoot, Sara Lawrence, 38, 58, 177
Likert, Jane G., 35
Likert, Rensis, 35
Little, Judith Warren, 36, 57, 155, 157, 176, 177, 181, 189, 195, 196
Livingston, Carol, 89
Lockwood, Anne Turnbaugh, 154
Lortie, Dan C., 58, 111, 112, 113, 114, 131, 133, 135, 136, 137, 195
Lotto, Linda S., 109
Loucks-Horsley, Susan, 155
Loughlin, Sally, 201, 202, 203, 209, 210
Louis, Karen Seashore, 138, 155, 156
Lutz, Frank W., 77

Madsen, Richard, 176
Maeroff, Gene I., 58
Mason, Danna, 145, 146
McCloskey, Gary N., 135, 136, 137, 156
McClure, Robert M., 79, 88, 89, 211
McDiarmid, G. Williamson, 195
McDill, Edward L., 77
McDonnell, Lorraine M., 58, 89
McElliott, Karen, 185, 186, 194
McGoldrick, Carolyn, 206, 207, 208, 209, 210
McGregor, Douglas, 97, 98, 107, 109
McKenzie, Floretta Dukes, 38, 58
McLaughlin, Milbrey W., 10, 37, 137, 154, 176, 177, 178, 195
McNeil, Linda M., 35, 177
Measor, Lynda, 178
Metz, Mary Haywood, 138, 139, 154, 156
Meyer, M. S., 235
Miles, Matthew B., 142, 156
Miller, Lynne, 10, 89, 195, 197, 211
Miskel, Cecil, 136
Mitchell, Douglas, 154
Mittman, Brian S., 77
Montag, Carol, 10
Moore, John H., 195
Murray, Lynn, 155

Natriello, Gary, 59, 77
Necco, Edward, 77
Neufeld, Barbara, 178

NAME INDEX

Newmann, Fred, 154, 156
Nias, Jennifer, 164, 177

O'Connor, Mary Jo, 198, 199, 200, 201, 209, 210
O'Shea, Cynthia, 197, 211
O'Toole, James, 155
Oakes, Jeannie, 96, 108

Page, Reba, 154
Pallas, Aaron M., 77
Paris, Scott G., 35
Pascal, Anthony, 89
Pasmore, William A., 155
Penning, Nick, 77
Peshkin, Alan, 173, 178
Phelan, Patricia, 178
Pomfret, Alan, 36
Powell, Arthur, 178
Proller, Norman, 137
Provenzo, Eugene F., Jr., 135, 136, 137, 156
Purkey, Stewart, 154, 156

Ralston, Anthony, 58
Raudenbush, Stephen W., 177
Rauth, Marilyn, 79, 88
Raywid, Mary Anne, 156
Reagan, Ronald, 99, 100
Resnick, Lauren B., 6, 10, 35
Reyes, P., 155
Richert, Anna, 194
Rosenblum, Sheila, 154, 155, 156
Rosenholtz, Susan, 155, 178
Rossmiller, Richard, 154, 156
Roth, Jodie L., 35
Roth, Robert A., 77
Rothkopf, Ernst Z., 78
Rowen, Brian, 177
Rutter, Robert A., 155

Sarason, Seymour B., 90, 91, 98, 101, 108, 109
Schaeffer, Robert J., 89
Schlechty, Phillip, 35, 36
Schlossman, Steven, 78
Schweitzer, John, 155
Scott, W. R., 177
Sederberg, Charles H., 156
Sedlak, Michael, 78
Sergiovanni, Thomas J., 195
Shakespeare, William, 96, 147
Sharkan, Diane, 57
Shedd, Joseph B., 58
Sherwood, John J., 155

Shields, Patrick M., 10
Shulman, Lee S., 19, 35, 181, 195
Sikes, Patricia, 178
Sirotnik, Kenneth A., 35, 36, 77, 195
Siskin, Leslie S., 177, 178
Sizer, Theodore, 178, 235
Smith, BetsAnn, 154, 155, 156
Smith, Donald, 195
Smith, Gregory, 155
Smith, Julia L., 155
Smith, Louis M., 135
Smith, Mary Lee, 18, 35
Snyder, Jon, 11
Soder, Roger, 77
Sosniak, Lauren, 135
Sternberg, Robert, 202
Sullivan, William M., 176
Swidler, Ann, 176
Sykes, Gary, 35, 195

Tabachnik, B. Robert, 194
Talbert, Joan E., 154, 177, 178, 195
Tanner, Laurel N., 35
Teichler, Ulrich, 155
Thompson, Charles L., 89
Timar, Thomas, 36
Tipton, Steve, 176
Tobin, Kenneth, 195
Tom, Alan R., 136
Turner, Julianne C., 35
Tyack, David, 10
Tyre, Alex, 156

Valli, Lina, 154
Van Maanen, John, 163, 167, 177
Vollrath, David A., 155

Wasley, Patricia A., 212, 235
Watts, Gary D., 88, 89
Weaver, W. Timothy, 77
Webb, Arnold, 77
Wehlage, Gary, 155
White, Paula A., 58
Whitford, Betty Lou, 36
Wigdor, Alexandra K., 35
Wigginton, Eliot, 10
Williams, Martha, 155
Wilson, Choya, 58
Wineburg, Sam, 194
Wise, Arthur E., 24, 35, 36, 135, 137
Wisenbaker, Joe, 155
Witte, John, 155
Wittrock, Merlin C., 194
Woods, Peter, 162, 177, 178

Zeichner, Kenneth, 194
Ziko, Wally, 204, 205, 206, 209, 210, 211

Zumwalt, Karen K., 35, 59, 77
Zwerg, Marilyn, 58

Subject Index

Accountability in education: model of learner-centered system for, 26-29 (fig., 28); need for new approach to, 11-12; purposes of systems for, 14; responsibilities of states, school districts, and teachers for, 25-26; strengths and limitations of various types of, 15-16; types of, 14-15

Aguilar Elementary School (pseud.): description of, 214-15; ongoing programs in, 221-22; peer evaluation in, 222, 226; plan for teacher management of, 218-19; steps in securing approval of management team for, 220-21; teacher reaction to change of principals in, 215-17; *see also* Teacher management

Alternate route teachers (in New Jersey): characteristics of, as compared to graduates of college-based programs, 62-73; comparison between English and mathematics teachers in program for, 73-74; *see also* New Jersey Provisional Teacher Program

Alternate routes to certification for teaching: challenges to, 59-60; general characteristics of, 59

American Federation of Teachers, 79, 87, 100

A Nation at Risk, 1, 83, 110, 122, 139

Basic skills, limitations of dominant emphasis on, in schools, 4, 130-32

Brooklyn New School (New York City), example of learner-centered accountability in, 29-33

Bureaucratic accountability: assumptions of, 16-17; criticisms of, 17-18; importance of, in achieving equity in schools, 23; uses of tests in, 18

Carnegie Commission, 1

Carnegie Task Force on Teaching as a Profession, 80

Center for the Study of Effective Secondary Schools (University of Wisconsin), 138

Coalition of Essential Schools, 34, 143, 147, 214, 222

Coleman report, 101

Collaborative work, in schools: importance of emphasis on, for students and teachers, 8-9; relevance of, to quality of worklife of teachers, 149; structural change for facilitation of, 9-10; unquestioned optimism regarding, 159; use of teacher teams to facilitate, 146

Colleagueship, among teachers: contrived forms of, 181; criticism of, 161; questions regarding, 162

Collective bargaining, in schools: beginnings of, 82-83; broadened scope of, 83

Commission on the Reorganization of Secondary Education, 82

Community, sense of, among teachers: presence of, in religious schools, 172-73; typical lack of, in public schools, 172

Computerized portfolio project, in Narragansett School, 205-6

Curriculum and instruction, teachers' sense of loss of control over, 126-27

Educate America, 93

Education, dubious economic assumptions about, in U.S., 99-100

Education Commission of the States, 214

Educational bureaucracy, as impediment to reform, 37-38

Educational Development Center (Boston), 41

Educational Policies Commission, 82

Educational policy, knowledge of, as source of empowerment for teachers, 47-49

Educational reform: erroneous assumptions as blocks to, 91-102; incrementalism in, 103; teachers as keys to success of, 37, 98-99; *see also* School reform

Education Summit (Charlottesville, 1989), 93

Evaluation, of teachers, 127-28, 222, 225-26

Ford Foundation, 41

Holmes Group, 1, 34, 68

241

SUBJECT INDEX

Individualism, as core value in American society, 160
In-school learning, in contrast to out-of-school learning, 6-7
Instruction, criticism of subject-matter organization for, 94

Learner-centered accountability system: example of, in Brooklyn New School, 29-33; features of, 26-29; model for (fig.), 28
Legislated learning, as approach to school reform: flaws in, 133; teachers' criticism of, 130-32

Market accountability, choice as a mechanism for, 25
Mastery In Learning Project (MIL): emphases in, 86; initial opposition to, in NEA, 85

Narragansett Elementary School (Gorham, Maine), see Teacher leadership in Narragansett School
National Assessment of Educational Progress, 19, 93
National Board for Professional Teaching Standards, 34
National Center for Innovation (NEA), 87
National Commission on Testing and Public Policy, 18
National Council of Teachers of English, 19
National Council of Teachers of Mathematics, 19, 43, 48
National Education Association: changing labels for, 79; emphases of, on site-based management, in school renewal, 85-86; Mastery In Learning Project of, 84-85; National Center for Innovation of, 87; new role for, in school reform, 87; professional associations linked to, through 1960s, 82; stimuli for broadening scope of activities of, 83-84
National Governors' Association, 80, 96
National Research Council, 19
New Jersey Provisional Teacher Program: conclusions from study of, 75-77; effectiveness of, in attracting professionally oriented persons to teaching, 68-72; effectiveness of, in enhancing pool of teachers, 62-66; effectiveness of, in retaining teachers, 72-73; effectiveness of, in staffing urban schools, 66-68; features of, 60-61; study of, 61-62

Occupational community: definition of, 163; "consciousness of kind" as feature of, 163-65

Parents, teachers' comments on lack of support from, 119-21
Political accountability, site-based management as a mechanism for, 25
Preservice teachers, program for, in Puget Sound Development Center: core seminar in, 183-84; opportunities and constraints for teachers' learning in, 183-93; roles of cooperating teachers, site supervisors, and teaching associates in, 184-193; structures provided in, to facilitate teachers' learning, 191-93
Professional accountability, in schools: assumptions of, 19; changes needed in schools in support of, 22-23; collective problem solving in relation to, 22-23; importance of enforcing standards for practice in, 21-22; importance of preparation and socialization of teachers for, 20-21; need for, to achieve productivity, 24; requirements of, 20
Professional community (of teachers): knowledge of and involvement with as source of empowerment for teachers, 42-47; sense of, among teachers, 172-73
Professional development schools, 182-83
Professional Links with Urban Schools (PLUS), in Los Angeles, 41
Puget Sound Professional Development Center, 179-83

Rand Change Agent Study, 133
Re:Learning, 34, 214, 222
Restructuring of schools: conclusions regarding effects of, 39-40; minimal effect of, on empowerment of teachers, 39, 150-51

School choice, as mechanism to achieve market accountability, 25
School improvement, testing as inappropriate tool for achieving, 103-4
Schooling: changes required by a learner-centered view of, 11-12; socioeconomic trends calling for new mission for, 12-13

SUBJECT INDEX

School reform: calls for, in 1950s and 1960s, 81; conflicting messages in proposals for, 2; legislated learning approach to, 130-33; need for, 90-91; need for open participation in, 134; waves of, 1; *see also* Schools

Schools: assumptions about, as blocks to reform, 91-102; bureaucratic structure of, 91-92; criticism of subject-matter organization of instruction in, 94-95; debates about responsibilities of, 100-1; debates over determinants of success in, 101-2; difficulties with centralized planning in, 93-94; disadvantages of summer vacations in, 95-96; dysfunctional consequences of enforced standards in, 96-97; key assumptions for authentic reform of, 105-8; need for radical reform of, 90-91; questionable assumptions about teachers and students in, 97-98; responsibility for effective performance of, 92-93

Site-based management, 24, 85-86, 134; criticisms of, 103-4; minimal effects of, on teacher empowerment, 39

Socioeconomic changes, 1-3, 110-11; as context for establishing a new mission for schooling, 12-13

Societal problems, response of school system to, 4

Staff development: assumptions (about teachers' learning) undergirding approaches to, 7; features of plans for, that contribute to quality of worklife for teachers, 149

Student-centered teaching: changes required by, 11-12; heavy demands of, on teachers, 8; nature of, 5

Students: decline in motivation and interest of, 115-17; erroneous assumptions about, as blocks to reform, 97-98; impact of changing family structures on, 118-19

Subject matter, knowledge of, as source of empowerment for teachers, 49-55

Supervision, bureaucratic model of, 81

Teacher Assessment and Development System (TAD) in Dade County, Florida, 127-28

Teacher-centered teaching, nature of, 5

Teacher certification, *see* Alternate routes to certification for teaching

Teacher empowerment: authority-based conception of, 38; beginnings of, 81; definition of, 38; minimal effects of restructuring and site-based management on, 39; necessity of, for enhanced professionalism of teachers, 37; types of professional knowledge needed as basis for, 40-41; teachers' knowledge as important source of, 55-57

Teacher leadership: conditions required for effectiveness of, 210, 212-13; diverse paths to, 209; four portraits of, in Narragansett Elementary School, 197-209; future prospects for, 234-35; mistrust of those in positions of, 213; nature of roles for, 209-10; questions pertaining to, in Aguilar Elementary School, 231-34; sharing of authority required in, 213; various forms of, 197-98

Teacher management (in Aguilar Elementary School): benefits, challenges, and lessons of, 223-31; communication as a problem in, 225; difficulties with decision making in, 225-26; faculty participation in, 229; lack of time for teachers in, 228; lessons learned in first year of, 230-31; need for role clarification in, 226-28; overlapping committees in, 229; questions pertaining to teacher leadership in, 231-34; stress arising from, 224-25

Teacher/scholar, role of, in Narragansett Elementary School, 198-201

Teachers: approaches to professional development of, 7; complaints of, regarding record keeping and paperwork, 124; deterioration of working conditions for, 139; differing demands on, in child-centered and teacher-centered schools, 8; diminished role of, 124; dissatisfaction of, with teacher evaluation system, 127-28; loss of control by, in curricular and instructional matters, 126-27; optimistic views of collaboration among, 159; pessimistic view of privacy and independence of, 158-59; view of, as independent artisans, 159-60

Teachers' unions: potential of, for assisting with school improvement, 87-88; Rand study of, in relation to educational reform, 87

Teachers' identity and consciousness of kind: departmental affiliation as source of, 168-70; instructional assignment as source of, 167-68; students as resources for, 165-67; subject-matter specialization as source of, 170-72

Teachers' job satisfaction: decline in, 112; impact of administrative attitudes and demands on, 129-30; impact of students' and parents' attitudes on, 121-23; teachers' reasons for decline in, 114-30

Teachers' learning: assumptions about, in programs for staff development, 7; contexts supportive of, 181-82; definition of, 180; need for better understanding of, 7; opportunities for and constraints upon, in participation in preparation of future teachers, 183-93; research on, 180

Teachers' privacy and independence: defense of, 160; skeptical views of, 158-59; predominance of, in secondary schools, 163

Teachers' professional knowledge, components of, to enhance empowerment of teachers, 40-41

Teachers' work, changes in teachers' description of, 113-14

Teachers' worklife: care for students as factor in, 152; empowerment of teachers in relation to, 150-51; factors contributing to quality of, 148-51; general conclusions regarding quality of, from two studies, 153-54; indicators of quality of, 140-42; leadership of principal as factor contributing to quality of, 151-52; principal as catalyst for changes in, 143-44; restructuring as factor in, 153-54; social class of community as dominant influence on quality of, 138; two case studies of, 142-48; uncertainty about proposals for improving, 139

Teaching: changed conception of, 11; decline in teachers' satisfaction with, 112; dual agenda for, 4-5; effects of social and demographic changes on, 3; low status of, in early twentieth century, 80-81; privacy and colleagueship as important issues in, 157-58; study of changes in teachers' perceptions of, 110-12; two forms of individualism in, 160

Testing, in schools: costs of, 18-19; criticism of, 18, 104-5

Urban Mathematics Collaboratives (San Francisco, Los Angeles): description of, 41-42; value of, in extending teachers' knowledge, 43-44, 47-49, 51-53, 55-57

Winter Exploration program (WE), at Aguilar Elementary School, 214, 217, 221, 229, 232

INFORMATION ABOUT MEMBERSHIP IN THE SOCIETY

Membership in the National Society for the Study of Education is open to all who desire to receive its publications.

There are two categories of membership, Regular and Comprehensive. The Regular Membership (annual dues in 1992, $25) entitles the member to receive both volumes of the yearbook. The Comprehensive Membership (annual dues in 1992, $48) entitles the member to receive the two-volume yearbook and the two current volumes in the Series on Contemporary Educational Issues. For their first year of membership, full-time graduate students pay reduced dues in 1992 as follows: Regular, $21; Comprehensive, $43.

Membership in the Society is for the calendar year. Dues are payable on or before January 1 of each year.

New members are required to pay an entrance fee of $1, in addition to annual dues for the year in which they join.

Members of the Society include professors, researchers, graduate students, and administrators in colleges and universities; teachers, supervisors, curriculum specialists, and administrators in elementary and secondary schools; and a considerable number of persons not formally connected with educational institutions.

All members participate in the nomination and election of the six-member Board of Directors, which is responsible for managing the affairs of the Society, including the authorization of volumes to appear in the yearbook series. All members whose dues are paid for the current year are eligible for election to the Board of Directors.

Each year the Society arranges for meetings to be held in conjunction with the annual conferences of one or more of the major national educational organizations. All members are urged to attend these sessions. Members are also encouraged to submit proposals for future yearbooks or for volumes in the series on Contemporary Educational Issues.

Further information about the Society may be secured by writing to the Secretary-Treasurer, NSSE, 5835 Kimbark Avenue, Chicago, IL 60637.

RECENT PUBLICATIONS OF THE NATIONAL SOCIETY FOR THE STUDY OF EDUCATION

1. The Yearbooks

Ninety-first Yearbook (1992)
    Part 1. *The Changing Contexts of Teaching.* Ann Lieberman, editor. Cloth.
    Part 2. *The Arts, Education, and Aesthetic Knowing.* Bennett Reimer and Ralph A. Smith, editors. Cloth.

Ninetieth Yearbook (1991)
    Part 1. *The Care and Education of America's Young Children: Obstacles and Opportunities.* Sharon L. Kagan, editor. Cloth.
    Part 2. *Evaluation and Education: At Quarter Century.* Milbrey W. McLaughlin and D. C. Phillips, editors. Cloth.

Eighty-ninth Yearbook (1990)
    Part 1. *Textbooks and Schooling in the United States.* David L. Elliott and Arthur Woodward, editors. Cloth.
    Part 2. *Educational Leadership and Changing Contexts of Families, Communities, and Schools.* Brad Mitchell and Luvern L. Cunningham, editors. Paper.

Eighty-eighth Yearbook (1989)
    Part 1. *From Socrates to Software: The Teacher as Text and the Text as Teacher.* Philip W. Jackson and Sophie Haroutunian-Gordon, editors. Cloth.
    Part 2. *Schooling and Disability.* Douglas Biklen, Dianne Ferguson, and Alison Ford, editors. Cloth.

Eighty-seventh Yearbook (1988)
    Part 1. *Critical Issues in Curriculum.* Laurel N. Tanner, editor. Cloth.
    Part 2. *Cultural Literacy and the Idea of General Education.* Ian Westbury and Alan C. Purves, editors. Cloth.

Eighty-sixth Yearbook (1987)
    Part 1. *The Ecology of School Renewal.* John I. Goodlad, editor. Cloth.
    Part 2. *Society as Educator in an Age of Transition.* Kenneth D. Benne and Steven Tozer, editors. Cloth.

Eighty-fifth Yearbook (1986)
    Part 1. *Microcomputers and Education.* Jack A. Culbertson and Luvern L. Cunningham, editors. Cloth.
    Part 2. *The Teaching of Writing.* Anthony R. Petrosky and David Bartholomae, editors. Paper.

Eighty-fourth Yearbook (1985)
Part 1. *Education in School and Nonschool Settings.* Mario D. Fantini and Robert Sinclair, editors. Cloth.
Part 2. *Learning and Teaching the Ways of Knowing.* Elliot Eisner, editor. Paper.

Eighty-third Yearbook (1984)
Part 1. *Becoming Readers in a Complex Society.* Alan C. Purves and Olive S. Niles, editors. Cloth.
Part 2. *The Humanities in Precollegiate Education.* Benjamin Ladner, editor. Paper.

Eighty-second Yearbook (1983)
Part 1. *Individual Differences and the Common Curriculum.* Gary D Fenstermacher and John I. Goodlad, editors. Paper.

Eighty-first Yearbook (1982)
Part 1. *Policy Making in Education.* Ann Lieberman and Milbrey W. McLaughlin, editors. Cloth.
Part 2. *Education and Work.* Harry F. Silberman, editor. Cloth.

Eightieth Yearbook (1981)
Part 1. *Philosophy and Education.* Jonas P. Soltis, editor. Cloth.
Part 2. *The Social Studies.* Howard D. Mehlinger and O. L. Davis, Jr., editors. Cloth.

Seventy-ninth Yearbook (1980)
Part 1. *Toward Adolescence: The Middle School Years.* Mauritz Johnson, editor. Paper.

Seventy-eighth Yearbook (1979)
Part 1. *The Gifted and the Talented: Their Education and Development.* A. Harry Passow, editor. Paper.
Part 2. *Classroom Management.* Daniel L. Duke, editor. Paper.

Seventy-seventh Yearbook (1978)
Part 1. *The Courts and Education.* Clifford B. Hooker, editor. Cloth.

Seventy-sixth Yearbook (1977)
Part 1. *The Teaching of English.* James R. Squire, editor. Cloth.

The above titles in the Society's Yearbook series may be ordered from the University of Chicago Press, Book Order Department, 11030 Langley Ave., Chicago, IL 60628. For a list of earlier titles in the yearbook series still available, write to the Secretary, NSSE, 5835 Kimbark Ave., Chicago, IL 60637.

2. The Series on Contemporary Educational Issues

The following volumes in the Society's Series on Contemporary Educational Issues may be ordered from the McCutchan Publishing Corporation, P.O. Box 774, Berkeley, CA 94702.

Boyd, William Lowe, and Walberg, Herbert J., editors. *Choice in Education: Potential and Problems.* 1990.
Case, Charles W., and Matthes, William A., editors. *Colleges of Education: Perspectives on Their Future.* 1985.
Eisner, Elliot, and Vallance, Elizabeth, editors. *Conflicting Conceptions of Curriculum.* 1974.
Erickson, Donald A., and Reller, Theodore L., editors. *The Principal in Metropolitan Schools.* 1979.
Farley, Frank H., and Gordon, Neal J., editors. *Psychology and Education: The State of the Union.* 1981.
Fennema, Elizabeth, and Ayer, M. Jane, editors. *Women and Education: Equity or Equality.* 1984.
First, Patricia F., and Walberg, Herbert J., editors. *School Boards: Changing Local Control.* 1992.
Griffiths, Daniel E., Stout, Robert T., and Forsyth, Patrick, editors. *Leaders for America's Schools: The Report and Papers of the National Commission on Excellence in Educational Administration.* 1988.
Jackson, Philip W., editor. *Contributing to Educational Change: Perspectives on Research and Practice.* 1988.
Lane, John J., and Epps, Edgar G., editors. *Restructuring the Schools: Problems and Prospects.* 1992.
Lane, John J., and Walberg, Herbert J., editors. *Effective School Leadership: Policy and Process.* 1987.
Levine, Daniel U., and Havighurst, Robert J., editors. *The Future of Big City Schools: Desegregation Policies and Magnet Alternatives.* 1977.
Lindquist, Mary M., editor. *Selected Issues in Mathematics Education.* 1981.
Murphy, Joseph, editor. *The Educational Reform Movement of the 1980s: Perspectives and Cases.* 1990.
Nucci, Larry P., editor. *Moral Development and Character Education.* 1989.
Peterson, Penelope L., and Walberg, Herbert J., editors. *Research on Teaching: Concepts, Findings, and Implications.* 1979.
Pflaum-Connor, Susanna, editor. *Aspects of Reading Education.* 1978.
Purves, Alan, and Levine, Daniel U., editors. *Educational Policy and International Assessment: Implications of the IEA Assessment of Achievement.* 1975.
Sinclair, Robert L., and Ghory, Ward. *Reaching Marginal Students: A Prime Concern for School Renewal.* 1987.
Spodek, Bernard, and Walberg, Herbert J., editors. *Early Childhood Education: Issues and Insights.* 1977.
Talmage, Harriet, editor. *Systems of Individualized Education.* 1975.
Tomlinson, Tommy M., and Walberg, Herbert J., editors. *Academic Work and Educational Excellence: Raising Student Productivity.* 1986.
Tyler, Ralph W., editor. *From Youth to Constructive Adult Life: The Role of the Public School.* 1978.

Tyler, Ralph W., and Wolf, Richard M., editors. *Crucial Issues in Testing.* 1974.

Walberg, Herbert J., editor. *Educational Environments and Effects: Evaluation, Policy, and Productivity.* 1979.

Walberg, Herbert J., editor. *Improving Educational Standards and Productivity: The Research Basis for Policy.* 1982.

Wang, Margaret C., and Walberg, Herbert J., editors. *Adapting Instruction to Student Differences.* 1985.

Warren, Donald R., editor. *History, Education, and Public Policy: Recovering the American Educational Past.* 1978.

Waxman, Hersholt C., and Walberg, Herbert J., editors. *Effective Teaching: Current Research.* 1991.